TORY RADICALISM

TORY RADICALISM

Margaret Thatcher, John Major, and the Transformation of Modern Britain, 1979–1997

Earl A. Reitan

ROWMAN & LITTLEFIELD PUBLISHERS, INC.
Lanham • Boulder • New York • Oxford

ROWMAN & LITTLEFIELD PUBLISHERS, INC.

Published in the United States of America
by Rowman & Littlefield Publishers, Inc.
4720 Boston Way, Lanham, Maryland 20706

12 Hid's Copse Road
Cummor Hill, Oxford OX2 9JJ, England

British Library Cataloguing in Publication Information Available

Library of Congress Cataloging-in-Publication Data

Reitan, E. A. (Earl Aaron), 1925–
     Tory radicalism : Margaret Thatcher, John Major, and the
transformation of modern Britain, 1979–1997 / Earl A. Reitan.
         p.   cm.
     Includes bibliographical references and index.
     ISBN 0-8476-8524-1 (cloth : alk. paper). — ISBN 0-8476-8525-X
(paper : alk. paper)
     1. Conservative Party (Great Britain)   2. Political planning—
Great Britain.   3. Great Britain—Politics and government—1979–
I. Title.
JN1129.C7R45   1997
324.24104'09'048—dc21   97-18649
                                                    CIP

ISBN 0-8476-8524-1 (cloth: alk. paper)
ISBN 0-8476-8525-X (pbk. : alk. paper)

Printed in the United States of America

⊗ ™ The paper used in this publication meets the minimum requirements of American
National Standard for Information Sciences—Permanence of Paper for Printed Library
Materials, ANSI Z39.48-1984.

To Carol

Contents

Preface

The focus of this book is Margaret Thatcher and the principles that came to be called "Thatcherism." The book has been written by an American historian for North American readers. For British readers it will provide an American point of view.

The Labour government that came to power in Britain at the end of World War II was determined to respond to the challenges posed by the war and the failures of the 1930s. From 1945 to 1951 Labour established a polity based on a planned economy, socialism, trade union power, and an expanded welfare state. The Conservative Party accepted what had been done and sought to improve upon it. A consensus developed that lasted until the 1970s when the system began to break down, culminating in 1979 with the disastrous "winter of discontent."

Margaret Thatcher came to the office of prime minister in May 1979. Two years later she described her government as "one of the most truly radical Ministries of postwar Britain." Indeed it was. For eleven years she displayed remarkable leadership, courage, and conviction as she led Britain out of an economic crisis and introduced a series of wide ranging reforms that transformed modern Britain. Her successor, John Major, led a ministry that completed the process. Acceptance of the Thatcherite reforms by Tony Blair, leader of "New Labour," indicates that Thatcherism has become the basis of a new consensus.

This book is not a personal biography of Margaret Thatcher and John Major, although necessary biographical information is included. Nor is it an analytical study of the workings of the political process. It is not a work of academic scholarship, although the author is an academic historian. It is based upon readily available sources. It is intended to be a fair-minded account of the policies of Margaret Thatcher and John Major and the ideas behind them.

During more than four decades as a scholar and teacher of British history, my family and I have always been well treated on our visits to Britain. We have enjoyed Britain's many splendid public facilities as well as the hospitality of individuals. Special thanks are due for the help and encouragement of British historians, who share with American scholars in the joint enterprise of learning, teaching, and writing about British history.

1

The Rise of Margaret Thatcher, to 1979

Britain Victorious, 1945

Margaret Thatcher came of age during World War II, and was forever marked by the spirit generated in Britain by that great conflict. On 8 May 1945, Britain rejoiced at the end of the war in Europe. Britain was a victorious power—an integral part of the alliance, dominated by the United States and the Soviet Union, that had won the greatest and most complete victory of modern times.

In Grantham, a small city in eastern England, Margaret Roberts, daughter of a local grocer and councillor, joined in the celebrations. Born in 1925, her adolescence had been shaped by six years of war in which Grantham had been directly involved. There were many Allied airbases in the area, including Bomber Command Group No. 5. She had seen, on the streets and in her family shop, soldiers and airmen of many nations, including Americans. Grantham had experienced air raids, and as a schoolgirl she had learned how to take shelter when the warning sounded. In important ways Margaret Thatcher's political career was shaped by her early experience of Anglo-American cooperation in World War II.

When he came into office in the dark days of 1940, Prime Minister Winston Churchill had formed a coalition government that included the leaders of all three political parties: Conservative, Labour, and Liberal. When the war in Europe ended, Churchill wanted to preserve the coalition government to complete the war against Japan, but the Labour members refused. Public opinion overwhelmingly favored an election, which would begin the process of putting Britain back on a peacetime footing.

During the war, parliamentary elections had been suspended. The election which took place in June, 1945 was the first in ten years. Churchill had led Britain through her darkest hours and to her greatest victory, but the British people did not see him as the man who could fulfill their aspirations for the postwar world. The Labour Party offered a specific platform: a planned economy, nationalization of major industries, full employment, extensive building of houses, a national health service, and a comprehensive system of social security.

Although the Conservative Party manifesto included many similar items, Churchill campaigned poorly, railing against the dangers of socialism. The result was a landslide victory for Labour, which gained a strong majority of the seats in the House of Commons.

The Labour Revolution

The polity that turned to Margaret Thatcher in 1979 was shaped in the years following World War II by the British Labour Party. A new and vastly expanded role for government was justified by two vivid memories: World War II had shown the capacity of the state to organize and direct the resources of the nation to the achievement of national objectives; and the depression of the 1930s had made clear, it seemed, the faults of capitalism and private enterprise.

The Labour Party combined two main groups: well-educated, middle-class socialists and the trade unions. It was an unstable mixture, and socialist ideology consorted uneasily with trade union pragmatism concerning jobs and wages.

The economic policy of Labour was based on planning, which was regarded as superior to the capitalistic, market-oriented economy that had failed dramatically in the 1930s. Planning would give priority to rebuilding Britain's industrial base, badly damaged by the war and the failure of private enterprise to modernize in the decades before. National ownership of the major industries ("the commanding heights of the economy") was seen as essential to making economic planning work. It was also thought that nationalization would improve labor relations, since workers would be working for the good of the nation, not for "the bosses" or remote shareholders.

Nationalization of the Bank of England, which had long served as a quasi-public institution, was intended to give the government better control of the supply of money and credit, but in practice little changed. Nationalization of the fragmented and inefficient coal industry was expected to improve the production of the most important source of energy. Other industries taken into public ownership were the railroads, electricity, gas, seaports, overseas cables, buses, and most long-distance trucking. The iron and steel industry was nationalized in 1951, just as the Labour government was coming to a close.

The nationalized industries were organized in corporations under the control of boards that were expected to run them as a business while performing a better public service. In reality, ministers often interfered for political reasons and some of these industries required heavy subsidies from the Treasury.

Apart from the change of ownership, the nationalized industries continued to be operated pretty much as before. The Labour government lacked the will and know-how needed to modernize them, and the Labour politicians had their hands full dealing with Britain's crushing postwar problems. Most of the industries that the Labour government nationalized were old and inefficient, with a dubious future. Despite the Labour Party's commitment to socialism, Britain remained a free-enterprise country and approximately 80 percent of the economy was privately owned and operated.

Labour's plans for centralized economic management required the cooperation of organized labor, the bedrock of the Labour Party. In turn, the Labour government promised to end the scourge of the depression years—mass unemployment. Full employment would be accompanied by social services that would make possible a decent life for all.

The British labor movement was fragmented into hundreds of craft unions, loosely united under an umbrella organization called the Trades Union Congress (TUC). With a Labour government in power, organized labor became an active participant in the political process—"an estate of the realm"—dominant in the Labour Party and participating prominently in the shaping of public policy.

The welfare state was the major accomplishment of the Labour government. An improved national insurance system, based on contributions from employers and employees, paid benefits for unemployment, sickness, retirement, maternity, widows, and death. There was also a means tested program of national assistance for those who needed help for other reasons.

Labour had promised health care for everyone, and fulfilled its promise by establishing the National Health Service (NHS), which essentially took over the medical facilities of the country. The NHS provided free medical, dental, and hospital care as well as free drugs, eye glasses, and dentures. Individuals registered with family doctors, who provided primary medical services, referring them to specialists if necessary. Doctors, usually organized in partnerships, received a basic payment to maintain their facilities and a flat amount for each patient, whether ill or not.

Most specialists practiced in hospitals, treating patients referred to them by the doctors. Doctors and specialists were permitted to supplement their incomes by treating private patients for fees, and beds were set aside in the hospitals for patients willing to pay personally.

In the boldest move of all, the local-authority hospitals were nationalized and funded out of general revenue. They were managed by regional hospital boards. The hospitals became the greatest problem for the National Health Service. Most were old and expensive to replace, and their staff experienced low pay, long hours, and poor working conditions.

In its early years, the National Health Service was swamped by a vast backlog of unmet medical needs and there were great shortages of medical resources. Despite some abuses, the NHS gave the British people far better medical care than they had received under private medicine.

One of the most pressing needs of the postwar period was to provide more housing. People had been badly housed in prewar Britain, and bombing had wreaked great destruction of homes. Returning veterans were ready to marry and settle down. The Labour Government committed substantial sums to subsidize the building of houses by the local authorities. Although labor and materials were scarce, in its sixth year the Labour government built more than a million houses. The quality of these council houses, by the standards of that time, was good, and they continue to be attractive to buyers today.

Under Labour, education did not receive high priority. The Education Act of 1944, passed by the wartime coalition government, promised free primary and secondary education for all, with an eventual school-leaving age of sixteen. Progress in this direction was limited by the existing stock of school buildings, many of them old and run-down, and the more pressing need for construction of housing and hospitals.

Within the Labour Party, strong differences of opinion existed concerning the class orientation of most schools. Normally, students were segregated by examination at age eleven, a practice that tended to separate middle-class and working-class children. Many Labour leaders had risen through the system and wanted to preserve and extend it. Others advocated "comprehensive schools" where all children would attend together, thus breaking down the class consciousness of Britain. This dispute, in one form or another, has continued to agitate the Labour Party to the present time.

Foreign Policy

With the end of World War II, the United States and the Soviet Union emerged as superpowers. Britain had been an important factor in World War II, especially in the early years, but after the war British foreign policy faced an uncertain future, as "the Cold War" came to dominate world affairs. Britain, having outlasted Hitler, was faced with a new struggle against the brutal dictatorship of Stalin.

Foreign Secretary Ernest Bevin was a dominant figure in the Labour Party. He was a strong opponent of domestic communists, whom he had long battled in the labor movement, and of the Soviet Union, their spiritual home. Bevin persuaded the United States to come forward as the leader of the West. Under the Marshall Plan, the United States provided extensive economic aid to the countries of Western Europe, including Britain. The United States led in the formation of the North Atlantic Treaty Organization (NATO), which maintained large forces in Europe to resist possible Soviet military expansion.

Through NATO, Britain made a long-term commitment of ground forces to the defense of Europe. To support the role of a great power sitting at the diplomatic head table, Britain maintained more than a million troops and began to develop an atom bomb—drains on human and financial resources that Britain could ill afford. The first British atom bomb was detonated in 1952.

Britain faced an important decision in her relations with Western Europe. In 1951, France, Germany, the Netherlands, Belgium, Luxembourg, and Italy began a process of economic integration by forming the European Coal and Steel Community. Britain was invited to join but refused; the global role took precedence over close involvement with Europe.

Continuance of Britain as a world power was essential to preserving her empire, which had become a commonwealth of independent nations (Canada, Australia, New Zealand, and South Africa) and dependent colonies that were in various stages of self-government. Reluctantly the Labour government was forced to recognize that in some places Britain's empire was slipping away. India was the "crown jewel" of the empire, but Britain's postwar weakness and strong local independence movements made it necessary to grant independence to India, Pakistan, Burma, and Ceylon (Sri Lanka).

Britain's position in the volatile Middle East was also crumbling. In 1947, the United States took over British responsibilities for the defense of Greece and Turkey. At the end of World War II, a large Jewish immigration into Palestine led to clashes between Jews and Arabs, and British troops were unable to maintain order. In 1948, Britain pulled out of Palestine. War broke out between the Arabs and the Jewish settlers, which led to the establishment of the state of Israel.

Although British resources were greatly overstretched, Britain was determined to maintain a position of influence in the Middle East. Her principal base was the Suez Canal Zone, which she held from Egypt on a lease until 1956. A backup base was established on the island of Cyprus. Other British forces were stationed in the Persian Gulf to protect Britain's oil interests, which at that time were 30 percent of her overseas investments.

Britain also maintained a presence in the Far East with bases at Singapore and Hong Kong. When a communist insurgency broke out in Malaya, Britain became involved in a long, drawn-out conflict that pitted thirty-five thousand soldiers against eight thousand guerrillas. In 1952, British troops were sent to Kenya to put down a rebellion there.

A New Era Emerges

In Britain an election must be held within five years of the previous election, but the prime minister (with the formal consent of the king or queen) may call it sooner. Labour's five-year electoral mandate expired in 1950 and it was necessary to go again to the voters. By that time, most of Labour's agenda had been completed and some leaders were calling for a policy of consolidation. Labour won a narrow victory, but its modest manifesto indicated that the period of fundamental reform had ended.

In 1951, the crumbling ministry of Clement Attlee called another election in an effort to get a clear mandate to rule. Although Labour had a slim majority of votes, the Conservatives won more seats in the House of Commons. Winston Churchill returned to No. 10 Downing Street as the leader of a Conservative government.

In the 1950s, Britain's postwar problems began to disappear. There was a sense of optimism. King George VI, who had remained in Buckingham Palace with his family throughout the war, died and was succeeded by his eldest daughter, Queen Elizabeth II. Her coronation in 1953 seemed to inaugurate a new era. In 1955 Winston Churchill retired, laden with honors and the symbol of Britain's "finest hour."

Growing Up

In the meantime Margaret Roberts was coming of age. She grew up in an apartment over her parents' grocery, where she developed the Victorian virtues of honesty, work, cleanliness, and Christian service. She and her sister helped in the shop, waiting on customers, shelving stock, and packaging bulk products. She enjoyed the general sociability of retailing. Her father was an avid reader, and once a week Margaret brought home books from the public library.

The Methodist chapel was the center of their social life. In contrast to the elegant worship and social cachet of the established Church of England, Methodism offered ordinary working people a plain Gospel message, a firm morality, and peppy hymns. Another important institution in Margaret's life was school. She was a scholarship student at the Kesteven and Grantham Girls' School, where she was consistently at the top of her class.

Despite their modest life, the Roberts family owned that totem of middle-class respectability—a piano. Margaret took lessons and won several local prizes. The piano on which she played had been made by her great uncle, a skilled builder of pianos and organs.

She gained her interest in politics from her father, a respected citizen of Grantham, who was a member of the town council for twenty-five years and eventually became mayor—in Britain an honorary office. She described her father as an "old-fashioned liberal" and an advocate of "individual responsibility and sound finance." In national politics he was "a staunch Conservative." In the election of 1935 (the last until after the war), Margaret was given the task of carrying messages between the polling place and Conservative Party headquarters.

In 1943, Margaret entered Oxford, where she studied chemistry. While she was a student she realized that her true interest was politics, but she had already embarked on her chemistry major and she needed to complete it for future employment. She was heavily involved in extracurricular activities, especially student political organizations. In her last year, she was elected president of the Oxford University Conservative Association, which enabled her to meet visiting Conservative politicians.

After graduating, Margaret worked as a research chemist while continuing her involvement in Conservative politics. In the election of 1950, at age twenty-four, she was selected to run as a Conservative for a parliamentary seat in Dartford, a Labour constituency where she could gain experience, although she had no chance of winning. She campaigned vigorously, and, as a good-looking young woman, she received considerable attention, including having her picture published in *Life* magazine. A German magazine described her as "a young woman with charm."

At her nomination dinner, Denis Thatcher, a prosperous businessman who was a partner in a paint factory, volunteered to drive her to London to catch her train home. During her campaign he drove her around in his Jaguar, cheering her on. The attraction was mutual, and in 1951, after another unsuccessful campaign, Margaret and Denis were married. Denis Thatcher gave Margaret the personal and financial support that she needed to pursue a new career by beginning the study of law. In 1953, she passed the bar exam and gave birth to twins. For the next few years she was occupied with the busy life of a mother and a lawyer.

The Conservatives in Power, 1951 to 1964

Churchill wished to preserve the national unity that had carried Britain through the war to victory, and he admired the efforts and sacrifices that had been made by ordinary people. He wanted to make good on the wartime promises of a better life for everyone. He and the Conservative Party accepted the principles of the Labour Revolution: central planning, full employment, and cooperation with the trade unions. The iron and steel industry and long-distance trucking were sold back to private enterprise, but the other nationalized industries remained as before. The National Health Service and other aspects of the welfare state were kept, and the Conservative ministry continued building council houses. A national consensus had been achieved that lasted for the next quarter century.

As prosperity returned, the Conservative Party won two more elections, and it seemed that Labour's moment had passed. In 1955 Churchill retired and was succeeded by Anthony Eden, foreign secretary during World War II and again in Churchill's second ministry. Eden called a snap election to strengthen his support in Parliament, but this time Margaret Thatcher was not a candidate.

In 1956 Eden faced a crisis, when Col. Gamal Abdul Nasser, the charismatic leader of Egypt, nationalized the Suez Canal, Britain's vital link with the East. At that point Israel, in collusion with Britain and France, attacked Egypt. The Israelis routed the Egyptian army, while the British and French sent troops into the former Canal Zone. When the United Nations and the United States denounced the attack on Egypt, the British withdrew in humiliation. Eden had a nervous breakdown and resigned. It seemed clear that Britain's attempt to maintain the role of a world power had crashed.

Eden's successor, Harold Macmillan, restored public confidence and the image of the Conservatives as "the natural party of government." In the 1930s, Macmillan had been one of a group of progressive young Conservatives who had advocated a "middle way" between *laissez-faire* capitalism and socialism. Now a poised and mature leader, Macmillan was the embodiment of the paternalistic "One Nation" Toryism of Disraeli, which saw the elite as responsible for the well-being of the country, and especially for those at the lower end of the economic scale.

Macmillan was the first British political leader to make effective use of television, projecting a calm, confident image in interviews and on talk shows. In the general election of 1959, he skillfully used television and national prosperity in his campaign, reminding the voters that "You've never had it so good." The Conservatives won almost 50 percent of the popular vote and a majority in the House of Commons.

That year, Margaret Thatcher returned to politics. The twins were six, and she decided to run for Parliament again. The selection committee in her own constituency turned her down, saying that she should stay home and look after her children. She was then selected for Finchley, a suburb north of London. She was a beneficiary of the Macmillan landslide of

1959 and took her seat in the House of Commons as Conservative member for Finchley, a seat that she held until 1992, when she was elevated to the House of Lords.

As a new MP (member of Parliament), Margaret Thatcher was fortunate to receive a post as a junior minister in the Ministry of Pensions. She worked hard at her job, where she learned how difficult it is to maintain a balance between helping people who need help and avoiding welfare dependency by people capable of taking care of themselves.

After the Suez fiasco, Britain faced a painful reappraisal of her place in the world. The American rebuff at Suez made a closer relationship with the European Economic Community (EEC) look more attractive. The EEC joined the Western European nations (France, West Germany, Italy, the Netherlands, Belgium, Luxembourg) into a single economic system, but the purpose of the EEC went beyond economics. Powerful idealism was also at work: after World War II, the peoples of Western Europe shared an idealistic desire to rid themselves of the national rivalries that had torn the continent apart.

Britain could not afford to be excluded from the European market, but she did not wish to give up her national sovereignty, "special relationships" with the United States and the Commonwealth, and her global interests in finance and trade. The British were an insular people, conscious of their national identity, and they did not share the idealistic motivations that had contributed to the movement for European unity. To the British, membership in the EEC was not a mission, but a matter of practical economics.

By 1960, however, the growing strength of the EEC was evident, and Macmillan applied for membership. A rising young Conservative, Edward Heath, was put in charge of the negotiations. The British application was vetoed by President Charles De Gaulle of France, who was convinced (perhaps rightly) that the British could never be good Europeans.

Close relations with Europe were also important due to the declining importance of the Commonwealth and the movement for independence throughout the British colonies. In 1960, Macmillan warned white South Africans that "the wind of change is blowing through this continent, and, whether we like it or not, this growth of national consciousness is a political fact." Ghana became independent in 1957, followed by Nigeria and other African colonies, Jamaica and other Caribbean possessions, Singapore, and Malaysia.

In 1963, Kenya was given independence and a black controlled government took over; white and Asian inhabitants left in large numbers. When black-majority governments came to power in Northern Rhodesia (Zambia) and Nyasaland (Malawi), a white-controlled government took over in Southern Rhodesia (now Zimbabwe) and declared its independence from the Commonwealth.

Time ran out for Macmillan in 1963. Restlessness among younger Conservatives had led him to dismiss one-third of his Cabinet the previous year, giving him a new nickname "Mac the Knife." Later in the year, ill health convinced Macmillan that he must resign as prime minister and leader of the Conservative Party. From his hospital bed, Macmillan kept firm control of the choice of a successor, and the queen came to the hospital to receive the verdict.

Macmillan informed the queen that the choice of the party leaders was the foreign secretary, the Earl of Home (pronounced Hume). A recent change in the law enabled Lord Home to renounce his peerage, which he did. As Sir Alec Douglas-Home, he was elected to the House of Commons in a bye-election and became prime minister.

The choice of the party leader and new prime minister by a few insiders aroused so much criticism that the Conservative Party decided that in the future the leader would be chosen by the Conservative MPs. On the first ballot a winner would require a majority plus 15 percent. A second ballot, if necessary, would require only a simple majority.

Sir Alec was capable and likable, but a mature landed gentleman was not right for "the swinging sixties." Home called an election the next year, in which he was defeated by Labour led by the forty-eight year old Harold Wilson. Wilson promised to bring to Britain "the white heat of the technological revolution." He won a narrow victory and organized a Labour government committed to new initiatives. Despite the Conservative defeat, Margaret Thatcher managed to carry her constituency of Finchley.

Harold Wilson, 1964–70

Harold Wilson was educated in a state-supported grammar school rather than in a prestigious private school. Wilson, like Edward Heath and Margaret Thatcher, represented the meritocracy of men and women who had climbed the scholarship route from grammar school to university. In 1966 he called an election to strengthen his support in Parliament and was rewarded with a comfortable majority.

Wilson maintained the postwar consensus while turning Labour in a new direction. He won the allegiance of Labour loyalists by renationalizing steel, but he left behind Labour's commitment to public ownership and the planned economy. Wilson undertook to manage the economy through monetary and fiscal policy. He abandoned Labour's preoccupation with the declining industries of the past in favor of high-tech industries such as engineering and aircraft. Taking blue-collar workers for granted, he sought to extend Labour's appeal to people in white-collar and service jobs.

Modernization of the economy would require advanced education. The *Robbins Report* (1964), initiated by the Conservatives, called for increased public investment in higher education to provide places for all who qualified. This was a proposal that both parties could accept, and a process of expansion began, including the establishment of many new universities. By the end of the decade, the number of university students had increased by 75 percent.

Wilson took pride in the growth of the polytechnics, institutions of higher education with career-oriented programs. Another innovation was the Open University, which enabled employed people to obtain degrees through correspondence, radio, and television. Wilson's commitment to high-level knowledge as the basis for a new kind of British economy was institutionalized by establishment of the Department of Education and Science.

Under Wilson, Labour strengthened the welfare state in the interests of social justice. Pensions, family allowances, and supplementary benefits were improved. Additional resources were granted to the National Health Service. Energetic efforts were made to provide modern housing by building tall blocks of flats that later became ghettos for the poor.

In the meantime, the pillars of the postwar settlement—the nationalized industries and trade union power—were failing. The most visible sign was inflation, as the British economy was unable to sustain the burdens placed on it. One reason was the low productivity of British manufacturing, which was characterized by sluggish management, restrictive unions, and badly designed products. Other countries pitied the former workshop of the world, now debilitated by "the British disease."

Wilson realized that the trade unions were part of the problem. Union power rested on the shop-room floor, where shop stewards contended with management and competed with each other in jurisdictional disputes. They called disruptive "unofficial strikes" that were not approved by the national union leadership.

In a publication entitled *In Place of Strife* (1969) Wilson proposed active involvement of the state in industrial relations. A Commission on Industrial Relations would be established to resolve differences before they led to strikes. The powers of national union leaders would be strengthened to reduce the number of unofficial strikes. A strike would require approval by the workers in a secret ballot. The assumption was that most workers did not want strikes, which reduced their income and might threaten their jobs. The proposal was so objectionable to the union leaders that it was dropped.

Wilson was forced to cut back on Britain's high-cost role as a world power. The British nuclear deterrent continued, and Britain stationed large forces in Western Europe, the Mediterranean, and scattered bases around the world. But Wilson announced that Britain would abandon the effort to maintain military forces "east of Suez." Small garrisons would remain in Gibraltar, Cyprus, Hong Kong, and the Falkland Islands, with a modest naval force in the Persian Gulf.

Britain's declining role as leader of the Commonwealth was dramatized by a crisis in Rhodesia. The white minority government, led by Ian Smith, had declared independence rather than yield to British insistence on granting political rights to the black majority. The Wilson government declared that this action was a rebellion and supported United Nations' economic sanctions, but British weakness and "kith and kin" sentiments at home foreclosed any stronger actions.

The Commonwealth connection contributed to another issue, immigration. In the 1950s full employment attracted many West Indians to Britain where they filled low-paid jobs in London Transport, the National Health Service, and elsewhere. In the 1960s, large numbers of East Indians and Pakistanis settled in Britain, and were joined by Asian minorities from Kenya and Uganda.

Labour's socialist leaders were idealistically sympathetic to racial minorities, but the union rank and file feared the threat of immigrants to jobs and the stability of their neighborhoods. From time to time racial disturbances broke out in cities where immigrants had settled in large numbers. In 1968, the Wilson government responded by restricting immigration from Commonwealth countries to persons with close connection to Britain by birth, descent, or naturalization.

While public opinion favored limiting immigration from the nonwhite Commonwealth countries, there was also strong support for equal treatment of immigrants who had already arrived and settled in Britain. The Race Relations Act prohibited discrimination in jobs, housing, or commercial services. This pattern of restriction *cum* nondiscrimination was to characterize British immigration policy until nonwhite Commonwealth immigration was virtually shut down by Margaret Thatcher.

The breakdown of the Commonwealth and the decline of the world power role led some in the Labour Party to advocate joining the European Community. Bending with the wind Wilson agreed, supported by both parties in the House of Commons. Another application was made for membership. Once again President De Gaulle imposed his veto.

In the meantime, the Conservative Party was also undergoing a change of leadership and direction. The party looked to the younger generation when it chose Edward Heath as its leader. Like Wilson and Margaret Thatcher, Heath came from a modest background. Son of a small builder of houses, Heath attended Oxford on a scholarship, supplementing his income by playing the organ. He served in the army in World War II, rising to the rank of colonel.

In Britain the parliamentary opposition maintains "shadow" ministers who are responsible for giving special attention to their counterparts in the Cabinet. Under Heath's leadership, Margaret Thatcher served her apprenticeship by holding several shadow offices: housing and land, opposition spokesperson on taxes under the shadow chancellor of the Exchequer, and shadow minister of education.

Opposition gave the Conservative Party the inducement and opportunity to reconsider its policies. The Conservatives began their departure from the consensus with a package of proposals: institutional reform in the interest of economy and efficiency, lower taxes, elimination of many regulations, some of which went back to wartime, limitation of trade union power, a strong attack on crime and public disorders, and an end to large-scale immigration. These ideas foreshadowed the policies that Margaret Thatcher would adopt a decade later.

In 1970 Wilson sought a fresh mandate by calling an election that he expected to win. The Conservatives promised to bring to government the fresh ideas of a new generation. Heath's campaign managers made good use of television, while Wilson was content to run on his reputation and look thoughtful while sucking his pipe.

Heath and the Conservative Party won an upset victory and Heath became prime minister, leading a Conservative government. Margaret Thatcher was reelected for Finchley and took a seat in the Heath Cabinet as minister for education and science.

The Ministry of Sir Edward Heath, 1970–74

Heath's first priority was British membership in the European Economic Community (EEC), to which he was strongly committed for idealistic as well as economic reasons. When President Charles De Gaulle of France retired in 1969, the way was open for British membership. Heath's application was accepted and Britain entered the EEC on New Years Day, 1973.

The main advantage of joining the EEC was access to a large and growing European market for British products. Heath minimized the effects that the political goals of the EEC might have on British sovereignty. In his overeagerness to join, Heath paid a high price, agreeing to a British financial contribution that was out of line with the resources of the British economy.

Both political parties were divided on the issue, and on the crucial division the treaty was ratified by only eight votes. Many Conservatives disliked the sacrifice of national sovereignty that membership entailed. Others emphasized the importance of relationships with the United States and the Commonwealth. Within the Labour Party, the socialists objected to joining a capitalistic economic entity, while trade unionists feared their established powers and work rules would be eroded.

The British people did not feel a strong sense of identity with continental Europe; polls showed no more than one-third of the voters in favor. Heath insisted, and the decision to join was accepted more as a practical matter of economics than as a full acceptance of the European ideal. In January 1973, great "Fanfare for Europe" celebrations were held to observe the occasion.

When Heath came to office, he announced that his would be a government of change. He was determined to modernize British government and society by implementing the new Conservative agenda. He declared his opposition to central planning, control of prices and wages, and subsidies for floundering nationalized industries. To stimulate the economy, income tax rates were cut and the lowest paid workers were exempted entirely. Interest rates were reduced and credit controls were removed.

Heath's "dash for growth" soon foundered on the same problems of productivity and inflation that had stymied Harold Wilson. Much of the money released into the marketplace by Heath's tax and monetary policies did not go into productive investments but into real estate speculation. With money and credit easily available, people plunged into real estate, borrowing at rising interest rates to finance their purchases. House prices rose by 50 percent in eighteen months as others entered the market, thinking that prices would continue to rise. Money also went into a consumption binge. Spending for foreign goods and holidays increased. Imports rose, the balance of payments turned unfavorable, and the pound again came under attack.

With the boom getting out of hand, Heath reverted to the former policies of state planning and control of the economy. As inflation mounted to 9 percent, Heath abandoned his faith in the free market and imposed statutory controls on prices and wages (the "U-Turn"). Public spending was cut and interest rates were raised to a record 13 percent.

The twin problems of inflation and the balance of payments were aggravated by the Arab–Israeli war of 1973. The Arab oil-producing states imposed an embargo on oil shipments, which dramatically increased the price of oil. The embargo hit hard the economies of advanced and developing nations alike. In Britain, unemployment rose to more than a million and inflation reached 24 percent.

The expansion came to a grinding halt, the brief boom in commercial real estate ended, and housing prices plummeted, leaving many people with mortgages greater than the value of their houses. The middle class, the core of the Conservative Party, was hard hit by the "stop-go" policies that Heath had criticized so severely under Harold Wilson.

Heath believed that modernization of the economy required fundamental reform of British industrial relations. It was generally agreed that irresponsible trade union power was an important factor in Britain's poor economic performance. The major problem was to end wildcat strikes and compel organized labor to live up to its contracts, especially in industries with a direct impact on the public, such as the railroads or electrical power generation.

Shortly after taking office, the Heath government passed the Industrial Relations Act, which established in Britain a comprehensive code to regulate relations between employers and employees, with an industrial court to resolve disputes. Unions were required to register and adhere to approved rules. The employment secretary was authorized to impose a "cooling-off period" in strikes that endangered the national interest, and could require approval by the workers in a secret ballot before a strike could go into effect. The right to strike was not infringed, but when these procedures were violated, the employer could sue the union for damages.

Heath's attempt to reform labor relations was overcome by a rash of strikes, led in 1972 by the coal miners, whose wages had fallen behind inflation and who saw jobs disappearing due to closures of unprofitable pits. The miners organized bands of "flying pickets" to prevent coal from being transported to the power stations. Among the leaders was Arthur Scargill, who a decade later would attempt similar tactics against Margaret Thatcher.

The miners were aided by the railwaymen and truckers, who refused to haul coal past the pickets. Soon it would be necessary to cut power generation and industry would come to a halt.

Not for the last time, the principle of collective bargaining was pitted against public needs. Faced with disaster, the Heath ministry established a commission to report on the miners' grievances. When the commission sided with the miners and recommended large wage increases, the ministry caved in. From her seat in the Cabinet, Margaret Thatcher looked on and learned.

As part of its commitment to modernizing Britain, the Heath ministry undertook a fundamental reform of local government, establishing a two-tier system. The upper tier consisted of counties, including the Greater London Council and similar "metropolitan counties" created for areas of urban sprawl. The lower tier consisted of two hundred and ninety-six rural and urban districts. Some of the latter were called boroughs and kept the honorary office of mayor. The districts had the principal responsibility for schools.

These local government units had important and extensive functions for roads, transportation, sanitation, schools and social services. They spent approximately 30 percent of all public money. Although most local government funding came from the Treasury, a considerable amount was based on "the rates," taxes on houses and commercial property. Home-owners, most of whom were Conservatives, had long complained about the rates. The Heath ministry considered a variety of reforms, but nothing came of that cause until Mrs. Thatcher took it up again a decade later.

In Office

Margaret Thatcher had come to the attention of Conservative Party leaders by her obvious intelligence and energy, and her ability to win elections. She clearly deserved a ministerial post. She plunged eagerly into her job as minister for education and science and gained valuable experience from it.

British secondary schools were of three kinds: grammar schools for students bound for university, secondary modern schools for the general student population, and technical schools providing training for students with specialized aptitudes or interests. Labour's policy had been to reduce the academic and social inequalities characteristic of British education by bringing students of all abilities and social backgrounds together in large "comprehensive schools."

Thatcher was determined to preserve the grammar schools that prepared the more able students for university admission. She issued Circular 10/70, which abrogated the commitment to comprehensive schools, leaving the matter to local education authorities. By that time the movement toward comprehension could not be stopped. More comprehensive schools were established during her time as minister of education than under any other minister. By 1979 more than 90 percent of secondary schools were comprehensive.

Mrs. Thatcher came to public attention as a result of the decision of the Heath ministry to cut spending, including spending on schools. Facing cuts, she decided to give priority to academic needs at the expense of school meals and free milk. She argued that families that were comfortably off could afford to pay for lunches and milk, while those who could not afford them should be helped by the Department of Social Services.

When the Heath Ministry introduced her bill to end free milk in the schools, a furor arose in the Labour Party and the press. Mrs. Thatcher was called "Thatcher, the milk snatcher," and her reputation for hard-heartedness was established, never to be lost. In November 1971, the popular tabloid, the *Sun*, at that time a left-wing newspaper, described her as "the Most Unpopular Woman in Britain."

In her autobiography she wrote: "I learned a valuable lesson. I had incurred the maximum of political odium for the minimum of political benefit."

Heath met his downfall in a another confrontation with organized labor. In 1973, the National Union of Mineworkers took advantage of the energy crisis precipitated by the Arab oil embargo and demanded wage increases far beyond the guidelines. To enforce their claim they refused all overtime work. They were supported by the electrical workers and the railwaymen, who had pay claims of their own.

Heath was determined not to give in so easily this time. He proclaimed a state of emergency. To save electricity, business was limited to a three-day week; darkened shop fronts reminded people of wartime. Street lights were turned off and television broadcasting was reduced. The miners responded with an all-out strike.

Early in 1974, Heath, driven to desperation, called for an election to determine "who governs Britain." Public support of the government did not appear. Heath had not changed the direction of the economy, controlled inflation, or resolved his disputes with organized labor.

The British people, tired of confrontation and crisis, turned back to the imperturbable Harold Wilson, who won a plurality of seats, although Labour lacked a clear majority and was second to the Conservatives in total votes. The two major parties each won 37 percent of the popular vote, to the benefit of the Liberals, who made a startling comeback with almost 20 percent. Nationalist parties in Scotland and Wales also made gains.

Later in the year, Wilson called another election, which gave him a slim majority of three seats, with Labour winning almost 40 percent of the vote and the Liberals holding their own with 18 percent. The Conservatives hit rock bottom, receiving only 36 percent of the votes.

In her autobiography Margaret Thatcher wrote: "I was upset at the result. We had finally squared up to the unions and the people had not supported us. . . . I knew in my heart that it was time not just for a change in government but for a change in the Conservative Party."

The Foundations of Thatcherism

After two electoral defeats in 1974, Heath found himself vulnerable within his own party. His "U-Turn" in 1972 and his failure to deal effectively with trade union power led many Conservatives to look elsewhere. Determined to change the direction of the Conservative Party, Margaret Thatcher stepped forward to wrest the leadership of the Conservative Party from Heath.

In her autobiography, she writes that she went to Heath's office, where she found him at his desk.

"I must tell you," she said, "that I have decided to stand for the leadership."

"He looked at me coldly," she continues, "turned his back, shrugged his shoulders, and said: 'If you must.' I slipped out of the room."

Her main support came from the Conservative 1922 Committee, a body of backbenchers (MPs who are not party leaders). They introduced a new rule for the choice of the Conservative leader, who was required to seek reelection every year. Other Conservative leaders had no desire to provoke a party fight by challenging Heath, but the new rule gave Margaret Thatcher—the maverick—the opportunity she needed.

As an outsider she promised a fresh start, and the backbenchers rallied behind her. She narrowly missed election on the first ballot. Heath, recognizing that he had lost the confidence of his party, stepped down and Mrs. Thatcher won comfortably on the second. To the amazement of the press, the public, and many Conservatives, Margaret Thatcher was now leader of the Conservative Party and prime minister in waiting.

Next she had to find Conservatives willing to follow her leadership in a party where she had little standing. One of the first to join her shadow Cabinet was William Whitelaw, who had stood against her in the second ballot of the leadership contest. "Willie" was an astute politician noted for his ability to reconcile differences and smooth troubled waters. Another was Sir Geoffrey Howe, a capable and hardworking lawyer who shared her views on free-market economics. Michael Heseltine, a forceful and ambitious younger member, was made shadow minister for industry, where his vigor was focused on blocking Labour's proposals for further nationalizations. Heath refused her invitation to join the shadow Cabinet.

When she became leader, Mrs. Thatcher's political views were not well formed, and many who voted for her did not know what they were getting.

She claimed to have been influenced by the works of F. A. Hayek, whose *The Road to Serfdom* condemned intervention of government in the economy as leading to authoritarianism in other ways. She gave special credit to her friend and mentor, Sir Keith Joseph, for helping her define a set of principles that she would carry into the next election. His experience as a minister in the Heath government had led him to the view that government intervention in society and the economy, no matter how well-intended, exacerbated the very problems that it was intended to resolve or created new problems that would lead to further government involvements.

Joseph's purpose was to restore to Britain the enterprise culture, weakened by Labour collectivism and Conservative paternalism. His solution was to cut taxes, spending, and borrowing, and give more responsibility to businesses and individuals for their own well-being. He advocated selling off the nationalized industries, leaving them to sink or swim in a competitive environment.

In respect of individuals and families, Joseph was a compassionate man, realizing the enormous adjustments that return to a free-market economy would cause. For that reason, he saw the need for a safety net in a period of economic change, but one that would not become a hammock. His main concern was to break "the cycle of deprivation" that kept families in poverty for generations. To break the cycle, he advocated improvements in education and an end to welfare dependency, especially among the growing number of unwed teenage mothers.

It was Margaret Thatcher's task to translate the theoretical ideas of Sir Keith Joseph into proposals that would be accepted by her party and resonate with the voters. The core support of the Conservative Party came from the middle class, and Mrs. Thatcher appealed especially to them.

"I believe we should judge people on merit and not on background," she said. "I believe that person who is prepared to work hardest should get the greatest rewards and keep them after tax. That we should back the workers and not the shirkers: that it is not only permissible but praiseworthy to want to benefit your own family by your own efforts."

She also sounded another powerful refrain in British conservatism: law and order. As crime, drug use, hooliganism, and illegitimacy increased, she offered a return to "traditional values" and "the smack of firm government."

Mrs. Thatcher had a strong interest in foreign policy, and she was by no means willing to accept the view that Britain could no longer be a force in international affairs. As leader of the opposition and a prospective prime minister, she had the opportunity to become acquainted with world leaders and problems. During the next four years she visited leaders in France, West Germany, Italy, Rumania, and Yugoslavia, the Middle East, India, Singapore, China, Australia, New Zealand, and the United States.

In foreign affairs, her main concern was the cold war, which had taken on new intensity as a result of technological advances in nuclear weapons. She recognized that the leadership of the United States was essential to European security and world peace. She believed that the Soviet Union had entered a new phase of aggressiveness in world affairs. It was her militant attitude that led a Russian journalist to give her the name: "The Iron Lady."

The Emergence of a Crisis

When Harold Wilson returned to office in 1974, he had no new ideas about how to deal with Britain's problems. He was there to hold power for Labour until something turned up. He ended the coal strike with a settlement favorable to the miners. Heath's Industrial Relations Act and pay policy were repealed.

Wilson was faced with the task of making a declining socialist economy work at a time of worldwide inflation and recession. He was trapped by his own party. Over time, the responsible socialists and trade union leaders of the Attlee era had been replaced by radicals who wanted to undermine capitalism and create a socialist state. Wilson owed his leadership of the Labour Party to them, and he was on a tightrope trying to reconcile their views with the broad public support needed by the leader of a major party.

Labour continued to offer its established solutions to the problems of a new age. Taxes and expenditures were increased to subsidize nationalized industries, provide for the growing number of the unemployed, and expand the welfare state. It was clear that many of Britain's problems were the result of a lack of investment and low productivity. Labour's answer was for the state to step in, and an "industrial strategy" was adopted. The National Enterprise Board was established to invest in new industries, such as electronics and biotechnology. Predictably, in many instances it dissipated its resources in futile efforts to keep failing private sector companies afloat.

Wilson attempted to deal with the problems of labor by making a "social contract" with the trade unions. In return for a promise of wage restraint, organized labor received legislation that strengthened the powers of the unions. The promise was an empty one; in the next year wage increases averaged 30 percent.

Labour's commitment to the welfare state was again demonstrated by increases in retirement pensions (which were indexed) and a supplemental pension plan based on earnings. New benefits were provided for the disabled and infirm. The special needs of women were addressed with maternity leave for pregnant women and the requirement of equal pay for equal work. An additional entitlement was introduced called "child benefit," which was paid to the mother regardless of income, giving many working-class mothers the first dependable income they had ever known.

Wilson's ability to finesse controversial issues was seen on the issue of British membership in the European Economic Community. There were opponents of the EEC in both parties: in the Labour Party they were left wingers, who were primarily concerned to establish socialism at home, and in the Conservative Party they were nationalists who objected to the loss of British sovereignty.

To settle the matter once and for all, Wilson proposed a referendum on the issue. Although the British people felt little commitment to European unity, they gave overwhelming approval to continuance in the EEC. The referendum marked the high point of British popular support for membership.

In 1976, Harold Wilson announced his decision to resign. He had brought about the revival of the Labour Party, but it was clear that its prescriptions for the country had either been discredited (nationalization) or accomplished (the welfare state). The consensus that had been established after World War II was running out.

Wilson's successor as prime minister was James Callaghan, a man of long and varied experience in Labour politics. By that time the anxieties of the 1960s had ripened into a sense of crisis, a condition with which the genial Callaghan and his disputatious party were poorly equipped to deal.

The decade of the 1970s was a time of economic turbulence throughout the industrialized world, aggravated by large increases in the price of oil in 1973 and 1979. Great masses of capital flowed through the emerging world economy as multinational companies transferred huge investments and cash balances from one place to another. Vast sums of Arab money generated by high oil prices flitted through the international money markets.

The British economy was especially hard hit. Inflation remained higher than in most industrial countries. Unemployment rose to over a million, and the pound fell to record lows on foreign exchanges.

The other members of the European Economic Community were facing similar problems. They agreed that the primary consideration in economic policy must be to control inflation. In 1978, the EEC established the Exchange Rate Mechanism (ERM), which required the member countries to adopt interest rates that would keep their currencies in a close relationship with the strong German mark.

The Callaghan government refused to join the ERM. Labour opposed external control of British monetary policy, for it would end Labour's vision of a socialist economy.

Nevertheless, the Callaghan ministry was forced to adopt tight money policies by the International Monetary Fund in return for a loan to support the international value of the pound. Callaghan had no choice but to increase taxation, cut spending and borrowing, curtail the availability of credit, raise interest rates, and sell some shares in British Petroleum, now becoming valuable due to North Sea oil.

As inflation soared to an average annual rate of 15 percent, workers' wage demands rose proportionately. Desperately Callaghan attempted to stabilize the economy by imposing wage controls, despite the assumption of the "social contract" that organized labor would itself maintain restraint. At first the Trades Union Congress (TUC) declared its support, but it was unable to check the pay demands of its member unions. In 1978, the Labour Party conference rejected all restraints on pay. The Callaghan ministry had lost control of the economy and a free-for-all resulted.

With no good way to fight back, managements agreed to wage demands that they passed on to consumers in higher prices, thus contributing to more inflation, which led to more demands for higher pay. When the end of the line was reached, factories shut down, and in 1977 unemployment mounted to 1.4 million. Labour's claim to a superior capacity to maintain industrial peace was shattered.

Although the Labour government was led by moderates like Callaghan, Labour's left wing had seized control of the party and forced Callaghan to pursue its agenda. Labour's commitment to socialism was extended by nationalizing the bankrupt automaker, British Leyland, and the aircraft and shipbuilding industries. Other legislation in harmony with Labour's left wing would remove from the National Health Service all doctors and hospitals engaging in private medicine. Legislation was passed to require state-supported schools to become comprehensive and to end the hated eleven-plus examination.

For some time, immigration—and race relations—had been a political issue. Both parties had struggled to reduce racial tensions by limiting immigration and passing legislation to prevent racial discrimination. The comfortable middle classes in their all-white suburbs could deplore racism, but poor people in run-down parts of major cities found their neighborhoods dramatically changed by immigrants, who were clearly identifiable by race.

Margaret Thatcher made clear her firm opposition to racial discrimination against people who had already settled in Britain, but she also took a strong stand against further immigration from the nonwhite Commonwealth countries. In a television interview she stated: "People are really rather afraid that this country might be rather swamped by people with a different culture. We do have to hold out the prospect of an end to immigration except, of course, for compassionate cases." Almost immediately the Conservatives shot up 10 percent in the polls.

The immigration issue was intensified by the rise of a nationalist organization called the National Front. The National Front was ostentatiously patriotic and strongly anticommunist. It opposed British membership in the EEC and favored capital punishment and a crackdown on crime. Above all, it was openly racist and opposed to nonwhite immigration, which it claimed took jobs away from true-born Englishmen. It took its cause to the streets, winning attention by ostentatious marches that usually led to violent confrontations. The National Front showed growing strength among white voters in East London and in other towns where immigrants had settled in large numbers.

Nevertheless, all parties came together on the need to reduce tensions with policies that would reduce racial prejudice. In 1976, the Race Relations Act widened the definition of discrimination and established the

Commission for Racial Equality to investigate complaints and support local authorities in enforcing the law on racial matters.

Devolution

Callaghan's problems were compounded by dissidence in "the Celtic fringe." The United Kingdom is comprised of four main nationalities: the English, the Welsh, the Scots, and the Irish of Northern Ireland. The English have long been dominant, politically and economically, and the English language is used throughout the country. Nevertheless, the smaller nationalities have preserved some of their traditional culture, and as Britain floundered in the 1970s, they began to look to their past to imagine a different future for themselves.

In the middle 1970s, nationalist movements arose in Scotland and Wales seeking "devolution," meaning delegation of some powers of the central government to elected assemblies established for those regions. Devolution was weak in Wales, for Welsh nationalism centered on a language that few spoke and the poverty of Wales made the notion of a separate political structure impractical.

Scotland was different. Scottish nationalism was strengthened by a long national history, separate administrative, legal, educational, and religious institutions, and a national culture that included such distinctive elements as kilts and bagpipes. Furthermore, Scotland's economic prospects looked good with the development of off-shore oil and natural gas, most of which was landed on the Scottish coast.

In both places political parties emerged to agitate for devolution. In the election of 1974, the Scottish Nationalist Party won seven seats and 30 percent of the Scottish vote. Always the opportunist, Harold Wilson came out in favor of devolution, although the left wing of his party saw devolution as a threat to a socialist economy and a reversion to the loyalties of the preindustrial age.

The Conservative Party was the party of the Union. Mrs. Thatcher was a strong Unionist but her party was divided on the issue. A major problem was that the devolved areas would be represented in both the Parliament of the United Kingdom and their own assemblies, which, to the English, seemed palpably unfair. Opinion in the Conservative Party began to solidify against devolution and Thatcher decided to oppose Labour's devolution plan.

As Callaghan's problems mounted, he sought to strengthen his position in Parliament by making an alliance with the Liberals, agreeing at their insistence to referenda in Scotland and Wales on devolution, a proposal that also assured him the support of the Scottish and Welsh Nationalist Parties. Labour backbenchers opposed to devolution countered by amending the bill to require that devolution be supported by 40 percent of those eligible to vote.

In Scotland, the referendum passed by a slim majority, but a low turnout meant that those in favor were well below the required 40 percent of the total electorate. The majority of the voters in Wales were opposed. The Scottish Nationalist Party was furious and abandoned its support of the Callaghan ministry.

The Fall of Callaghan and Labour

Margaret Thatcher's rise to power was as much a result of Labour's failures as her own leadership and persuasiveness. In the disastrous winter of 1978–1979, the British economy ground to a virtual halt. The effects of the world depression were aggravated by strikes, often accompanied by mass picketing that disrupted normal activities. Unemployment was at 1.3 million workers. There was growing recognition that inflation was at the root of many of these problems.

Buffeted by inflation, many workers felt they had no choice but to fight the guidelines of their own Labour government. The remnants of the social contract gave way in November 1978, when the Ford Motor Company ended a nine-week strike by giving its workers pay raises of 16 percent. Truck drivers called a national strike demanding similar raises. British Rail was afflicted with numerous one-day strikes. Britain suffered severely from the shutdown of road transport, aggravated by secondary picketing of factories and docks.

The winter was unusually cold, and for the first time since 1963 the entire United Kingdom was covered with snow, disrupting transportation and communications. As strikes spread, violent mass picketing took place in many parts of the country. Britain seemed to be falling apart.

The ultimate disaster of the "winter of discontent" came when more than a million public employees, hard-hit by inflation, went on strike. Now equipped with television sets, the British public was appalled by scenes of garbage piling up in the streets, sick people (including children) turned away from hospitals, schools closed, and the dead unburied. The tabloid newspapers printed screaming headlines: "Pickets Rule," "No Mercy." It was a political and moral defeat from which the Labour Party could not recover.

Callaghan knew that the tide had turned against him and the policies of the Labour Party. Opinion polls showed a strong swing against Labour. Callaghan realized that anything his government attempted to do would be resisted by his own party and would not be credible, either to the international financiers, who held Britain's fate in their hands, or to the British people.

Mrs. Thatcher as leader of the opposition called for limitations on picketing, secret ballots before calling strikes, and no-strike agreements with workers in vital services. "There will be no solution to our difficulties," she declared, "which does not include some restriction on the powers of the unions."

In March 1979, the Scottish Nationalists vented their frustration by moving a vote of No Confidence, and Mrs. Thatcher leaped into the fray. On the night of the vote, even the catering staff in the Houses of Parliament was on strike, so that the members had to provide their own meals. Mrs. Thatcher feared that some of her Conservatives might wander off to nearby restaurants and miss the crucial division. The smaller parties would be crucial in the final decision.

It was a tense moment as the members filed through the lobbies to register their votes. The Conservatives, facing the prospect of a return to power, held fast behind their leader. The Liberals, the Scottish Nationalist Party, and most of the Ulster Unionists voted against the government. When the tally was announced the opposition motion had won, 311–310.

The five-year maximum between elections was coming to an end, and Callaghan was forced to go to the country at the worst possible time. Parliament was dissolved in April and an election was called for May.

Polls showed that Margaret Thatcher was well behind the likable Jim Callaghan in personal popularity. She won because the Labour government and the Labour Party had been discredited while she offered new leadership and a fresh start.

In her campaign speeches, Mrs. Thatcher advocated a strong foreign policy and increased defense spending, reduction of the income tax to encourage investment, cuts in public spending and strict limits on public-sector pay, and vigorous efforts to control inflation. She was committed to free enterprise, a competitive market economy, and restricting the powers of the unions. She presented Labour as the party of inflation, wage controls, and strikes. She promised that Labour's legislation requiring local authorities to establish comprehensive schools would be repealed. Foreign policy was not an issue, and both parties called for reduction of Britain's payments to the European Economic Community.

Mrs. Thatcher reiterated her familiar appeals to personal responsibility instead of reliance on the state. She made clear her commitment to Victorian middle-class values: strong families, home ownership, personal savings, educational opportunities, law and order.

As the campaigns unfolded it became clear that the key issue was trade union power, which most of the British public felt had become too great. Mrs. Thatcher stated emphatically her determination to confront the problem by establishing "a fair balance between the rights and duties of the trade union movement." She promised legislation to limit trade union privileges, including restrictions on picketing and strikes in essential services.

Within the Conservative Party, there was great anxiety at provoking a confrontation with the unions that might result in the kind of disastrous defeat inflicted on Sir Edward Heath in 1974. Immune to such fears, Mrs. Thatcher charged ahead.

Another issue was immigration. The National Front decided to make a major effort, fielding over three hundred candidates and claiming access to the free party-political broadcasts on radio and television. Opponents of the National Front mobilized large demonstrations against it. In a working class area of south London, a violent clash took place, with three hundred people arrested and one person killed. Firm police control of parades prevented most of the confrontations from which the National Front derived much of its publicity.

The major change in voting patterns was a massive swing of skilled workers, formerly the core of the Labour Party, to the Conservatives. As they prospered, they had developed middle class lifestyles and aspirations. They had had enough of high taxation, inflation, and wage controls. They looked for leadership that would restore a sense of national unity and bring order to the workplace and the streets. They had been frightened by the radicals of the Labour Party and the industrial disruptions of the past winter.

With 44 percent of the popular vote in a 76 percent turnout, the Conservatives won a majority of forty-three seats over all other parties combined. Labour received 37 percent of the vote and the Liberals 14 percent, with the remainder going to candidates from the Scottish, Welsh, and Northern Ireland parties. Knowing that he was going to lose, Callaghan campaigned with dignity. He continues to enjoy the respect of his countrymen, now as a member of the House of Lords.

The National Front collapsed, winning less than 1 percent of the vote. It was apparent that many of its supporters had voted Conservative, largely on the basis of Mrs. Thatcher's strong stand on immigration.

The Conservative victory was by no means the result of Margaret Thatcher's personal popularity. In fashionable circles (including some Conservatives), she had the reputation of a strident, right-wing ideologue. The prospect of a woman prime minister was unwelcome to many. Her individualistic, free market principles were not widely held.

Mrs. Thatcher won because Britain was in a crisis with which the Callaghan government and the Labour Party seemed unable to cope. At that moment Margaret Thatcher stepped forward to display leadership, courage, and conviction, qualities to which the British people usually respond. For the next eleven years, those personal qualities made her one of Britain's great prime ministers.

2

The Beginnings of Thatcherism, 1979 to 1983

The Prime Minister

Margaret Thatcher came to power at a time of national breakdown that had resulted in widespread distress. She shared the public sense of crisis, and her election in 1979 was a result of her evident determination to do something about it.

Mrs. Thatcher saw herself as an agent of change—a "conviction politician" with no interest in trying to revive the failed consensus of the past. She advocated a diminished role for government, fiscal responsibility, free enterprise in a market-driven economy, reduction of the powers of the unions, tight management of the welfare state, tough control of crime and public disorders, and sturdy British patriotism. The piecemeal, hit-and-miss steps by which her reforms were implemented use pragmatic adjustment to the realities of leadership in a democracy, but did not change the underlying consistency of her purpose.

Several weeks were required before the Thatchers could move into No. 10 Downing Street. When Margaret and Denis occupied the small prime minister's flat at the top of the building, she was back where she came from—living over the shop!

Their daily life was simple. As much as possible she continued a practice of their earlier years, having breakfast together. Beyond that, her hours were irregular and she made a meal or a snack whenever time permitted. Like many busy people, there were times when she resorted to

31

the freezer and the microwave. She slept about four hours per night. Her time and energy were devoted to her work.

Mrs. Thatcher usually met with the queen once a week to discuss government business. Queen Elizabeth is intelligent, conscientious, and experienced, having met in her royal capacity with seven prime ministers before Mrs. Thatcher. Although these meetings are strictly private, it is said that Mrs. Thatcher and the queen did not get along well. A cartoon of the time showed Mrs. Thatcher saying to the queen: "You look after the weddings, and I'll look after the government."

When Margaret Thatcher began her ministry she had to establish herself in the eyes of her Cabinet, the Conservative Party, and the British public. She had to find Conservatives who shared her view that Britain needed a radical change of direction—not only from the policies of Labour, which were discredited by "the winter of discontent," but also from the "One Nation" Toryism of the past.

Initially, political realities dictated that she choose ministers who carried weight in the Conservative Party. Among these were Sir Geoffrey Howe, chancellor of the Exchequer, and Lord Carrington, foreign secretary. William Whitelaw, the home secretary, had not been politically close to Mrs. Thatcher, but he was noted as a conciliator and as such he became a valued member of her team.

During the years of opposition, Sir Keith Joseph had been the principal influence in defining Mrs. Thatcher's economic views. He was made minister for industry. Sir Edward Heath was passed over for foreign secretary, the post that he really wanted. He rejected her offer of ambassador to the United States.

Cabinet meetings were often stormy, as Mrs. Thatcher sought to impose her views on a Cabinet that was divided and often skeptical. She was opinionated and outspoken, and at times she revealed a shrewish nature as she shouted down those who disagreed with her. Unwilling to reply in kind to a woman, some of the men gave up and concentrated on their own departments. In 1981, she reshuffled her Cabinet, to bring it more in line with her ideas.

As an outsider in her own party, her support among Conservative members of Parliament was shaky. She gave considerable attention to the Conservative backbenchers, who had made her the party leader. She knew the importance of their good will. In her earlier years she was a frequent visitor to the Commons' tea room.

Getting Going

The Thatcher ministry took office at a time of worldwide inflation and recession, aggravated by sky-high oil prices resulting from the overthrow of the shah and the Islamic Revolution in Iran. Inflation peaked in 1980 at 18 percent, and the Gross National Product fell. Unemployment was at 1.3 million in 1979.

Mrs. Thatcher's immediate goal was to reduce inflation, which in her opinion discouraged business investment, led to short-term speculation and profiteering, and penalized saving. In that objective she was supported by public opinion; most people were not unemployed and were shocked by runaway inflation.

Her answer to inflation was to keep a tight rein on public spending, central and local, and to use high interest rates to reduce business and consumer borrowing. Stringent efforts were made to keep money growth within narrow limits. Interest rates were already at 14 percent when she took office. In November 1979 they were raised to 17 percent and remained at or near that level for the next year.

Mrs. Thatcher rejected the idea that inflation could be checked by controls on prices or wages. She made no effort to restore full employment by subsidizing failing industries. These she repudiated as the discredited policies of Labour. If the state managed its own finances properly, she believed, the market would make the necessary adjustments in prices, wages, and employment.

In the first three years the economic crisis overwhelmed all other concerns. Sir Geoffrey Howe, chancellor of the Exchequer, was a sensible, hard-working lawyer long identified with free market policies. Howe's 1979 budget was the first installment of Thatcherism. Income tax was sharply reduced: the base rate fell from 33 percent to 30 percent, and the top rate was cut from 83 percent to 60 percent. Although tax cuts poured more money into an already inflated economy, in Thatcherite ideology, this policy, so advantageous to the wealthy, would benefit the economy by encouraging entrepreneurship and investment.

To compensate for the revenue lost by the income tax cuts, the burden on consumers was increased. The value added tax (a kind of sales tax) and the gasoline tax were raised, as were national insurance contributions. The nationalized utilities were permitted to increase their artificially low prices, which cut government spending for subsidies and was a further addition to the cost of living. In the next year, consumer prices, to most people the most important economic indicator, rose by 18 percent.

Heavy cuts in public spending were announced in all branches of government except the police, defense, and the National Health Service. Tight cash limits were imposed on all departments. Cuts fell heavily on the civil service and local governments, where pay increases were kept well below the rate of inflation. Subsidies to housing and education were reduced, as were subsidies to the nationalized industries, leading to more unemployment. Pensions and other social security payments, however, were given increases in line with inflation.

At first the fiscal and monetary policies of the Thatcher ministry seemed to have aggravated the twin problems of inflation and recession. High interest rates choked off domestic investment and sucked in "hot money" from abroad, creating a strong pound that damaged exports. Economic output in the next two years fell by 3 percent. By 1983 unemployment had risen to three million, with few prospects for new jobs to replace those irretrievably lost. With the tax cuts and the social costs of the recession, the deficit increased by 30 percent in the first year of Thatcherite finance.

Despite double-digit inflation, Mrs. Thatcher rejected calls for price and wage controls, clinging firmly to her belief that only the market could resolve the problem in a manner that would last. From 1979 to 1981, the retail price index rose an average of 14 percent annually. Wage inflation kept pace: the unions got wage increases averaging 16 percent in 1979 and 20 percent in 1980. People with jobs were holding their own; the blow fell heaviest on people living on fixed incomes and the unemployed.

The early policies of the Thatcher ministry were devastating to British business. Large private companies and the nationalized industries showed heavy losses. By November 1982, industrial output had fallen to the lowest level since 1965. Employment in manufacturing dropped from seven million in 1980 to about five million in 1990, most of that drop coming in the first three years of the Thatcher ministry. Many of Britain's languishing industries in the Midlands and the North never did recover, and many who lost their jobs in the shakeout never regained employment.

After this disastrous beginning, Mrs. Thatcher realized the contradiction between cutting taxes and fighting inflation. The decision was made that the fight against inflation must take precedence over tax cuts intended to stimulate economic growth. Inflation could be checked only by reducing public borrowing, and the way to do that was to raise income taxes and cut spending further. Much as she regretted giving up her premature tax cuts, Mrs. Thatcher had the courage to raise taxes in a recession, an unorthodox policy that eventually succeeded.

Accordingly, Sir Geoffrey Howe's budget for 1981 included increases in the income tax (actually not adjusting for inflation, then running at about 18 percent), an increase in national insurance contributions, and a wide variety of new consumption taxes and other charges. The main burden of these increases fell on people earning below the national average; their taxes and national insurance contributions were greater than in 1979.

Since Margaret Thatcher rejected price and wage controls, the public sector was the only place she could act to reduce inflationary forces. Public employees received raises below the rate of inflation, although higher than Thatcher wanted. The nationalized industries, which had been heavily subsidized by the Labour government to save jobs, were informed that subsidies from the government would be reduced. National Health Service charges were increased. Higher education took severe cuts, and university expansion was stopped in its tracks.

As part of the battle against inflation, Thatcher was determined to cut the spending of local governments, which received about 60 percent of their financial resources from the Treasury. Investment by central government and local authorities in public facilities was cut by 40 percent between 1979 and 1982, most of that taken from public housing. Council house rents were increased to reduce local subsidies. Despite mounting needs, the capacity of local governments to respond to the twin pressures of inflation and recession was crippled.

The Local Government Act (1980) strengthened central control by fixing the spending of each unit of local government at the level it needed to maintain uniform national services. Defying the government, the Labour controlled Greater London Council adopted a "municipal socialist budget," an example followed by the Inner London Education Authority and the councils of the metropolitan counties. They increased the rates, a step that fell heavily on owners of businesses and homes, most of whom were Conservatives. In 1983, the government responded with the Rates Act, which authorized capping of the rates.

In 1980, local authorities were no longer required to provide school meals. "Thatcher, the milk snatcher" had won in principle, although most schools continued milk and meals for low-income pupils.

Eventually tight money and unemployment brought inflation down. In 1982 the inflation rate began dropping and reached 4.5 percent in 1983. For the next five years inflation remained around 5 percent, a level that undergirded a period of strong economic growth.

"Fortune favors the brave," said the Roman statesman, and in one respect Margaret Thatcher had Fortuna on her side. By 1979, the discovery of large amounts of recoverable oil in the North Sea had made Britain an important oil producer. High oil prices provided additional financial resources that eliminated the balance of payments problem, strengthened the pound, enabled the government to maintain unemployment benefits, and eased some of the strains of the recession. By 1981, Britain had become a net exporter of oil.

Oil revenues and the strong pound made possible a free market step of the greatest consequence: abolition of the exchange controls that had been in place since World War II. Sterling was freed to become a world currency again, and British investors could seek the best possible returns anywhere in the world. The role of London as a financial center was enhanced, and the growth of overseas investments made Britain an integral part of the emerging world economy.

During this period of inflation and unemployment, the safety net held. Although Mrs. Thatcher gained a reputation for hostility to social programs, she continued the main commitments to social security, the National Health Service, and schools. Training programs for young people were introduced, to assist them in preparing for the changing world of work. In some cases the training was a valuable investment in the future; in others the programs may have done little more than keep restless youth off the streets, in itself an accomplishment of some social utility.

One factor in Margaret Thatcher's electoral victory was her commitment to a reduction of immigration. An English nationalist to the core, she shared the uneasiness of many of her countrymen at pockets of poorly assimilated immigrants in major cities and the possible effects of unchecked immigration on the national character. The problem was to prepare legislation that was undeniably racist without appearing to be racist.

The solution adopted was a new definition of British citizenship that sloughed off the long-standing claims of Commonwealth residents. The Nationality Act of 1981, for the first time, defined British citizenship as something other than being a subject of the queen. Full British citizenship went to people who resided in the United Kingdom or were closely related to citizens. The eligibility of Commonwealth immigrants for citizenship was narrowly restricted.

The Nationality Bill had considerable support in both parties: the Conservatives were strong nationalists, and Labour wanted to protect jobs and keep wages up. The bill was strongly opposed by immigrant groups and the churches. It faced strong opposition in the House of Lords, where the archbishop of Canterbury was a prominent opponent. Passage of the Nationality Act terminated the right of millions of former imperial subjects to settle in Britain. Essentially, the question of Commonwealth immigration was settled. Margaret Thatcher had fulfilled her campaign promise.

By 1982, the economy was in a position to revive, but a heavy price had been paid in unemployment and bankruptcies. Most of the burden had been borne by industrial workers, retired people, and the poor. Inflation and spending restraints had damaged public services, both national and local. Margaret Thatcher's popularity had reached a low point. A poll showed that only 25 percent of the British people were satisfied with her performance as prime minister, and only 18 percent were satisfied with the Conservative government.

The Trade Unions

The first three years of the Thatcher ministry were tormented by strikes. In 1979, Britain had its worst year ever, with 4.5 million workers on strike at one time or another and almost thirty million workdays lost due to strikes. Mrs. Thatcher's policy was to keep the government out of private-sector strikes, allowing the workers to face the loss of their jobs if they priced their employer out of the market.

She believed that workers were more concerned with preserving their jobs than in engaging in political and industrial confrontations. "Millions of British workers," she said in 1979, "go in fear of union power." Polls showed that she was right: up to 80 percent of workers favored the government's proposals to reform and limit the unions.

The major problem was strikes in the nationalized industries, which had been sheltered by Labour from market competition. Almost immediately the Thatcher government was challenged by the leadership of the National Union of Mineworkers (NUM). Substantial sums had been invested in improving the best mines, which could produce all the coal that Britain needed, and many less-efficient pits faced closure. Mrs. Thatcher was not prepared for the kind of confrontation that had destroyed the Heath ministry. The "hit list" of mines to be closed was withdrawn, and the National Coal Board was given an additional subsidy.

However, she realized that a confrontation with the miners was likely to take place eventually, and she did not want to be caught unprepared, as Heath had been. When she investigated she found that neither the Coal Board nor the main users of coal had stockpiled coal at the plants where it would be needed. She insisted that preparations be made to make it possible to withstand a coal strike in the future.

In 1982, the moderate president of the NUM retired and was succeeded by Arthur Scargill, a militant firebrand who was a bitter enemy of the National Coal Board. Scargill immediately demanded a 31 percent pay raise. The rules of the NUM required a ballot prior to calling a strike.

Scargill campaigned hard for a "Yes" vote, but the miners, fearful of losing their jobs, voted 61 percent against. Foiled, Scargill bided his time and waited for a better opportunity.

The most damaging strike was at British Steel. In 1980 the steelworkers went on strike for higher wages. In addition to picketing British Steel plants, pickets were also posted at private steel companies that were trying to remain open. Attempts were made to block imports of steel, although some steel was getting through.

Unlike users of coal, users of steel had accumulated large stocks in anticipation of the strike. One way or another, the major steel users, such as the auto industry, were able to get the steel they needed. Once again Mrs. Thatcher avoided an all-out confrontation with a major nationalized industry. After three months, the strike was settled with a compromise. The government agreed to an 11 percent raise in exchange for a productivity agreement that closed some old, inefficient plants.

With British Steel back in production, it was necessary to take the steps needed to make it profitable in the future. Mrs. Thatcher brought in Ian MacGregor, a toughminded American manager (born in Scotland) to lead the corporation. MacGregor began cutting jobs and closing inefficient plants. At that point, Mrs. Thatcher was willing to provide additional investment capital for British Steel, which changed from being the least efficient producer in Europe to one of the best.

Margaret Thatcher faced another test at the nationalized auto manufacturer, British Leyland (BL). From a market share of 33 percent in 1974, BL cars had fallen to 20 percent in 1979. The unions at BL were notoriously disruptive, and under Labour governments they had usually gotten their way. The company had steadily lost market share to private competitors like Ford, whose models were more attractive and costs were lower. It was a sad day for car lovers in 1980 when BL ended production of the MG sports car.

In 1980, a strike for higher wages was threatened at BL. In this instance, management simply announced that it would begin paying the wages it had proposed—take it or leave it!—and urged the workers to show up. At a time of high unemployment, almost all employees reported for work, and the strike did not take place. When a similar crisis arose in 1981, the workers voted to accept BL's offer rather than face closure of the plants.

BL was rewarded with an infusion of cash from the government, despite Mrs. Thatcher's general principle that nationalized industries must stand or fall on their own merits. The political and social consequences of shutting down BL were too much to accept. People have strong emotional feelings about cars, and the British public wanted to preserve the last large British carmaker.

Workers in the public sector had been left behind by galloping inflation. In 1981, the civil service unions responded with a series of strikes that interrupted the Inland Revenue (the British equivalent of the IRS), issuance of passports and driver's licenses, air traffic controllers, and other essential public services. Eventually they settled for the government's offer of 7.5 percent. The general public had shown little sympathy for the civil servants, with their secure jobs and comfortable pensions.

More serious was a nationwide strike in 1982 at the National Health Service, whose many low-paid workers had suffered severely from inflation. Unwilling to leave the British people totally without health care, the union called for "rolling disruptions" from one hospital to another. After eight months, the Health Service workers, making little headway with the government and seeing the backlog of patients mounting, gave in and accepted a modest increase. The Thatcher ministry had won a victory, but it was not a victory to be proud of.

Unlike Sir Edward Heath, Margaret Thatcher moved cautiously to limit the powers of the unions. Her step-by-step approach seemed reasonable to the unions, compared to what they had been led to expect, nor did they think that her government would last long enough to accomplish its purpose. They did not realize what was happening to them until it was too late.

The Employment Act of 1980 required 80 percent approval to establish a closed shop, restricted sympathy strikes, and limited picketing to the worker's place of employment. The Employment Act of 1982 provided that unions engaging in illegal labor practices could be sued for civil damages and fined or held in contempt of court. The problem of wildcat strikes and other shop-floor disruptions was dealt with by making the national unions responsible for local violations of the law or the labor contract.

The acts of 1980 and 1982 brought into labor relations a new element—the judges, a group typically unsympathetic to the unions. By offering a remedy in the civil courts, strikes would be depoliticized, since government intervention would be replaced by complaints brought by employers, except where violence erupted, in which case the police and the criminal justice system would become involved.

The newspaper business had some of the most powerful and combative unions, for the printers were determined to preserve the obsolete methods and work rules that were threatened by new technology. For more than a year, the *Times* and the *Sunday Times*, the most prestigious British newspapers, had been shut down due to conflict between the owners and the employees concerning this matter.

Although a compromise settlement was reached in 1981, the owners decided to sell out to Rupert Murdoch, the Australian tycoon, who was the owner of two tabloid newspapers, the *Sun* and the *News of the World*. Much as they disliked Murdoch and his insistence on efficient labor practices, the unions decided to come to terms with him to save their jobs. Murdoch, however, had more tricks up his sleeve, which were revealed in due time.

The Conservative victory in 1979 marked the beginning of the end for the political influence of organized labor, tied as it was to the Labour Party. At first the Trades Union Congress (TUC) was unconvinced that the Thatcher government meant what it said about taming the unions. As unemployment grew, the TUC assumed that a crisis of such dimensions would require the government to change its policies. When Margaret Thatcher held to her course, it became clear that the government had abandoned the historic goal of full employment. A hostile government, an unsympathetic public, and mass unemployment brought to an end the political and economic power of organized labor.

Political Parties

The Thatcher ministry got off to a turbulent start, and the Cabinet and House of Commons were filled with contention and acrimony. Led by Sir Edward Heath, some of the former leaders of the Conservative Party criticized her financial and economic policies, which they declared were doctrinaire and disruptive. They belonged to the "One Nation" Conservative tradition of Disraeli and Macmillan, but their moderate, pragmatic approach was swept aside by the ideologically driven policies of Thatcherism.

By 1981, the strain of the Thatcherite economic policy was beginning to show. Sir Edward Heath had consistently attacked the Thatcher-Howe budgets, complaining that the cost of unemployment was far greater than the benefits of fighting inflation. In 1980, the backbench 1922 Committee had supported the government's policy, but by 1981 even the backbenchers were calling for a change.

Mrs. Thatcher insisted that the worst was over. Britain, she said, is like a patient "who for a time is suffering from both the illness and the medicine." When the suggestion was made that it was time for a "U-Turn" like Sir Edward Heath's in 1972 she replied: "You turn if you like. The lady's not for turning."

Defeat in the election of 1979 brought a dramatic change in the Labour Party. In 1980, James Callaghan retired from the party leadership. He was succeeded by Michael Foot, a scholarly intellectual lacking leadership ability or experience in the higher offices of government. Bitter differences broke out between the Labour MPs who had supported Callaghan's moderate policies and the left wingers, who felt that Callaghan had sacrificed the principles of the Labour Party to the forces of international capitalism. Usually identified with the left, it was Foot's task to hold his contentious party together.

Within the Labour Party, the left wing was now dominant and in a position to assert its policies: withdrawal from NATO and the European Economic Community, unilateral nuclear disarmament, price controls, increased public expenditure to restore full employment, renationalization of certain industries, abolition of the House of Lords, and an end to private education and medicine. These policies had little support among the British people and contributed to the precipitous decline of the Labour Party.

In 1981, the Labour Party broke wide open. Four moderate leaders decided to leave the party to establish the Social Democratic Party, a party with a strong agenda of social reform but not dominated by the unions. Led by Roy Jenkins, one of Labour's most distinguished and experienced members, they argued that Britain needed a party of moderate reform that would strike a balance between Thatcherism and socialism. Public opinion polls seemed to support that idea.

The rebels were joined by more than twenty Labour MPs. A major reason for their defections was the opposition of Michael Foot and Labour's left wing to membership in the European Economic Community. The Social Democrats advocated a mixed economy with extensive public investment, decentralization of government, an improved welfare state, a firm commitment to Europe, support of NATO, and efforts for multilateral disarmament. With four leaders who were experienced and well regarded, the Social Democratic Party had instant credibility. The media, with their incessant search for novelty, gave extensive attention to the new party, which hired a public relations firm to help the process along.

In June, the Social Democrats allied with the Liberal Party led by David Steel to form a centrist force that would be attractive to moderate voters who rejected both Thatcherism and socialism. Jenkins became the leader of the SDP–Liberal Alliance in the House of Commons and the country, with Steel in a subordinate role. Their stated purpose was to "break the mould of dogma and class conflict" that characterized the two major parties.

At first the SDP–Liberal Alliance achieved remarkable success, reaching 44 percent in the opinion polls in the fall of 1981, the Conservatives and Labour sinking to 27 percent each. Despite the blaze of publicity, support for the SDP–Liberal Alliance was shallow and based mainly on dissatisfaction with the two major parties. As the Thatcher government took hold the Alliance began to slip, and by April 1982, the three parties were virtually even at 33 percent in the polls.

During those grim days of inflation, recession, and unemployment, the monarchy provided a bright spot. In July 1981, His Royal Highness, Charles, Prince of Wales and heir to the throne, was married to Lady Diana Spencer. The wedding took place in St. Paul's cathedral with great pomp and ceremony and was televised throughout the world. On that grand occasion, the magic of the British monarchy was seen at its most bewitching. The next year the birth of a son seemed to secure the future of the dynasty.

In July 1986, the royal family added Miss Sarah Ferguson, who was married to Prince Andrew, Duke of York, the Queen's second son. Few anticipated the unhappy outcomes of these royal marriages.

Privatization

Margaret Thatcher was devoted to the principles of free enterprise, competition, and the market economy. In her view, public ownership of major industries meant that they became politicized: without the test of the free market, they became inefficient and uncompetitive; for political reasons, they were not permitted to fail and required subsidies to preserve jobs and votes. Selling off the nationalized industries was a logical outcome of Thatcherism, but it began tentatively, almost as an afterthought.

The first privatizations were of industries that did not have strong political constituencies and were not widely known to the public. These included the government's shares in British Aerospace (1981), Cable and Wireless (1981), British Oil (1982), British Rail Hotels (1981), and Associated British Ports (1983). The entire National Freight Corporation was sold to its employees. The price of the shares rose so rapidly that opponents of privatization who had not taken up their quota of shares soon regretted their adherence to principle.

The privatizations had the additional advantage that they brought much-needed funds into the Treasury, a consideration that became increasingly important as privatization moved on to larger industries. In 1979–1980 the income from privatizations was £377 million; by 1988–1989 it was more than £6 billion. Harold Macmillan compared privatization to selling off the family jewels to pay current expenses. Apart from any economic merit that privatization might have, it became an important factor in the finances of government.

The Cold War

Margaret Thatcher was a child of the World War II era, and in her early years she had been imbued with the World War II spirit of democracy versus dictatorship. When the war ended and the cold war began, she saw the tensions between the Western democracies and the Soviet Union in the same light.

She recognized the importance of American political leadership, economic strength, and military power as embodied in the North Atlantic Treaty Organization (NATO). She saw the United States as the guarantor of free flowing global trade, so vital to the island kingdom. She held firmly to the idea of a "special relationship" between the United States and Great Britain, with Britain serving as a link between the United States and its allies on the European continent.

Mrs. Thatcher brought a new assertiveness into British foreign policy. Although Britain could not rival the superpowers, she was convinced that Britain could play a significant role in world affairs and should be able to defend herself and her remaining dependencies. Despite the fiscal squeeze, she supported the NATO decision for a five-year program of increased military spending. And she blew the trumpet of British nationalism loud and clear!

Her reforming zeal did not extend to the Foreign and Commonwealth Office or the Ministry of Defence. A review of defense needs was undertaken in 1981, but it had little effect other than a recommendation to reduce the navy, which proved embarrassing the next year when Argentina invaded the Falkland Islands. The five-year NATO buildup was sustained until it ran out in 1985, when military expenditures began to decline.

Mrs. Thatcher was determined that Britain would maintain its own nuclear deterrent. When the Soviet Union began installing medium-range nuclear missiles that could reach targets in Western Europe, NATO decided that it had to be prepared to retaliate in kind. The decision was made to place powerful, accurate American cruise missiles (a medium-range missile) in Germany and Britain.

The new missiles were politically controversial, for a strong antinuclear movement had come into existence that rejected entirely the use of nuclear weapons. In addition to those who opposed nuclear weapons on military and moral grounds, others questioned whether Britain could afford the high cost of being a nuclear power, especially since NATO already had access to powerful American nuclear forces.

Britain's nuclear deterrent was opposed by the Campaign for Nuclear Disarmament (CND). The objective of the organization was to eliminate nuclear weapons throughout the world, and to make Britain the leader of the antinuclear movement by abandoning nuclear weapons without waiting for others. The Labour Party had shown its sympathy with the organization, and many prominent Labour figures were members.

The antinuclear cause was dramatized by large numbers of women who established a "peace camp" at Greenham Common, north of London, where the cruise missiles were to be installed. In April 1983, the CND organized a vast demonstration with participants linking arms from Greenham Common to an ordnance factory fourteen miles away. Although there were gaps in the chain, the demonstration was proclaimed a success.

In 1983, the first cruise missiles arrived at Greenham, despite violent demonstrations at the base. The general public thought otherwise. Polls showed that two-thirds of the British public favored retention of nuclear weapons along with strong conventional forces.

President Ronald Reagan

The inauguration of Ronald Reagan as president of the United States in January 1981, brought a kindred spirit to the White House. Margaret Thatcher was eager to restore "the special relationship" that had faded during the 1960s and 1970s. President Reagan responded favorably, for they had much in common. They shared similar ideas about reducing the role of government, cutting taxes and spending, and firm opposition to Soviet militarism and expansion.

Despite their personal friendship, the Reagan foreign policy was at times embarrassing to Mrs. Thatcher. In 1982 Israel, stung by Palestinian attacks from Lebanese territory, invaded south Lebanon to destroy the settlements of the Palestinians. This invasion provoked an invasion by Syria into northern and eastern Lebanon, and the Lebanese government fell apart.

The Reagan administration, with much fanfare, sent American troops to Lebanon to preserve the unity of that small country. The president called upon America's allies for support in forming a multinational force for this purpose. Mrs. Thatcher assessed the chances for success in this venture as almost nil, but she wished to preserve her relationship with the president. For this reason she sent a small contingent of troops, as did France. The multinational force accomplished nothing, and the American and other troops remained stationary in their positions.

In October 1983, 241 American marines housed in the Beirut airport were killed by a terrorist who drove a truckload of explosives into the building. Shaken by this disaster, Reagan pulled American troops out of Beirut, leaving his allies to deal with the situation. British and French troops were withdrawn the next year and the Lebanon fiasco came to an end.

When the Americans left Lebanon, some American forces were rerouted to attack the small West Indian island of Grenada, which had come under the control of a communist leader. The ostensible reason was to destroy an airfield that the Grenadans were building with Cuban assistance. The Reagan administration claimed that Grenada was becoming a threat to hemispheric security. Some American students on the island were portrayed as potential hostages.

When she got wind of this plan, Mrs. Thatcher endeavored to restrain the Reagan administration. Britain had an important interest, for Grenada was part of the Commonwealth and the queen was the formal head of state. Mrs. Thatcher urged the Reagan administration to hold back until a serious threat (if any) emerged.

Needing a public relations "victory" to offset his fiasco in Beirut, Reagan invaded the tiny island without warning. The United States vetoed a Security Council declaration that the invasion was a violation of international law. A heavily armed American force landed and easily overpowered six hundred Cuban construction workers armed with rifles. Although the Grenadans had no airpower, the U. S. Air Force was brought into the fray, and American "precision bombing" struck a hospital killing fifty patients.

The British public viewed this made-for-TV war as an irresponsible exercise of superpower might, and the British press expressed its resentment that a part of the Commonwealth had been attacked without obtaining British consent. Margaret Thatcher was embarrassed that her efforts to maintain a "special relationship" with President Reagan had been ignored.

The European Community

While showing her determination to maintain good relations with the United States, Margaret Thatcher displayed readiness for confrontation with the European Community (EC). She was determined to challenge the domination of the European Council of Ministers by France and Germany, and to resist the bureaucratic regulations of the European Commission in Brussels. She was accused of "handbagging" at ministerial meetings: making her point by whacking those vexatious foreigners with her handbag.

"The Iron Lady" insisted that the terms negotiated by Sir Edward Heath for admission to the EC were inordinately expensive. In her first meeting with the European Council, she made it clear that the existing situation could not continue. In 1980, the EC leaders recognized the justice of her claim, and the British contribution was substantially reduced. Mrs. Thatcher was satisfied, and remarked: "We are trying to be good Europeans."

At the root of Britain's continuing problems with the European Community was a difference of opinion concerning its purpose and character. Breaking down national borders within the Community had led to remarkable economic growth, but in the process the Community had developed a complex regulatory system managed by a large bureaucracy in Brussels. Within the Community, the system worked to regulate competition among members and protect established interests. In relation to other countries, the Community was protectionist, especially in respect of agriculture.

With her belief in free enterprise and market competition, Mrs. Thatcher's economic philosophy ran counter to that of the European Community. Britain was a country with important Atlantic and global interests. The EC had adopted tariffs and other obstacles to imports from nonmembers, which threatened Britain's economic ties with other parts of the world. When Thatcher complained to President Mitterand of France that the Community was protectionist he replied: "That was the point of it."

Economic integration required predictable exchange rates among the member states. To achieve this objective the Community had established the Exchange Rate Mechanism (ERM), which required each member of the EC to follow policies that would keep its currency in a stable relationship with the others. Mrs. Thatcher flatly refused to join the ERM. She believed in free markets, including free exchange rates among national currencies. The strongest currency in the ERM was the West German mark, and Margaret Thatcher, nationalist that she was, did not want the British currency tied to West Germany.

The European Community had also developed a strong movement toward political unity, which Margaret Thatcher staunchly resisted. She was determined to protect British sovereignty, especially in respect of foreign policy, defense, and the national currency. Although Britain was unquestionably part of Europe, for four centuries the British people had also looked outward and found a destiny overseas. Her efforts to push the EC in a direction more congenial to Britain were unsuccessful. Under Mrs. Thatcher, Britain was always the misfit in the EC.

Britain cooperated with the Community in one respect—the establishment of a European Parliament, directly elected by the voters in each member country. The United Kingdom has seventy-eight members. Concerned as she was with preserving national sovereignty, Thatcher was determined that it would be nothing more than a "talk shop," and such it has remained, albeit an expensive one.

The Falklands War

Just as Mrs. Thatcher's popularity had reached its lowest point, she was given a new lease on her political life by General Leopoldo Galtieri, the president of Argentina, whose regime was noted for its disdain for human rights and the "disappearances" of thousands of its people. In April 1982, the Argentines invaded the Falkland Islands, a barren, windswept archipelago located off the southeastern coast of Argentina. The claims of Britain and Argentina to the islands were lost in obscurity and the islands had little economic value, but there could be no question that the eighteen hundred people who lived there were British and had no desire to be ruled by General Galtieri.

Negotiations concerning the fate of the islands had been taking place since 1965 and continued right up to the day of the invasion, but Britain felt no sense of urgency about the matter. Despite reports of unusual Argentine military activity, the Foreign Office and the British public were totally surprised when reports arrived that Argentine naval and ground forces had arrived at Port Stanley, the only city of the Falklands, and were landing troops.

Mrs. Thatcher reacted like a lioness whose cubs were threatened. A hastily improvised armada was sent on a fifty-day voyage to the rescue. There were forty-four warships and ten thousand ground troops. The *Queen Elizabeth II* and other cruise ships were requisitioned as troop ships. The queen's second son, Prince Andrew, was a helicopter pilot on one of the aircraft carriers and went off to the South Atlantic with his mates.

In Parliament, there was general agreement that a firm response was necessary, but the government was heatedly attacked for its failure to anticipate the Argentine action. There was strong criticism of a defense policy that emphasized NATO and missiles at the expense of the navy. Lord Carrington, Foreign Secretary, took the blame for the debacle and resigned.

Led by Margaret Thatcher, a Cabinet committee was established to serve as a war cabinet. The war was supported by all parties, although the Labour Party hoped that a display of British willingness to use force would lead to a resolution of the dispute without actual fighting. Public opinion rallied to support the war. Britain was no longer a major power, but the British people still had their national pride and a glorious history. They were not going to be pushed around by a second rate country like Argentina, especially one ruled by an unsavory dictator.

Through it all Mrs. Thatcher held to her course with Churchillian determination. Now it was the turn of the Argentines to be surprised, for they had not expected such a prompt and vigorous response. The members of the European Community and the Commonwealth promised their support immediately and imposed economic sanctions on Argentina. After intense debates, the United Nations Security Council passed a resolution condemning Argentina's invasion and demanded immediate withdrawal as a preliminary to negotiations.

Despite Mrs. Thatcher's efforts to establish a "special relationship" with President Reagan, the first response of the United States was to attempt to mediate the dispute. The Reagan administration looked to Latin American dictators as bulwarks against communism. They did not want a humiliating defeat for the Argentines, which would probably bring the downfall of the Galtieri regime. While the British force was heading southward at full speed, Secretary of State Alexander Haig shuttled between Washington, London, and Buenos Aires with a proposal for a neutral administration of the islands until a permanent settlement could be reached.

When Secretary Haig's efforts got nowhere, the United States belatedly imposed economic sanctions on Argentina. From the outset, the U.S. Department of Defense gave the British task force support in the form of weapons, fuel, ammunition, weather forecasting, and communications that contributed significantly to the success of the operation.

As the armada proceeded southward, there were many who had second thoughts. The Labour Party urged further efforts at a settlement through the United Nations. Even some members of the Cabinet were getting cold feet. An amphibious landing on a defended shore in the stormy South Atlantic eight thousand miles from home was by no means a sure thing.

There were two main islands, East and West Falklands, and about one hundred smaller islands. Linked with the Falklands were the island of South Georgia and the Sandwich Islands. By the end of April, South Georgia, eight hundred miles eastward, had been captured, and the British naval task force was approaching the Falklands. A two-hundred mile exclusion zone around the Falklands was declared, within which any Argentine ship or plane would be attacked.

When the Argentine cruiser *General Belgrano* approached the zone in a threatening manner, she was torpedoed by a British submarine and sank, with the loss of almost four hundred lives. Although they were not under attack, the escorting Argentine destroyers fled the scene at full speed, not remaining to pick up survivors. The *Sun*, the most popular of the tabloid newspapers, filled its front page with a picture of the *Belgrano* sinking and a screaming headline: GOTCHA!

The Argentines fought back with land based fighter bombers firing air launched Exocet missiles that sank several British warships. Later, Argentine pilots, flying at the extreme limit of their range, attacked British ships engaged in landing troops.

In mid-May, with winter approaching in the southern hemisphere, British commandos established beachheads despite fierce Argentine air attacks. After more troops were landed, British forces advanced on Fort Stanley. The Argentine soldiers proved to be cold, frightened, ill-trained recruits. They put up token resistance, well aware that they were no match for British regulars and had been abandoned to their fate.

On 14 June the Argentine forces surrendered and the Falklands War ended in a triumph that thrilled the nation. Britain lost two hundred and twenty-five men killed with almost eight hundred wounded. Six British ships were sunk and ten damaged, and nine carrier planes were lost. The Argentines had six hundred and fifty-two men killed. The Argentine junta fell from power, and Margaret Thatcher had won a classic military victory.

The Election of 1983

In her first three years Mrs. Thatcher had been one of Britain's most unpopular prime ministers. Polls had shown her approval rating as low as 20 percent, and at times the Conservative Party was rated lower than Labour or the SDP–Liberal Alliance. With the victory in the Falklands War, that changed. Public approval of her handling of the war soared from 60 percent in the first few weeks to 84 percent as victory came into view. At the beginning of the war the three major parties were virtually even in the polls. When the war ended the Conservatives were at 52 percent.

By 1983, the polls showed the Conservatives at 44 percent, Labour at 35 percent, and the SDP–Liberal Alliance at 20 percent. The economy of Britain was improving and with it public confidence. In January, 22 percent of the public said they expected the economy to improve; by April, just before the election, that figure had risen to 36 percent. Steps had been taken to bring the public finances under control and to curb the power of the unions. Inflation had fallen to 4 percent and wages were increasing at double that figure, although unemployment was still at three million.

Taking advantage of these favorable omens, Mrs. Thatcher announced that a general election would take place in June 1983, although Parliament still had a year to go. The Conservative election manifesto indicated that the reforming spirit of Thatcherism would continue. Income taxes would be further reduced. The manifesto promised to continue privatization of nationalized industries and trade union reform, especially in respect to strikes in essential services. The most important new thrust was reform of local government, limitation of increases in the rates, and abolition of the Greater London Council and the other metropolitan counties.

With the left wing in command, Labour's election manifesto was a declaration of war on Thatcherism: increased spending to reduce unemployment, exchange controls to reduce the influence of international capital movements, repurchase of nationalized industries that had been privatized, expansion of public ownership to new industries such as electronics and pharmaceuticals, repeal of Tory legislation restricting the powers of the unions, improved social benefits, increased spending on the National Health Service and the building of council houses, and withdrawal from the European Economic Community. Defense was an important issue, as Labour committed itself to unilateral nuclear disarmament and withdrawal from NATO.

The bookish Michael Foot was respected within the Labour Party, but his bumbling inability to control his own party diminished any claim he might have to leading a government. Labour was embarrassed by the Militant Tendency, a small extremist group that advocated abolition of the monarchy and other institutions of central government, and predicted civil war if its demands were not met. Expulsion from the Labour Party did not remove the public's identification of the militants with Labour's left wing.

Saddled with policies rejected by most of the public, the Labour Party faced an electoral disaster. One Labour MP called the party's manifesto "the longest suicide note in history." Labour's support in the polls dropped from 36 percent to 28 percent over the four-week election period.

The SDP–Liberal Alliance had become an important factor in electoral politics as nonsocialist alternative to Thatcherism. The Liberal leader, David Steel, was an attractive campaigner, and Roy Jenkins, leader of the Social Democrats, provided intellectual power and a sense of strong leadership. Its main promise was to launch an all out attack on unemployment through public works and special programs for the long-term unemployed.

Labour's losses were the Alliance's gains. From 15 percent in the polls at the beginning of the campaign, the Alliance rose to 26 percent. Polls showed that if both opposition parties were combined Mrs. Thatcher would probably lose.

The election gave the Conservatives 42 percent of the vote, Labour 28 percent, and the Alliance 25 percent. The Thatcher ministry was still a minority government in terms of the popular vote although it had a strong majority of the seats in Parliament.

The realignment of British politics that had begun with Margaret Thatcher's victory in 1979 was now becoming evident. The Conservative Party had the support of the middle class, homeowners, and white-collar workers in the growing financial and service-industry sectors. Mrs.

Thatcher's ability to win and hold a large body of working-class voters (especially skilled workers) was an important factor in her electoral victory and contributed significantly to the decline of Labour. Furthermore, all these groups were growing, especially in the south of England, which went heavily Conservative.

Labour was the big loser. With 28 percent of the vote, Labour narrowly escaped coming in third. Over the previous twenty years the industrial working class, the bedrock of the Labour Party, had declined to less than half the labor force. Union membership had fallen, and union leadership had been discredited by the excesses of the 1970s.

Labour still had strength in the declining industrial areas of the north of England and Scotland, where factories were closing and unemployment was high. With the exception of the high-rise, low-income housing estates, Labour was virtually wiped out in the prospering south of England, which contained most of the population and wealth of the United Kingdom.

In the previous twenty years the white-collar, suburban middle class had grown, and such people were not attracted to a political party advocating socialism and dominated by the trade unions. The SDP–Liberal Alliance had done well and could looked forward to becoming the main opposition party. The Conservatives and the Alliance were both middle-class parties, and the future seemed to lie with them.

3

The Heyday of Thatcherism, 1983 to 1987

Established Leader

Margaret Thatcher worked hard to maintain a strong public image. She presented her ideas and policies through carefully prepared speeches, which were reported and commented on at length in the newspapers and presented in briefer form on television news broadcasts. She made effective use of television interviews. The Tuesday/Thursday periods for "Prime Minister's Questions" provided an opportunity for her to provide the brief statements beloved by the press, and later television.

Not everybody liked her public personality. One commentator was annoyed by her "hectoring style, know-it-all manner, and quasi-regal airs," but conceded that "she is undeniably crisp and clear, the confident mistress of the facts and figures which underpin her simplistic world view." (Quoted in Jones and Kavanagh, 112).

Like many leaders of modern democracies, Margaret Thatcher was not primarily a party politician. She dominated her Cabinet, although she could not ignore their advice and risked serious embarrassment if she pushed them too far. Nor could she take for granted the support of the Conservative MPs, who normally maintain a kind of tribal unity behind their leader. Her style and policies appealed to the Conservative backbenchers, and she was especially effective among the party activists who attended the annual Conservative Party conferences. She was, in some ways, a populist, who appealed beyond her Cabinet and party to the people.

While Mrs. Thatcher made herself widely visible in the United Kingdom and in world affairs, she rarely spoke in the House of Commons, apart from the obligatory "Prime Minister's Questions." On the average, she gave a speech in Parliament about every forty-five days. Although she was quick witted and well informed, she never intervened in the debates.

She steadfastly opposed televising the Commons' debates until 1989, when public pressure made it necessary to give way. Then the public discovered that she was very good at "Question Time" and usually came out the winner.

Having established herself politically, Mrs. Thatcher was ready to move aggressively to establish a team whose views were more in accord with her own. Sir Geoffrey Howe moved to the Foreign and Commonwealth Office and was replaced as chancellor of the Exchequer by Nigel Lawson, a rising star. Michael Heseltine moved from Environment to Defence. Another Cabinet shuffle in 1985 brought Douglas Hurd, a Conservative Party stalwart, into the Cabinet as home secretary. John Major, a pleasant young man of humble background who had entered Parliament in 1979, began his march up the ladder by serving as one of the Conservative whips (party managers) in the House of Commons.

The Economy

Mrs. Thatcher's economic goal was to make Britain competitive in the emerging world economy, and to a considerable extent she succeeded. Bringing the finances of government under control was essential to stabilizing the pound. Priority was given to low inflation, on the assumption that it was essential to growth. Full employment, the goal of British governments for forty years, fell by the wayside.

In 1983, the British economy began a period of economic growth, admittedly from a depressed level. In the four year period, 1983 through 1986, the Gross Domestic Product increased by 8 percent, industrial production by 7 percent, productivity per worker by 13 percent, and exports by 21 percent.

With inflation at 5 percent, consumer confidence and spending rose and a demand-side upswing began, strengthened by similar growth in the United States and other countries. Employed persons benefited. During the four-year period, the retail price index rose by an annual 4.7 percent while earnings grew at an average of 7.7 percent per year. Imports increased by 30 percent as British consumers went on a binge, buying foreign cars, television sets, and cameras, and enjoying holidays abroad. North Sea oil helped keep the balance of payments in balance and sterling remained strong.

At the Exchequer, Nigel Lawson continued the Thatcherite fiscal policy: shift taxation from incomes to consumption, control spending, reduce public borrowing, and keep inflation down. Revenues were growing, bolstered by income from North Sea oil and sales of nationalized industries. Expenditure was tightly controlled and the rate of increase was well below the growth of the revenue, gradually whittling down the need to borrow.

In 1984, Lawson cut the tax rates on corporations, balancing the losses incurred with new revenue gained from removing a cluster of unwarranted corporate tax exemptions. Employers' contributions to the national insurance system were abolished, removing a tax on jobs and making a welcome addition to corporate balance sheets.

In 1985, the basic exemption for the personal income tax was substantially raised, thus relieving many low-income people of the burden of the income tax. Homeowners were given a boost by increasing the tax deduction for mortgage interest. As revenues grew, Lawson promised to cut the income tax base rate from 30 percent to 25 percent, beginning by knocking off 1 percent in 1986 and another 2 percent in 1987. The top rate remained at 60 percent until 1988.

Deregulation proceeded, as banks were permitted to lend on mortgages, and building societies (S&Ls in the United States) were permitted to act more like banks. Deregulation of hire-purchase (installment buying) encouraged consumer spending and debt. An unsettling reminder of the Heath ministry was the rapid increase in the price of houses, which rose by 75 percent in London in three years. Lending institutions were flush with cash; mortgage loans were easily available at 100 percent of value and moderate interest rates. As house prices soared, people were willing to take on large mortgages in the expectation of further rises.

Under Margaret Thatcher, London expanded its role as one of the world's great financial centers. Thatcherism meant a return to Britain's image of itself as a country with a global perspective. North Sea oil generated cash that became part of the worldwide flows of capital. Britain was close behind Japan in total overseas investments.

The commitment of the Thatcher ministry to free enterprise and the market economy was dramatically demonstrated in October 1986, when the stock market was opened up in what was called "the Big Bang." Legislative limitations on the Stock Exchange were removed, and the Exchange itself was required to remove trading restrictions that it had imposed on its members, including fixed commissions. The stock trading, merger, and takeover boom in the United States spread to Britain, with much of the activity financed with borrowed money.

Of course, the boom could not last, and a sudden drop on the New York Stock Exchange in October 1987 brought the party to an end. People with big money and good advice ran for cover; those who did not get out quickly enough took losses. The volume of shares traded declined dramatically, leading to mergers and layoffs in brokerage firms. Computerization, after a few glitches, further reduced the need for personnel.

Despite excesses, the boom unleashed by "the Big Bang" was valuable to British financial institutions. The stodgy, tradition-bound ways of the past were replaced by a new, aggressive mentality that made the City (the financial district) a center of money and investment in the emerging world economy. It has been estimated that 50 percent of the increase in the national wealth during the 1980s came from financial services.

The weak spot in the British economy was manufacturing, where employment continued to fall. Investment in manufacturing did not keep pace with the growth in the rest of the economy, and British firms failed to put enough money and effort into research and development. British banks preferred short-time loans to established firms rather than the long-term commitments needed to build an industry. Industry response to growing demand was sluggish, and imports took advantage of the opportunity.

The result was continuing high unemployment, which averaged 3.1 million from 1983 through 1986, a figure previously unheard of. The high point was 1986, when it peaked at 3.3 million, most of the unemployed coming from manufacturing industry. There was some increase in employment in the next several years, but the new jobs were mainly for women or part-time workers, and the number of employed adult male breadwinners declined.

Housing

One of Mrs. Thatcher's objectives was to reduce the involvement of the government in housing. As much as possible, she wanted housing to be provided by private enterprise and owned by the inhabitants. As part of the effort to control expenditure, funds for construction of council houses were greatly reduced as were subsidies to hold down the rents on existing council houses. For the next decade, housing was the spending area receiving the largest cuts.

Housing helped to ease financial stringency in another way: by sale of public housing units to their occupiers. In 1980 the Housing Act was passed, giving tenants of council houses the right to purchase their houses at low prices and on easy terms. The longer they had been tenants, the greater the discount, up to a 50 percent discount on market value. Local governments were prohibited from subsidizing council house rents. The consequent increases in rents made it advisable for tenants to buy, if they could afford it.

In the first four years of the Thatcher ministry, almost half a million houses and flats were sold. Housing sales were an important source of income for the Treasury, rising from £472 million in 1979–80 to more than £2 billion in 1986–87. In 1979, 56 percent of all housing in Britain was occupied by the owner; in 1988 the figure was 64 percent. Most of the increase was due to sales of council houses to working-class people who had expected to rent all their lives. Michael Heseltine, at that time environment secretary, stated that the bill "lays the foundation for one of the most important social revolutions of our time." It also helped convert working-class voters into Conservatives.

Privatization

During Mrs. Thatcher's second ministry, privatization became a major feature of Thatcherism. Selling off the nationalized industries was politically advantageous in many ways: it brought money into the Treasury, it helped fund tax cuts, it relieved the taxpayers of costly subsidies, it eroded the political base of the Labour Party, and it forced the unions to deal with private employers (who might downsize or go out of business if costs became too high) rather than engage in political strikes against the government.

The initial privatizations had dealt with smaller or less-known firms. These continued with the disposal of the remainders of British Aerospace (1985), Cable and Wireless (1983, 1985), the National Bus Company,

Associated British Ports (1985), some naval shipyards (1985–1986), and the factories of the Royal Ordnance.

Privatization was acceptable in manufacturing industry where a competitive market existed, but public utilities such as telephones, gas, electricity, and water were another matter. People were reluctant to remove these basic services from public control, and competition was not considered to be a factor in their performance.

The Thatcher government argued that privatizing public utilities would bring in new management and private capital to extend and modernize them. It was recognized that privatizing the public utilities would require nonpolitical regulatory bodies to control rates and monitor service.

The telephone system had begun as part of the Post Office. The two were separated in the 1960s, but British Telecom continued the bureaucratic, unionized culture out of which it had arisen. The British telephone system was obsolete at a time when communications in other advanced countries were being revolutionized.

In 1984, the Thatcher ministry proposed the sale of British Telecom, the largest share offer ever made to that time. Nigel Lawson proposed mass-marketing the shares to the general public, rather than relying on bids from major investors. The shares were offered in lots of varying sizes with a modest down payment. More than a million people applied for the smaller batches—so many, in fact, that larger lots were broken up into smaller lots and institutional investors that had applied for the larger lots got nothing. The unions urged employees of British Telecom to boycott the sale, but 95 percent of them bought shares anyway.

By the end of the month, the part-paid shares were almost double the down payment, and many holders of the small lots sold out, taking a quick profit. Eventually, institutional investors (including union pension funds) ended up holding the lion's share anyway. Although the Labour Party criticized the government for selling the shares too cheaply, the Conservatives gloated that now 5 percent of the adult population was shareholding capitalists.

The effect of privatization was dramatic, as the clumsy, old-fashioned British telephone system was modernized. Investment was doubled; new up-to-date equipment was introduced; delays in installation declined; and prices fell. Telecom suddenly showed interest in its customers. Responding to complaints that there were not enough pay phones, and that too many of them were not working, the company quickly added 45 percent more pay phones and the number functioning rose from 77 percent to 95 percent. A regulatory body called Oftel was established that kept prices below inflation, and yet British Telecom flourished. It was a striking example of the benefits of privatization.

One of the shortcomings of private enterprise was revealed when Telecom began removing the beloved red payboxes, designed by the distinguished architect Sir Giles Gilbert Scott, that had been a familiar fixture on British streets since 1906. They were ripped out, shipped to the junkyard, and replaced by sleek, modernistic designs. The discerning public was appalled at the loss of a minor but ubiquitous part of the nation's public architecture. Loss of the red payboxes seemed an unnecessary price to pay for efficiency and modernity.

The successful privatization of British Telecom in 1984 led to the privatization of British Gas in 1986. British Gas had been nationalized shortly after World War II. It was a giant of British industry. It distributed gas to British factories and households, explored for gas in the North Sea oilfields, and sold and serviced gas appliances at retail.

The first North Sea gasfields were opened up in the 1960s. In the next twenty years, British Gas built an elaborate network of gas mains and pipes that provided cheap, clean energy to British homes and industries and ended the gloomy fogs and killing smogs that had been a feature of life in British towns. When privatization took place, natural gas provided 50 percent of British energy and coal was declining rapidly.

Seeing the success of Telecom, British Gas was more than willing to be privatized. The privatization plan gave British Gas a twenty-five year monopoly on the distribution of gas, with the exception of large industrial users, where competition was permitted. The monopoly was justified on the grounds that no competitor could compete with its unparalleled distribution system. A regulator of prices and services (Ofgas) was established.

The sale of British Gas was a deal even larger than British Telecom. An elaborate publicity campaign was undertaken to secure the maximum return, and 40 percent of the shares was reserved to be sold in small lots to gas customers on an easy payment plan. Almost four and a half million people applied for shares, including most of the employees of the company. The shares sold out immediately, and by the end of the year, holders of part-paid shares had a profit of 30 percent over their initial payment. Tony Blair, speaking for Labour, complained that the shares had been sold too cheaply.

Many who bought shares in Telecom and British Gas did so only to turn a quick profit. Nevertheless, from 1979 to 1989, the number of individual shareholders in Britain increased from three million to nine million. Mrs. Thatcher had added millions of new shareholders to her "people's capitalism" and perhaps to the Conservative Party.

A major problem was what to do with British Leyland, Britain's only large manufacturer of automobiles and trucks. The jewel in British Leyland's crown, Jaguar, was successfully privatized in 1984. Leyland's other products (Rover, Land Rover, Range Rover, and BL trucks) were losing market share to imported cars or cars manufactured by the British subsidiaries of Ford and General Motors. Leyland required large subsidies from the government to stay afloat and preserve jobs—a typical example of the inefficient nationalized industries that Margaret Thatcher was determined to get rid of.

In 1985, General Motors made a favorable offer for Land Rover, Range Rover, and BL trucks. Ford made an offer for Rover. Mrs. Thatcher discovered that powerful emotions could be aroused by the auto industry. An outcry arose in Parliament and the press that Americans were taking over Britain's last auto manufacturer. The main resistance came from rural and small-town England, the heartland of Conservatism, where Rover cars were popular and patriotism was at stake.

Anti-Americanism was part of the protest, although both American companies had long produced cars in Britain that were manufactured by British autoworkers. Workers at Rover welcomed privatization, which would help protect their jobs. Shocked at the reaction, the American companies abandoned the deal.

Bowing to public clamor, Rover was sold instead to British Aerospace, a formerly privatized company, for much less than was offered by the American companies. British Aerospace, in turn, entered into an arrangement with Honda to manufacture cars, giving Honda entry to the British car market. Leyland Bus was sold to Volvo, a Swedish firm. Leyland's van business was sold to a Dutch firm. So the foreigners won after all, but not the Americans.

In 1985, a surprising storm blew up that nearly brought the downfall of the Thatcher ministry. It concerned a company called Westland, which was Britain's only manufacturer of helicopters. Although Westland had good products, it faced bankruptcy unless taken over by a larger company that could provide additional capital. For some time, Westland had been cooperating with the American company, United Technologies, which manufactured Sikorsky helicopters. Some of Westland's products had been Sikorsky designs manufactured under license. United Technologies made an acceptable bid to purchase a share of Westland, and this offer was favored by the company.

Michael Heseltine, then minister of defence, was independent and strong willed. He had come to resent Mrs. Thatcher's domination of the Cabinet and pro-American foreign policy. Since Westland produced helicopters for the British armed forces, he declared that a company of strategic importance should not be permitted to come under American influence. Heseltine attempted to put together a European consortium to absorb Westland. The pro-Europeans in the Conservative Party insisted that Westland should find a European partner. Mrs. Thatcher felt that such a decision should be left to the company, especially since no firm offer from Heseltine's consortium had appeared.

Heseltine publicly challenged the ministry's position on Westland and impulsively resigned. The result was a big row in the Conservative Party and the press about Margaret Thatcher's alleged autocratic and devious methods. A considerable amount of anti-Americanism was involved, fostered by extensive American investment in Britain, which was thought to threaten Britain's economic independence. In all of this, the best interests of Westland and its employees were ignored. Eventually the storm passed, and the deal with United Technologies was completed.

By airing internal differences, the Westland affair weakened momentarily the public perception of the Thatcher ministry and slowed its momentum on other aspects of its agenda. Heseltine became the darling of the pro-Europeans, and his willingness to stand up to Margaret Thatcher made him seem like a future rival. He had brought out the growing division within the Conservative Party concerning relations with Europe.

The Trade Unions

The election of 1983 put Margaret Thatcher in a position to reduce further the power of the trade unions, which she held responsible for much of Britain's economic decline. The Employment Acts of her first ministry were strengthened in 1984 by legislation that ended the self-perpetuating power of union leaders by requiring that they be re-elected every five years. Furthermore, a strike could not be called without a secret ballot of all members that would be involved, and unions would be legally liable for damages from a strike held without a favorable vote.

The legislation of 1984 included an attack on another Thatcherite grievance: the use of union funds for political purposes, almost always for support of the Labour Party. The law required prior approval by secret ballot. In this instance, Thatcher had mistaken the attitude of the members, who supported the political use of union funds by large majorities. They had lost confidence in the efficacy of the strike, but they were still willing to take political action to advance their interests.

The crucial test of Mrs. Thatcher's determination was the coal strike of 1984. At issue was the decision of the National Coal Board to close money-losing pits. The coal industry had long been in decline. In 1914 there had been a million miners, in 1946 700,000, and by 1983 the number had shrunk to 200,000. New sources of energy, especially oil and natural gas, had cut the use of coal in half over the previous ten years. The deeper and more modern coal pits in the Midlands were still profitable, but in other parts of the country old and inefficient mines with thin seams of coal were a cost to the taxpayer.

By 1983, Mrs. Thatcher was ready to deal with the problems of the coal industry, knowing that the necessary cutbacks would provoke a strike of the kind that had brought down Sir Edward Heath in 1974. She prepared for a strike by moving Ian MacGregor, who had performed well in transforming British Steel, to the chairmanship of the Coal Board. MacGregor was a tough, resolute manager, and he began making plans to close unprofitable pits. The Coal Board quietly accumulated large stocks of coal and located them at the generating plants and steel mills that were the principal users of coal. Other major users were advised to accumulate inventories.

A fleet of tanker trucks was leased, painted in innocuous colors, and hidden away for use when needed. Anticipating major confrontations, Mrs. Thatcher established an agency that would mobilize police from all over the country to stop illegal practices such as secondary strikes, mass picketing, and violence.

It was important that the Coal Board divide the miners to prevent a complete shutdown. The mines of Nottinghamshire in the Midlands were efficient and profitable; those miners were unwilling to challenge the Coal

Board and possibly lose their jobs. Workers in the inefficient mines were offered generous terms to give up their jobs, and many of them decided it was better to take the payments than strike. The miners left to challenge the Coal Board were those who were most militant and who worked in the least desirable pits.

None of this deterred Arthur Scargill, feisty leader of the National Union of Mineworkers, who was determined to block all closures and force a confrontation with the National Coal Board over this issue. Apart from an understandable desire to keep up the membership of his union, Scargill was a fiery demagogue who carried deep resentments toward the government. His motives were as much personal and political as economic. He hoped to repeat the victory that the miners had gained in 1974, when shortages of coal had shut down the nation and ended the Heath ministry.

Scargill, however, was holding a weak hand, for the circumstances of 1984 differed greatly from those ten years earlier, when the OPEC oil embargo had made coal the essential fuel. After the excesses of the 1970s, many unions had become resigned to the changes taking place in British industry. The Thatcher ministry and the Conservative majority in Parliament, victorious in two elections, were hostile. The Labour Party was severely weakened and the public had lost sympathy with strikers.

Scargill called for a strike in March 1984. In so doing, he was limited by the requirement of his union that the decision be made by the miners voting in a secret ballot. He did not ballot his members because he knew that he would lose in a vote. Where regional ballots were taken, the strike was rejected.

To avoid a strike vote, Scargill persuaded militant miners in some regions to strike, and they were used as pickets to prevent other miners from working. Gangs of strikers called "flying pickets" went to mines in other parts of the country to seek support or compel it by intimidation. Their violence against fellow miners violated the law against secondary picketing, which brought the police into the conflict.

The British public was astonished to see on their television screens hundreds of police equipped with riot gear streaming into strike areas from other parts of the country, guarding power plants and protecting long lines of trucks bringing coal. Wives and children of the strikers appeared and engaged in angry confrontations with the police. Clashes between the miners and the police won public sympathy for the police and the rule of law. The archbishop of Canterbury, however, spoke up in support of the strikers.

The Central Electricity Generating Board was the government's command post, for it was essential to keep the generators operating and the lights on. The workers at the generating plants were persuaded that it was their job to keep the power flowing. As one of them said, his ninety-year-old mother depended on electricity to keep warm, and if "the electric's off, she's finished." High earnings due to extensive overtime strengthened his resolve.

Convoys of independent truckers brought coal from those mines that were still working to the power stations, making big money but facing threats, abuse, and sometimes danger from the pickets. The most important factor was the increased use of oil. Generating plants were hastily converted from coal to oil, and tank trucks were hired to bring the oil to the plants. Every tanker driver who owned his own truck made a fortune during the strike, hauling oil day and night until he or his truck collapsed. Nuclear plants operated constantly at hotter levels than ever before.

With high unemployment, Scargill's call for support from the rest of the labor movement was not answered. The steel workers declared that they would keep making steel with whatever coal they could get. Leaders of the transport workers and railwaymen expressed support, but their members continued working and moving coal. Scargill obtained financial support from some unions in other countries, but his overtures to Colonel Muamar Gaddafi of Libya were too much for most people to stomach.

When the Trades Union Congress (TUC) executive voted to support the strike, one of the members stated: "Our men will not obey, and the union leaders who voted for it know it will not stick."

Scargill had hoped for support from the dockworkers, who had their own grievances. In July, the dockworkers went out on strike in support of the miners. They were prepared to block imports of coal, but the Coal Board did not intend to import coal, to avoid alienating those miners who remained at work. The dockworkers' strike affected the importation of ore for British Steel and imports of food, but enough ports continued working to meet all needs.

The dock strike lasted only ten days, and then it collapsed. There was much featherbedding on the docks, and the dockers feared that after the strike their hiring system would be changed with extensive loss of jobs. A second dock strike in August was effective in only a few ports and soon ended. The failure of the dock strikes made it even more clear that Scargill was doomed.

Margaret Thatcher, as was her policy, stayed aloof from the strike, which she stated firmly was between the mine workers and the Coal Board. She made it clear that there would be no government bailouts and that profitable and unprofitable pits would go down together if a satisfactory settlement was not reached. She was prepared to call in troops to preserve order, but the Generating Board persuaded her that such action would only lead to sympathy strikes.

Efforts to reach a negotiated settlement were frustrated by Scargill's refusal to consider closure of any mines whatsoever. As more strikers returned to their jobs, coal production began to return to nearly normal levels. By March 1985, almost a year after it had begun, the strike had ended in total defeat for Scargill and the miners whom he had led into a disaster. The number of coalminers was reduced by 40 percent, but the reduced number produced 85 percent of the coal that had been produced before the strike.

The effects of the coal strike on Britain were great. The Falklands War and the coal strike were the decisive events in establishing Margaret Thatcher as a national leader. She had won the battle that Sir Edward Heath had lost ten years earlier.

Beyond the coal industry, it was evident to workers that strike action would not bring government intervention nor would it win public sympathy. It might not even bring support from other unions. At a time of high unemployment, workers were concerned about protecting their jobs, which might disappear if their factory or industry were needlessly disrupted. Public opinion had turned against strikes that were intended to secure gains for some by making everyone else suffer. The efficacy of the strike—labour's ultimate weapon—had been blunted, if not destroyed.

The decline of the trade unions was seen in another failed strike. The print unions were among the most militant elements in the British labor movement, and they were still smarting from the concessions they had made in 1981. They insisted on excessive numbers of printers, their work rules were highly restrictive, their paid hours grossly inflated, and the quality of their printing was low.

Rupert Murdoch, owner of the *Times*, the *Sunday Times*, the *Sun*, and the *News of the World*, was determined to introduce computerized technology into the newspaper business, making large numbers of printers redundant with a commensurate reduction in costs. He built a new, picket-proof building on cheap land in the former docklands, away from Fleet Street where newspapers had been located for more than two centuries. He installed the latest computerized printing equipment and recruited technical staff to operate it, many of them from the electricians union.

Murdoch knew that the printers would strike, as they had so often in the past. Since they were among the most literate and best-paid workers in Britain, they would be able to sustain a long and unified walkout. He also realized that the Employment Acts of 1980, 1982, and 1984, with their restrictions on sympathy strikes and picketing, gave him the leverage he needed to overcome the resistance of the unions, which would be desperate.

After a long period of negotiations, in January 1986 the unions declared a strike and Murdoch dismissed all the strikers. His new plant went into full operation, and it was evident that the new technology would revolutionize the printing business. The printers, living in the past, refused to accept the brutal fact that their skills had been rendered useless and their jobs had ceased to exist.

Murdoch had prepared for the strike as carefully as Mrs. Thatcher had for the coal strike. The printers union assumed they could count on the sympathy of the transport workers and railroad unions, who would refuse to deliver newspapers that had been printed while the workers were on strike. To counter this tactic, Murdoch had organized his own delivery system using independent truckers. He had built a second high-tech, computerized plant in Glasgow to serve Scotland and the north of England. He could deliver his morning papers overnight to every newsstand in the British Isles.

The legal prohibitions against secondary strikes left the printers without support from other unions. Some unions attempted to support the printers with sympathy strikes, but Murdoch obtained injunctions prohibiting them from picketing or other forms of strike action. When the printers attempted to shut down Murdoch's new printing plant, "the battle of Wapping" took place, as police struggled with mass pickets. In one confrontation at Murdoch's printing plant, one hundred and seventy-five police officers and demonstrators were injured.

Mrs. Thatcher adhered to her policy that strikes were a matter for management and labor. She refused to intervene, except to enforce the law against mass picketing. The strike failed and organized labor had taken another heavy blow. Murdoch's technology provided such profitable economies that the other papers soon followed suit. They moved out of Fleet Street to the docklands and built new, computerized plants that no longer needed the skills of the printers.

The trade unions continued to play an important role in British industrial relations, but the Thatcher years deprived them of their most potent weapon—the strike. A combination of Thatcherite legislation, long-term unemployment, and the failures of the miners' and printers' strikes convinced organized labor that strikes, apart from brief stoppages to underline a point, would not succeed and might recoil upon the workers involved.

The recession of 1979–1982 hit hardest the industries where the unions were strongest: manufacturing, mining, construction, docks, and railways. Privatization of key industries weakened their leverage. In 1979, British trade unions enrolled 13.5 million workers, or 57 percent of potential membership. In 1986 the figure was 10.5 million or 43 percent of potential membership, and in 1992 it was 35 percent.

Economic growth since that time has taken place largely in sectors that typically have been difficult for unions to organize—clerical, service industry, small business, and new factories in small towns and rural areas where unions have not been well established. Unions have remained strongest in the public sector.

Local Government

Mrs. Thatcher was a centralizer. She believed that irresponsible local governments jeopardized her efforts to control inflation, lower public spending (including local spending), and reduce taxes. Local governments were required to "contract out" many activities: garbage collection, building and vehicle maintenance, catering, and the like. Political partisanship was also involved, since Labour was strong in the cities and larger towns.

The great grievance of the Thatcherites was a long standing one: the rates—taxes on homes and businesses based on the presumed rental value of the property. The government subsidized local authorities with block grants based on population and other factors. In the past, these grants had provided 60 percent of the money for local government, but with the financial squeeze they had fallen to about 48 percent by 1988. Local authorities responded by raising the rates.

Approximately 60 percent of the local rates was paid by business. The remainder was paid largely by homeowners. Of thirty-five million voters in England, eighteen million paid rates and six million of those had their rates paid by housing benefit or otherwise reduced. Since most Labour voters were renters, Labour councillors in industrial towns did not hesitate to impose heavy rates on homeowners, who tended to be Conservatives. High rates were also imposed on business property, despite the negative effects on jobs.

The Greater London Council (GLC) and councils of some other industrial cities, among them Liverpool and Sheffield, had come under the control of left-wing extremists referred to by the tabloids as "the loony left." They raised the rates and increased spending on their pet projects. They filled local-government jobs with themselves and their friends, expanded welfare services for the poor and unemployed, and made grants of public money to special-interest groups such as feminists, public-housing tenants, gays, lesbians, minorities, and peace groups.

In 1981 the GLC, which had come under the control of Labour left-wingers, cut fares on the London Underground by 32 percent, a popular step, and raised the rates to make up the difference. Some London boroughs, where the ratepayers were strong, called for abolition of the GLC and establishment of a separate transportation authority for the London area.

In 1984, legislation was passed capping the rates of the GLC and seventeen others, most of them controlled by Labour. The GLC flatly rejected the cap. In Liverpool, the militant Labour councillors refused to submit a budget based on the legal limits. To show their dismay they issued dismissal notices to all city employees, which were later recalled. Then the council overspent its budget and pledged its reserves to borrow from international bankers.

Margaret Thatcher's answer to urban non-compliance was a demonstration of raw power, fuelled not a little by anger. In 1985 the Thatcher ministry proposed abolition of eighteen urban councils whose fiscal management was regarded as irresponsible. All but two were controlled by

Labour. The list included the six metropolitan counties established by the Heath ministry plus the GLC.

This step had considerable public support locally, but met resistance from members of both parties in Parliament. In addition to predictable opposition from the Labour Party, these proposals were criticized by many Conservatives, for local responsibility was an important part of the Conservative creed. Opposition also came from representatives of the arts, environmental protection, public health, and other special interests, who feared that dividing large local government units into smaller ones would weaken local support for their concerns.

The proposal came close to defeat in the House of Lords, where many Conservative peers objected strenuously. It seemed incredible that the vast, diverse sprawl that constituted greater London, and to a lesser extent the other metropolitan counties, would have no centralized government, but such was the case.

Despite resistance the bill became law and responsibility for managing these urban areas fell to the thirty-two London boroughs and the districts of the other metropolitan counties. One of the last acts of the GLC was to distribute its massive assets among favorite groups and causes, an action later reversed by the High Court. Twelve years later, the massive London County Council building across the Thames from the houses of Parliament was still vacant.

The European Community

In her second ministry, as the British economy improved and her reforms began moving forward, Margaret Thatcher was able to give more attention to foreign policy. Her victory in the Falklands War had given her a Churchillian aura and had made her a global celebrity.

Mrs. Thatcher's strong personality and nationalistic outlook involved her in frequent controversies within the European Economic Community (EEC), where her willingness to accept confrontation had earned her the nickname, "Attila the Hen." These clashes tended to strengthen the anti-European element in the Conservative Party and marginalized pro-Europeans like Michael Heseltine and Sir Edward Heath.

In the 1980s, the Community was expanded to include Greece (1981), Spain (1986), and Portugal (1986), economically weak and politically unstable countries that were admitted as a way to support their struggling democracies. At first the British thought that the new members would dilute the grip of France and Germany on Community affairs. Instead, those countries, sometimes lumped with Italy as "Club Med," needed the regional subsidies doled out by the Community, and they clung closely to their paymasters.

Mrs. Thatcher was supportive as the EEC moved toward an internal free market, which had always been Britain's reason for joining the Community. The crucial step was taken in 1986 with the Single European Act, which would eliminate all barriers to trade among the member states by 1992. The act also envisioned political and monetary union, a goal that came back to haunt the Conservatives a decade later.

By that time about half of Britain's trade was with the other members of the European Community, as opposed to 20 percent with those same countries twenty-five years earlier. Nevertheless, British trade still had a global dimension, as Britain traded more outside the EEC than any other member. Britain's major disappointment was that the single market did not include financial services and air transport, where Britain was strong. Although they claimed dedication to the Community spirit, other members were determined to support their own banks, insurance companies, and national airlines.

A major new undertaking in 1986 was the signing of an agreement with President François Mitterand of France to build a tunnel under the English Channel connecting England and France. The decision brought out ancient rivalries between the two countries, with reminders of the importance of the Channel in wars with Philip II of Spain, Louis XIV, Napoleon, and more recently Hitler's Germany. In reality, NATO and European unity had rendered these objections meaningless. The major problems were financing, much of which was expected to be provided by private capital, and the environmental effects of increased traffic in the congested southeast of England.

The Superpowers

The personal friendship of Mrs. Thatcher and Pres. Ronald Reagan was real, but its influence on the relations of the two countries was modest.

The "special relationship" was severely tested in 1986 when President Ronald Reagan decided to unleash a midnight bombing raid on Tripoli to punish Colonel Muammar Gaddafi, ruler of Libya, for his support of terrorism. Other European countries refused Reagan permission to dispatch bombers through their air space. They regarded the raid as a violation of international law, an action that could only injure innocent people, and a display of military force for domestic political consumption.

Despite these considerations, Mrs. Thatcher repaid Reagan for his support in the Falklands war by allowing him to use British bases for the raid. She insisted on a careful definition of targets, limiting them to places used to support terrorists. Despite American claims of precision bombing, when the raid was carried out bombs were scattered all over Tripoli, hitting friend and foe alike, including the French embassy.

When the news came to Britain of civilian casualties, the British press and public were shocked at scenes of physical destruction, weeping mothers, and angry mobs promising retaliation. The raid encouraged the view that the United States was a reckless superpower ready to use airpower against any weak country that aroused its ire. BBC coverage of the attack was so critical that the Conservative Party Central Office found it necessary to publish a rebuttal.

Reagan proclaimed victory, but Gadaffi continued to support international terrorism, although more discreetly. Two years later Gadaffi got his revenge when a terrorist bomb brought down a Pan-American Boeing 747 over Lockerbie, Scotland, killing 258 passengers and eleven inhabitants of the town.

Margaret Thatcher's most important contribution to the superpower relationship was her reaction to the rise of Mikhail Gorbachev to power in the Soviet Union. She early recognized that a new kind of Soviet leader had emerged who held out the prospect of an end to the cold war. In response to friendly British overtures, Gorbachev visited London in December 1984 and Mrs. Thatcher declared: "I like Mr. Gorbachev; we can do business together."

Gorbachev became general secretary of the Communist Party and *de facto* leader of the Soviet Union in March 1985. Mrs. Thatcher realized that Gorbachev did not represent fundamental change: his objective was to make the system work better through *perestroika* (restructuring) and *glasnost* (openness to criticism). It was evident that Gorbachev intended to continue the Soviet Union's role as a great power and rival of the United States.

The major issue between the two superpowers was nuclear weapons, where American technological advances were causing anxiety in the Soviet Union. The Soviet Union was most concerned by the American development of the Strategic Defense Initiative ("Star Wars"), a complex system in space intended to defend the United States against intercontinental ballistic missiles.

If successful, the Strategic Defense Initiative (SDI) would leave the Soviet Union exposed to American missiles without the ability to retaliate. Many in the West questioned whether the complex SDI system would ever work, but the Soviets took it very seriously. It seemed to them that the United States was gaining a technological edge that the crumbling Soviet economy could never match.

Mrs. Thatcher was a supporter of nuclear weapons, which she felt had maintained the peace in Europe by negating the vast Soviet superiority in conventional forces. But she was convinced that the key to nuclear deterrence was the nuclear balance. For forty years, fear of retaliation had prevented nuclear war. SDI held out the possibility that the nuclear balance would be upset, possibly provoking the Soviet Union to undertake a nuclear war before the "star wars" defense was in place.

Thatcher had the ear of President Reagan and she had won the respect of Chairman Gorbachev. Her most important influence in world affairs was probably her ability to explain Reagan and Gorbachev to each other. She made it clear to Gorbachev that the West would not let down its guard in respect of nuclear weapons and would continue to resist Soviet expansion in Third World countries. She visited Washington in December 1984 and again in February 1985, where she encouraged Reagan to continue with SDI research, but she insisted that its testing and implementation should be done in a measured manner that would not push the Soviet Union to desperate actions.

The climax arrived in October 1986, when Reagan and Gorbachev met at Reyjavik, Iceland, to discuss nuclear disarmament. Both were ready to make substantial cuts in their nuclear arsenals, but the Soviets insisted that the United States abandon SDI, which Reagan refused to do.

Reagan, carried away by enthusiasm for disarmament, proposed doing away with all nuclear weapons within ten years, a prospect that appalled Mrs. Thatcher. She hurried off to Washington to remind the president that nuclear weapons had preserved the peace for forty years and should not be abandoned. Reagan, who was having second thoughts about his proposal, agreed.

In March 1987, Mrs. Thatcher made a triumphant visit to Moscow as the guest of Chairman Gorbachev. In addition to public appearances, where she was well received, she talked frankly with Gorbachev about the Cold War, nuclear weapons, disarmament, human rights, and Gorbachev's plans for economic development.

As Gorbachev sought to work his way through the daunting problems of the Soviet Union, its Eastern European empire, and the super-power rivalry with the United States, perhaps Margaret Thatcher served as a useful and unthreatening interpreter of Western views.

The Election of 1987

In 1987, Mrs. Thatcher decided that the time was opportune for an election, a year earlier than required. The polls showed that the Conservative Party was rising after a slump. At the end of 1986, the Gallup poll found the Conservatives at 41 percent, Labour at 32 percent, and the SDP–Liberal Alliance at 23 percent. Mrs. Thatcher's former low ratings had risen to 38 percent favorable.

As she undertook to lead her party into a third election, Margaret Thatcher could state that her early goals had been achieved: the economy was humming, inflation was under control, the pound was strong, the banks were lending freely to businesses and individuals, the housing market was buoyant, consumers were spending, and exports were increasing. Her most popular policies had been the sale of council houses and limiting the powers of the unions. She indicated that she was now ready to give more attention to social problems: schools, health, and crime.

The Conservatives appealed to the middle class and those with middle-class aspirations. Professional and white-collar workers, the most likely Conservative voters, were now 40 percent of the workforce. Many skilled workers owned their own homes (formerly council houses) and were making good money in steady jobs. With the decline of manufacturing, Labour's working class, unionized constituency was melting away.

Unemployment was high and confined mainly to the north of England, while the south was thriving with new white-collar and white-coat industries. There was widespread concern with crime in the inner cities and the large housing estates. Douglas Hurd, home secretary, promised vigorous efforts to maintain "law and order," a goal also supported by the other political parties.

Within the Conservative Party, Mrs. Thatcher's policies underwent a drumfire of criticism from Sir Edward Heath and other "One Nation" Conservatives. One prominent Conservative urged the party to remember "its well established tradition of the protective role of the state." Harold Macmillan, now Lord Stockton, compared privatization to selling the family silver to pay tradesmen's bills. He recalled the human tragedies of unemployment in the 1930s, which he had seen firsthand as a young MP for Stockton. The archbishop of Canterbury called on the Church to be the conscience of the nation. He declared that "the costs of the present policies, with the continuing growth of unemployment, are unacceptable."

After its failure in the election of 1983, the Labour Party had chosen a new leader, Neil Kinnock, a charismatic Welshman who could arouse the Labour Party faithful but had never held any Cabinet office. Kinnock faced a constant struggle as he attempted to move his fractured party toward the center. Policies without public support, such as withdrawal from the European Community and ending the sale of council houses, were dropped. Opposition to privatization remained, although modified to appease the millions of new shareholders that had been created. As an indication of moderation, the Labour Party's symbol, the red flag, was replaced by a red rose (sans thorns) to suggest that the previous class-based radicalism had been replaced by a gentler spirit.

Labour had important issues on which to run: the decline of manufacturing industry, persistent high unemployment, and the shortcomings of the public services. Kinnock proved to be an effective TV campaigner, and he hit hard at the moral shortcomings of Mrs. Thatcher's "uncaring" leadership.

Labour's weak spot was its views on foreign policy and defense, where Margaret Thatcher was strong. Kinnock affirmed the commitment of Labour to NATO, but he continued his antinuclear stance, calling for unilateral nuclear disarmament and the closing of American nuclear bases in Britain. The Conservatives depicted Labour's defense policy as a British soldier with his hands in the air.

In the election of 1983, the Social Democrat–Liberal Alliance had shown signs of becoming a major party, and it had continued to achieve successes in by-elections. But it lacked an established power base. Its appeal to voters in the opinion polls was an expression of dissatisfaction with the two major parties that was unlikely to translate into votes in national elections. Its few members in Parliament were unable to influence policy or gain much attention in the media.

The Alliance also had internal problems. Roy Jenkins, one of the founders of the Social Democrats, retired from the leadership and was succeeded by David Owen. David Steel continued as leader of the Liberals, although incapacitated for a while by ill health. The individualistic members of the Alliance parties were inclined to be cantankerous and its party conferences were often contentious.

For the SDP–Liberal Alliance, the election of 1987 was vital: if the Alliance could pass Labour and become the second largest party it could begin to accumulate the votes of those who opposed Thatcherism. The Alliance parties, therefore, positioned themselves to the left of the Conservatives, supporting economy in government, a market economy, the European Economic Community, and NATO. They promised a more vigorous attack on unemployment, racial tensions, and regional disparities. They were divided on the nuclear deterrent.

When the election results were tallied, the Conservatives had won a commanding majority of seats with only 42 percent of the votes. Mrs. Thatcher's victory in 1987 was less a result of her own popularity, which was beginning to wane, than popular mistrust of the alternatives. The Conservatives lost some seats in the north of England, where unemployment remained high, but they dominated the south, where Labour won only three seats outside of London.

The Conservative Party gained 54 percent of the middle-class voters, who had increased to 40 percent of the population. They also held the support of the skilled workers. Conservative support among men continued to rise, although Labour gained among women, who saw Labour as the more "caring" party. The Conservatives were strong among the over fifty-fives, whose voting percentage is always high.

Labour improved slightly to 31 percent of the vote, but much of that came from the declining industrial areas of Scotland, unskilled workers, young voters, people dependent on pensions and public aid, and inhabitants of large council housing estates. The main strength of the Labour Party was in the public sector employees, the unions, and local government, and these were segments of the electorate hard-hit by Thatcherism.

The Alliance parties garnered a disappointing 23 percent. Eventually, the two parties merged to form the Liberal Democratic Party, conceived as "the natural alternative to Thatcherism."

Margaret Thatcher's three electoral victories indicated that a major political realignment had taken place. The electoral success of Thatcherite conservatism was based on something more than a strong leader or unattractive opponents. It was the result of demographic and economic developments that were changing the social structure and regional orientation of the United Kingdom. Thatcherism was based on political realities to which the the other political parties would have to adapt.

4

The Decline and Fall of Margaret Thatcher, 1987 to 1990

Thatcherism under Stress

After her victory in the election of 1987, Margaret Thatcher seemed to be at the peak of her power. Resistance within the Cabinet and the Conservative Party had been quelled, and her political opposition had once again tasted defeat. Three years later she would be out of office, brought down by the very qualities that had made her a strong leader.

Despite appearances, signs of political weakness were present. Many of the major figures in the Conservative Party disliked her personal assertiveness and disagreed with her free market philosophy. In 1989, at the height of her power, it was estimated that no more than 20 percent of the Tories were committed Thatcherites. Although she was widely respected by the British public for her courage and competence, her incessant activity was unsettling to many. She had never been a popular leader, and in three elections her party had never won more than 44 percent of the vote.

Her style can be described as "presidential," in that she was more a national leader than a party leader. A portent of future difficulties was seen in her domineering ways toward her Cabinet. Increasingly she relied on her own judgment and a "kitchen cabinet" of personal advisers in No. 10. Instead of working together to achieve agreed policies on major issues, Cabinet members found it best to devote their attention to the administration of their own departments. One of her former Cabinet ministers remarked that she promoted "a cult of personality" and conducted a "slightly authoritarian government."

Sir Geoffrey Howe continued at the Foreign Office, Douglas Hurd as home secretary, and Nigel Lawson at the Exchequer. John Major entered the Cabinet as chief secretary to the treasury, a responsible post that put him in charge of spending.

As a political leader, Mrs. Thatcher took for granted the support of Conservative voters, and she was still able to bring down the house at Conservative conferences. She charged ahead on her agenda, although many of her objectives were not popular. In a poll taken in 1988, it was found that 39 percent of the population said they were "Thatcherist" in that they favored a capitalist, market oriented society, while 54 percent said they were "socialist." Although 70 percent of the people polled saw Britain as "Thatcherist," only 40 percent wanted it to be that way.

By 1987, Margaret Thatcher was an established world figure who got attention wherever she went. Few political leaders have been able to resist the siren song of foreign policy, and in this respect she did not differ from others. In the TV age, the temptation to strut on the world scene is even stronger.

She enjoyed major TV successes when she entertained Reagan and Gorbachev in London, as well as when she visited Washington and Moscow. In 1988 she visited several African countries, Turkey, and Poland, attended the NATO summit in Brussels and the summit of the major industrial nations (G7) in Toronto, made an eleven-day tour of the Far East and Australia, and went to Washington for a farewell visit with President Ronald Reagan.

In 1989, she made a nine-day tour of Africa, met with Gorbachev in London, attended the NATO summit in Brussels, the European Council in Madrid, the G7 summit in Paris, and visited Japan and Malaysia. Perhaps she forgot the good example of her father and did not give sufficient attention to tending the shop.

In the meantime, the opposition parties were trying to get their acts together. After disputes about the leadership, the Liberal Party and the Social Democrats fused to form the Liberal Democratic Party led by Paddy Ashdown, a forceful speaker who performed well on television.

The electoral defeat of 1987 led Neil Kinnock to begin an extensive review of Labour Party policy in order to make the party more attractive to the growing middle class. He was supported in this project by Tony Blair, a brilliant young lawyer and MP, who shared Kinnock's view that the Labour Party needed to broaden its appeal.

Kinnock struggled with the unions and the left wing to bring a "new realism" to Labour in the interest of electability. A free-market economy, properly regulated to prevent abuses, replaced nationalization as the basis of Labour's economic policy. The battle against inflation would continue through tight but fair fiscal and monetary policies. The income tax would be made more progressive, providing revenue that would be used to increase benefits for children and the elderly.

Labour's commitment to full employment was affirmed, along with support for industrial modernization and training to create new jobs. No effort would be made to restore the former powers of the unions. As shadow employment secretary, Tony Blair persuaded the Labour Party to abandon support for the closed shop, arguing that it was an abridgement of individual rights to compel workers to join a union. In 1990, Kinnock declared that Labour's industrial policy would be justice for all, not favors to friends.

Membership in NATO was accepted, and the employment and social policies of the European Economic Community made membership in the EEC more acceptable to the unions. The most controversial step was dropping the pledge to unilateral nuclear disarmament, a cause to which Kinnock himself had long been committed. Thus armed, Kinnock set forth to transform a Labour Party still controlled by the unions and constituency activists.

Foreign Policy

In her third ministry, Mrs. Thatcher's involvement in world affairs increased to the point that it was almost her paramount interest and may have contributed to her failing grip on domestic politics. She had established a good rapport with Mikhail Gorbachev, cemented by the Soviet president's visit to London in 1987. Her views had some influence in the negotiations between Gorbachev and Reagan on the reduction of nuclear weapons in Europe. Gorbachev made a second stop in Britain in 1989, which Thatcher reciprocated later in the year.

In 1989–1990 the world scene was dramatically changed by events in the Soviet Union and Eastern Europe. The Soviet economy continued its precipitous decline, aggravated by President Gorbachev's reform policies. Within the Soviet Union, subject nationalities in the Baltic area, the

Ukraine, Georgia, and the Moslem regions claimed the right to manage their own affairs. The Soviet empire in Eastern Europe crumbled as one country after another threw off Soviet control and ejected its Communist rulers.

In November 1989, the Berlin Wall was breached, and in October 1990, the former communist East German state collapsed and was absorbed by the Federal Republic of West Germany to create the German Federal Republic. In November the Conference on Security and Cooperation in Europe declared that the Cold War had ended.

The inauguration of President George Bush in 1989 weakened the relationship with the United States that had been so important to Margaret Thatcher. The Bush administration decided that American foreign policy should draw closer to West Germany, which was seen as the new center of power in Europe. Bush and Secretary of State James Baker seemed to view Mrs. Thatcher as a tiresome woman proffering advice that was neither wanted nor heeded. They would soon find that they were mistaken.

Despite her resolution to be "a good European," Margaret Thatcher, with her free market views and global perspective, continued to be a troublesome factor in the European Community. In that respect she was in tune with the British public, which was slow to accept Britain's relationship with Europe. The European Community was more unpopular in Britain than in any other member state, with the exception of Denmark.

In 1990 only 50 percent of the public thought that membership in the European Community was "a good thing." Nevertheless, Britain derived substantial benefits from the single market: 53 percent of British exports went to member states in 1990, compared to half that amount twenty years earlier.

Movement toward greater European unity was promoted by the president of the European Commission, Jacques Delors, who acted, not as a civil servant, but as an independent statesman. In 1989, Delors outlined steps toward monetary union and a charter of rights, followed by proposals for political union within a federal system. He also advocated a "social Europe" with uniform social regulations and benefits.

Margaret Thatcher had already stated her objections in a speech at Bruges (September 1988) in which she declared: "We have not successfully rolled back the frontiers of the state in Britain only to see them reimposed at the European level, with a European super-state exercising a new dominance from Brussels." She echoed the views of President

Charles De Gaulle a quarter of a century earlier when she declared that the European Community should be a union of sovereign states: "France as France, Spain as Spain, Britain as Britain, each with its own customs, traditions, and identities."

In the same speech, she reiterated British internationalism. While asserting that Britain's destiny was in Europe, she added: "That is not to say that our future lies *only* in Europe." She insisted that "Europe should not be isolationist." She was determined to keep Britain and Europe open to the wider world.

With the breakdown of the iron curtain, Mrs. Thatcher saw Eastern Europe as a great new responsibility for the West. She urged expansion of the European Community to Poland, Czechoslovakia, Hungary, and other newly freed states. This proposal would necessarily mean a looser European Union, and would make the Common Agricultural Policy, uniform employment and social policies, and regional subsidies unworkable.

Expansion to the East threatened the tight condominium of France and West Germany within the European Community and the centralizing policies of Jacques Delors. For that reason it was, for the foreseeable future, unacceptable.

The Economy

In Mrs. Thatcher's third ministry, the results of Thatcherism began to be seen. From 1985 to 1989, the Gross Domestic Product expanded by 14.5 percent. The public revenue grew by 37 percent in that same period, while spending growth was held to 21 percent. The main spending increases were for health and community care (12 percent), education (8 percent), and law and order (14 percent). The main reductions were in defense (9 percent) and housing (40 percent). Savings in subsidies to council housing were to some extent offset by housing benefits to welfare recipients.

With the economy growing, tax cuts to stimulate investment finally became feasible. In 1988, Nigel Lawson, chancellor of the Exchequer, reduced the top rate of income tax from 60 percent to 40 percent and the basic rate to the promised 25 percent. Intermediate bands (brackets) were eliminated. In October 1987, Lawson boasted to the Conservative Party conference: "We have turned a budget deficit into a budget surplus. For the first time in living memory we are repaying the national debt." The media, always looking for fresh faces and striking personalities, hailed Lawson as "the miracle man."

Mrs. Thatcher attached high moral value to self-reliance and thrift. She wanted to reduce dependence on the state by encouraging people to save for retirement. Her ministry introduced tax-advantaged savings plans, offered by banks, building societies, and insurance companies, to supplement the basic state pension. These plans would encourage the middle class and the virtuous working class to accumulate wealth. They had the further advantage of bringing capital into the economy.

The British economy had long been led by financial services, and the boom was especially noticeable in banking, foreign exchange, and insurance. Manufacturing investment in plant and equipment belatedly began to increase, and industrial production rose. The principal growth was in the service industries, which in 1988 employed 68 percent of the workforce.

More than three million new jobs were created from 1983 to 1990. A large proportion of the new jobs that were created were filled by women, many of them in low-paid, part-time clerical or service jobs. Employment of women increased by 15 percent from 1985 to 1990 while male employment held steady. In 1990, 48 percent of employees were women. Approximately twenty million young workers entered the workforce in the 1980s and they were available to take the new jobs.

The main beneficiaries of Thatcherism were the wealthy and the middle class. From 1979 to 1989 the incomes (after taxes) of the wealthiest 10 percent increased by 65 percent per married couple. The income of the poorest 10 percent fell by 14 percent. The wealthiest also benefited most from the decrease in income taxes: from 1979 to 1989 their taxes fell from 52 percent to 36 percent of income, while the taxes of those with average incomes remained virtually the same.

Geographical divisions became pronounced. London and its great urban sprawl were generally well off; the East and the Southeast were doing well. The West of England was holding its own. Economic growth was almost entirely in the white-collar or white-coat industries, whose employees lived in neat little houses in the suburbs or in small towns where supermarkets, shopping centers, and schools were nearby. Often both husband and wife worked, needing two incomes to support the lifestyle to which they had become accustomed.

The dark side of Margaret Thatcher's Britain was unemployment. During "the winter of discontent" that had brought her to power, unemployment had been approximately 1.3 million, or 4.9 percent of the labor force. In 1981, unemployment was 2.5 million (9.4 percent); in 1986 it was 3.3 million (11.8 percent); and in 1990, when she left office, it had fallen back to 1.6 million (5.8 percent). Many of the unemployed had held jobs that would never return, or lived in areas that would not generate new jobs. One result was the emergence of a large underclass; from 1979 to 1987 the number of people below the poverty line doubled.

Legislation and mass unemployment had weakened the unions, leaving workers without recourse. An Employment Act of 1990 completed the declawing of Britain's trade unions. The closed shop virtually disappeared. Shop floor disruptions had been brought under control by holding national unions liable for damages resulting from "unofficial strikes" and allowing employers to dismiss the leaders. The welfare state, itself under attack, was all that stood between workers and the vagaries of the free market economy.

The centers of economic hardship were the Midlands, the North and Northwest, Scotland, Wales, and Northern Ireland. Some of the old industrial towns of the North and West, such as Birmingham and Manchester, were thriving as regional centers of banking, retailing, and services. Many others, however, had lost the industries that had provided jobs and there was little likelihood that new, high-tech industries would locate there.

Privatization

The Thatcher commitment to privatization had been strengthened by the successful sales of her second ministry, and the process continued with unabated vigor. Each privatization helped to fund tax cuts, won political support from business, and further weakened the Labour Party. As to creating a "share-holding democracy," most of the small purchasers regarded the undervalued shares as a chance to turn a quick profit, and the bulk of the shares were soon owned by large investors and institutions.

Before the industries could be sold they had to be made profitable, and in accomplishing this purpose Margaret Thatcher showed herself to be the best manager that the nationalized industries ever had. Good management made these industries salable, but in so doing Mrs. Thatcher refuted her own principle that nationalization was inefficient. The dilemma facing the government in all its privatizations was that the company could not be sold until it was profitable, but once profitable there was no good reason to sell it.

British Airways had been high on the privatization list, but for years the airline had been losing money and it could not be sold until that situation was changed. In 1983, a new chairman was appointed with the assignment of making the airline saleable. By 1987 he had succeeded by cutting its bloated staff while improving service, at which time the airline was successfully privatized.

Other privatizations that took place in 1987 were Rolls Royce (aircraft engines) and the British Airports Authority, which included Heathrow and Gatwick airports. Rolls Royce stock doubled the first day, giving a quick preelection profit to the two million people who applied for shares. Tony Blair, Labour's spokesman on economic matters, complained that it was a breach of trust "to undervalue shares for the purpose of attracting investors." It was notable, however, that Neil Kinnock said nothing, realizing the popularity of the shares among the voters.

The largest privatization of the year was the government's remaining 31.5 percent of the shares of British Petroleum in the largest stock offering ever made, anywhere. All the stock could have been sold to institutions without difficulty, but a significant portion was reserved for small investors and a massive advertising campaign was undertaken. However, the sale coincided with the stock market crash of October 1987, and thus the sale was less successful than expected.

Privatization of British Steel was another long-term goal, but the steel industry had to be made profitable before it could be sold. A vigorous program began to introduce modern technology, shed jobs, and close unprofitable plants. The costs in unemployment and disruption of communities was high, but by 1988 British Steel had become one of the largest and most profitable steel companies in the world.

In that year, British Steel was successfully sold to a consortium of British and overseas investors, with 23 percent reserved for an estimated 500,000 small investors. Once again the Labour Party complained that "British Steel is being offered at this bargain basement price for sordid political reasons."

The Thatcher ministry broke new ground with the privatization of the water and electricity companies, natural monopolies essential to public well-being. They needed massive amounts of new capital to keep pace with technology and changing needs. Furthermore, their long established managers and employees with their set ways of doing things were unlikely to respond to changes in those industries.

Britain's nationalized water system was organized into ten companies serving major river basins, such as Thames Water and Severn-Trent Water. In addition to providing water and sewer services, these companies had a variety of environmental responsibilities, including maintaining the purity of rivers, flood control, the management of wetlands, and protection of wildlife. A major obstacle to privatization was the influence of anglers, a numerous and dedicated lot, who did not want their favorite fishing spots to come under the control of private companies. This problem was dealt with by establishing the National Rivers Authority and limiting the privatized companies to water and sewerage.

Sale of the water companies to investors took place in 1989. To make the companies saleable, the government wrote off their debts, provided generous tax breaks, injected a considerable amount of cash for capital improvements, and offered the shares on easy terms. The shares were highly attractive, and the offer was five times oversubscribed. A regulatory office (Ofwat) was set up to regulate prices and monitor the quality of service.

The electricity industry was complex, and not all parts were attractive to investors. In 1988, a complicated privatization plan was proposed. Twelve regional electric companies delivered electricity to consumers. Shares in these companies were sold to the public in 1990 and were a popular investment. An office to regulate the industry (Offer) was established. As the first step toward privatization, the power stations were were organized into two separate generating companies.

The National Grid carried electricity from the generating companies to the regional electric companies. The National Grid was turned over to the twelve electric companies, but it was required to purchase electricity from the cheapest source, thus introducing competition between the two generating companies. Private companies were encouraged to enter the power generation business, selling electricity either to the twelve regional companies or to the National Grid.

Investors rejected privatization if it included Britain's outmoded nuclear power plants. There was considerable environmental opposition to nuclear power, especially in regard to the disposal of nuclear waste. Accordingly, the nuclear plants were withdrawn from the sale.

In 1990, the Ports Bill was passed to sell off the Port of London Authority and other ports owned by the government. The two major privatizations that still remained in the planning stage were British Coal and British Rail.

The Channel tunnel project proceeded, despite engineering difficulties and over spending. In 1990 the French and British segments of the Channel tunnel met under the Channel after three years of work, but vast overruns had been incurred.

Problems also arose with the new roads and the high speed rail system needed to connect the tunnel with London. The existing roads and rail network were clearly inadequate, but Britain insisted that it could not afford extensive new construction. Residents along the proposed route did not want increased road and rail traffic in their back gardens. Differences also emerged in deciding on the best route to bring the trains into London.

Margaret Thatcher was closely involved in efforts to promote the British armaments industry through exports. Her largest arms deal (£20 billion) was signed with Saudi Arabia in 1985. In 1988–1989 she made two trips to Nigeria and British foreign aid to Nigeria was greatly increased. Two years later a British manufacturer won a large contract to supply battle tanks that the Nigerian military used in 1992 for a political coup.

When British Aerospace had an opportunity to make large weapons sales in Malaysia, the Thatcher ministry sweetened the deal by promising economic aid to build a dam in the interior, although consultants had reported that the project was not viable. In 1988, the arms deal was signed, and in 1990 the agreed aid for the Pergau Dam was paid. Although this arrangement was not unusual in the highly competitive world of international arms sales, when revealed in 1994 it proved embarrassing to those involved.

In the 1980s Iraq, under Saddam Hussein, was seen as a bulwark of Western interests against Iran, which had come under the rule of the ayatollahs. Western countries, including Britain, were eager to sell weapons to Saddam, and Britain used its long established connections in the Middle East to advance the interests of British arms manufacturers.

In 1985, the brutality of the Iraq–Iran war led the United Nations to prohibit the export of weaponry to either of the belligerents, and Britain agreed to support the sanctions. In 1989, a British company, Matrix

Churchill, had an opportunity to sell machine tools to Iraq that could be used to make weapons. Several junior ministers joined to "interpret" the guidelines in a manner that would allow the sale, informing Mrs. Thatcher and the foreign secretary (John Major) in a perfunctory manner. Letters written by one of the junior ministers to Members of Parliament stated that the policy had not changed, when to some extent it had.

Although Mrs. Thatcher was not directly implicated in the Matrix Churchill affair, it seems likely that her determination to support the British armaments industry by making sales abroad influenced the decisions made by the junior ministers. They had reason to think that they were carrying out her policy although it was better that she not know too much about it. In this instance, as with the Pergau Dam, Mrs. Thatcher had contributed to a political scandal in waiting.

The Emergence of a Crisis

By 1989, the Thatcher ministry and its energetic leader were encountering criticism and resistance from a variety of sources, including the Conservative Party. The crucial problem was a financial crisis, as inflation revived. Nigel Lawson realized that the boom that he had unleashed had gotten out of hand. Wage settlements averaging 9.25 percent and a great expansion of consumer credit through hire purchase and credit cards fuelled inflation, which reached 8 percent in 1989. House prices rose steeply, but banks and building societies had money to lend and people bought at prices unimaginable a few years before. The boom sucked in foreign goods, and the balance of payments turned sharply against the pound.

In 1988, Lawson raised interest rates to 10.5 percent and then to 13 percent to fight inflation and correct a deteriorating balance of payments. He rejected other measures that might have moderated the boom, such as controls on mortgage lending and consumer credit. They smacked too much of Sir Edward Heath's "U-Turn."

The financial crisis gave new urgency to differences of opinion concerning Britain's relations with the European Community. As inflation took off, the financial community urged British participation in the Exchange Rate Mechanism (ERM). The ERM used the strong West German mark as its standard, and other countries were expected to stabilize their exchange rates with the mark. It was thought in the City that membership in the ERM would bring salutary discipline to the British economy and thus reduce inflation and improve the balance of payments.

Lawson was close to the financiers and sympathetic to this view. Sir Geoffrey Howe, the foreign secretary, was a strong advocate of full British participation in the European Community. He supported Lawson in urging membership in the ERM, which would be a clear signal of Britain's commitment to Europe. While this decision was pending, Lawson pushed interest rates as high as 15 percent to fight inflation and keep the pound in step with the mark.

Margaret Thatcher was appalled. She had come to office in 1979 determined to reduce inflation and the stifling effects of high interest rates. Ten years of painful effort and sacrifice seemed to be going down the drain. Observers noted increasing tension between the prime minister and "the miracle man." When Mrs. Thatcher brought back Sir Alan Walters, her former economic adviser, to give her independent advice, a showdown appeared imminent.

Tangling with Lawson and Howe put Mrs. Thatcher up against two strong-willed individuals with their own constituencies in the City and in the Conservative Party. As tensions mounted she backed off, and in June 1989, she announced her support for Lawson's policies. Lawson conceded that a decision concerning membership in the ERM could wait another year.

Nevertheless, Lawson continued the tight money policies that would keep the pound and the mark suitably aligned. Mrs. Thatcher disagreed. She believed in the rationality and inescapability of markets, in money as well as other items. "There is no way to buck the market," she said.

While wrestling with financial problems, Margaret Thatcher also faced controversies arising from her institutional reforms (see Chapter 5). In 1988 civil service reform entered a new and more drastic stage. An extensive review and reform of the social security system was undertaken. In 1988, the huge Department of Health and Social Security was split in two. Kenneth Clarke, an ambitious junior minister, became minister of health with a brief to reform the NHS. He promised to overhaul its "ramshackle bureaucracy" and run it in a businesslike manner. The Thatcher ministry also began implementing the school reforms planned by Sir Keith Joseph, which set off disputes with the teachers that lasted for several years.

Most people and powerful interests would be affected by these reforms. Civil servants, doctors, nurses, teachers, and social workers resisted reforms that were untested and ran counter to accepted ways of doing things. Pensioners, the unemployed, and others dependent on the welfare state were inclined to think that the reforms would not make life any better for them. The general public was uneasy at the pace of change. Mrs. Thatcher had pushed the country further and faster than it was willing to go.

The Poll Tax

Most disruptive of all was Margaret Thatcher's plan to abolish the rates and replace them by a tax on persons instead of property. By 1987, property values had risen dramatically. In 1985 a revaluation (reassessment) of property in Scotland produced large increases in valuations, resulting in steep increases in the rates that businesses and homeowners had to pay. Property owners in Scotland were in an uproar. No revaluation of business and residential property had been made in England in more than a decade, and it was recognized that sharply higher valuations would bring a similar reaction there.

The Conservatives were the party of small business and middle-class homeowners, who bore the burden of the rates. Approximately two thirds of the population paid no rates or had their rates paid for them by the welfare system. The Thatcherites charged that Labour-controlled councils in large cities imposed high rates on the well-off to provide services for the poor, advance the radical agenda of "the loony left," and keep their constituents voting "irresponsibly" (i.e., Labour).

With her victory in the election of 1987, Mrs. Thatcher felt strong enough to undertake a drastic reform of local government finance and get rid of the hated system of rates. Seeking a replacement, the decision was made that the only way to curb local government spending was to make the beneficiaries pay for at least part of it.

Early in 1988 a bill was introduced to replace the rates on homes with a uniform community charge (poll tax) on every person over eighteen years of age. There were lower charges for students and people with low incomes. If local governments spent excessively, they would have to increase the poll tax to cover the cost. It was expected that the general public (not just homeowners) would become a pressure group to restrain local government spending in order to keep the poll tax low. If local pressures were not effective, the central government would have the power to limit poll tax charges (capping).

Business property remained under the rating system, but a national level was set for business rates so that businesses would not be tempted to move from high-rated communities to those with lower rates. The income from business rates was assigned to communities on a per capita basis, so that local governments with large businesses would not have an advantage over those with none and councils would not be tempted to squeeze businesses for all they could get.

The Poll Tax was driven through the Cabinet and Parliament by Margaret Thatcher and none other. Likely political fallout was minimized. Problems of administration and collection were ignored, although people are considerably more mobile and easily concealed than houses. Within the Cabinet, Nigel Lawson cogently explained the faults of the poll tax, but Mrs. Thatcher would brook no resistance and the other members tamely signed on.

Tumultuous debates took place in the House of Commons, where Mrs. Thatcher faced a back-bench revolt reminiscent of the overthrow of Sir Edward Heath in 1975. When the final vote was held in January 1990, thirty-one Conservatives voted against it, including Heath and Heseltine.

After a trial in Scotland, the poll tax was introduced in England and Wales in March 1990. Although the system seemed logical in the abstract, it aroused a storm of protest when applied. Taxing the rich and the poor equally seemed so unfair that many Conservatives were critical and the general public was incredulous. A widely distributed photograph showed a nobleman with a large estate talking about the poll tax to a poor woman who paid him a modest rent for a small caravan (trailer) in which she lived. Both paid the same poll tax! Mrs. Thatcher's rivals, within and without the Conservative Party, had a field day.

Homeowners were glad to be relieved of the rates, but they were astonished at the size of their poll tax charges. Local governments, whose spending previously had been tightly controlled, seized the opportunity to increase their budgets. The poll tax rose proportionately, averaging £400 per person, rather than the estimated £200. It was found that 73 percent of households and 82 percent of individuals would pay more in poll tax than they had paid in rates.

People without children who owned expensive houses and paid high rates were better off paying the poll tax. Families with a modest house and several children over eighteen living at home paid more in poll tax than they had in rates, as did elderly ladies living in little old houses with a low valuation. Renters, especially those with large families, who had paid no rates at all, were hit hardest.

Margaret Thatcher had intended that people who objected to the poll tax would rise up against the spending of their local councils. Instead they blamed her!

It was not enough to say, as Mrs. Thatcher did, that the wealthy paid their share of taxes in other ways while renters received local government services and paid no rates at all. She tried to point out that local authorities set the level of the poll tax, and their ambitious spending plans were the cause of the problem. She declared that every citizen should be proud to make a financial contribution to the community, a view of taxes not commonly found among ordinary mortals.

Complaints rained down upon Conservative MPs, and Mrs. Thatcher faced a full-blown crisis in her own party. Business interests, to whom Thatcher was usually sensitive, opposed the new business rates. Local governments were up in arms against the new system, but that only confirmed her judgment that it was needed. In many places, people simply refused to pay. In March 1990, a demonstration in Trafalgar Square against the poll tax resulted in a riot where cars were burned and more than three hundred policemen were injured.

In a desperate effort to calm the situation the government funneled large subsidies to local governments to keep the poll tax down—-the very antithesis of Thatcherism.

The Fall of Margaret Thatcher

From the beginning of her ministry Margaret Thatcher had been unpopular among many Conservatives, and that continued despite the fact that she had won three elections. Within her Cabinet she met resistance from Geoffrey Howe and Nigel Lawson. Prominent Conservatives out of office, like Sir Edward Heath and Michael Heseltine, criticized her domineering manner and her evident willingness to run the whole show.

Disputes concerning Britain's relationship with Europe led to the breakdown of her long relationship with Sir Geoffrey Howe, who opposed her confrontational stance toward the European Community and refusal to join the ERM. In July 1989, Mrs. Thatcher decided that it was time to get Howe out of the Foreign Office.

She handled the matter badly. After various efforts to avoid an open breach, he was made leader of the Conservative Party in the House of Commons, where he was a popular figure and in an ideal position to intrigue against her.

As a successor to Howe at the Foreign Office, Mrs. Thatcher chose John Major, an agreeable young man who had risen to the office of chief secretary to the Treasury, where he had displayed a good head for numbers and a thorough grasp of detail. His appointment as foreign secretary astonished everyone. It was the chance of a lifetime for a young man on the make. Major's friend and colleague in the Treasury, Norman Lamont, took his place as chief secretary.

With Howe out of the Foreign Office, Nigel Lawson realized that his own position was slipping. Mrs. Thatcher was upset by the inflation and high interest rates unleashed by Lawson's expansionary policies. They differed on British membership in the ERM, and Thatcher resented Lawson's policy of shadowing the mark with a view to future membership. In October 1989, Lawson resigned when he discovered that Mrs. Thatcher was going behind his back for economic advice.

Politically, the Thatcher ministry had room only for one media star, and it could not be Nigel Lawson. Lawson was an articulate and colorful figure, who enjoyed public attention. He forgot that it was Margaret Thatcher who had brought him into the limelight, a fatal mistake in an underling. As prime minister, Mrs. Thatcher had to lead the Cabinet, the Parliament, the Conservative Party, and the country. She was determined to lead from the front, a fact of politics that Lawson had difficulty accepting.

John Major, who had scarcely had time to settle into the Foreign Office, replaced Lawson as chancellor of the Exchequer. It was left to this young, inexperienced politician to deal with the economic crisis that Lawson left behind. Douglas Hurd, another pro-European, replaced Major at the Foreign Office.

These surprising changes shook the Conservative Party and startled political observers. A warning shot was fired later in the year when a little-known backbencher, Sir Anthony Meyer, stood as a candidate in the annual leadership election to give Conservative MPs an opportunity to show their dissatisfaction. When Meyer received thirty-three votes, with twenty-seven abstentions, it was clear that Mrs. Thatcher was in trouble within her own party.

The year 1990 was decisive for Margaret Thatcher. When the year opened she was the most unpopular prime minister since polls had begun. In March 1990, polls showed that only 20 percent of the public were satisfied with her performance. Her belief in rugged individualism and a competitive market was not widely shared.

At the Exchequer, John Major continued Lawson's high interest policy, and by mid–1990 the full effects were being felt. Most British houses were bought with variable rate mortgages. Mortgage rates rose to 15 percent and house prices began to fall. Millions of people who had bought during the boom found themselves with negative equity: the mortgage was higher than the sale value of the house.

Consumers with high mortgage payments and other debts reined in their spending and retailing began to suffer. The shiny new office towers had high vacancy levels. The new shopping malls that were just coming on line had difficulty paying their way. The housing market collapsed.

Banks and insurance companies that had prospered during the boom found themselves faced with disaster as their profits from lending declined. Their portfolios were burdened with nonperforming mortgages and unsecured loans that were unlikely to be repaid. Construction slowed and workers drawn into the building trades by the boom were laid off.

The politicians and the public began to realize that Thatcherism and prosperity were not synonymous. The Conservative Party fell to 30 percent in the polls and suffered heavy losses in the local elections in May. Later in the year a by-election in Eastbourne, a Tory stronghold, was lost to the Liberal Democrats in a spectacular upset. The Conservative Party was stunned.

Crisis in the Persian Gulf

At this crucial moment a foreign policy crisis distracted Margaret Thatcher from her growing problems at home. In August 1990, Saddam Hussein, the brutal dictator of Iraq, suddenly invaded the adjacent mini-state of Kuwait, which he claimed should be Iraqi territory. When news of Saddam's invasion arrived, Mrs. Thatcher was in the United States attending a conference. Suddenly President George Bush realized that Britain was an important power after all, and he rushed to Colorado to meet with her.

The invasion brought back memories of the Falklands War, and Mrs. Thatcher again rose to the challenge. She was influential in encouraging Bush to organize an international alliance that would resist Saddam Hussein, defend the other states of the Arabian peninsula, and expel the Iraqis from Kuwait. She promised full British support, and immediately British forces were on their way to the Gulf.

"This was no time to go wobbly," Mrs. Thatcher told the president.

A legal basis for action was established when the United Nations Security Council condemned Iraq's aggression and demanded the restoration of the government of Kuwait. An embargo on Iraq was imposed and the Western powers were authorized to enforce it, but it seemed evident that overwhelming force would be needed to expel Saddam from his conquest. Neil Kinnock declared Labour's support for armed resistance to outright aggression.

With Saudi Arabia as a base, an allied force of half a million military personnel, with massive amounts of equipment and supplies, assembled to defend the Gulf states and restore the independence of Kuwait. The United States supplied most of the troops, support forces, and communications, but Britain sent almost fifty thousand well-trained troops. France and other countries also contributed. Margaret Thatcher's contention that a well-prepared, well-led power of medium rank could still play an important role in world affairs had been confirmed.

Resignation

While the Gulf crisis was in progress, the turmoil in the Conservative Party came to a head. The economic crisis continued and pressure increased to enter the ERM as a means of reducing monetary turbulence. Lacking strong views of his own, John Major was persuaded by the pro-European elements of the Conservative Party and the influence of the prestige press that it was necessary to join the ERM.

Mrs. Thatcher's anti-European and free-market instincts warned her against the ERM, but an election was due in 1992 and Major felt strongly the need to unite the party. Having lost Lawson over this issue, Thatcher could not afford to lose Hurd and Major too. With a political storm brewing, Thatcher found that she could not have everything her own way. In October 1990, Mrs. Thatcher agreed to join the ERM—a decision that both she and John Major would regret.

Many Conservatives were anxious about the unpopularity of their leader, which rubbed off on the party. The economy was in recession and inflation and interest rates remained high. The poll tax was a continuing aggravation. Neil Kinnock was beginning to look prime ministerial, and the changes he had made in Labour's policies made the party look ready for government. Newspapers that had previously supported the prime minister declared that she had become an electoral liability.

The poll tax gave her enemies within the party their opportunity, for Mrs. Thatcher would not abandon the poll tax, and with the poll tax in place Conservative chances in the next election were dim indeed. The Conservative conference in October was gloomy, for it was evident that the poll tax spelled doom with the voters.

Sir Geoffrey Howe precipitated Mrs. Thatcher's downfall. At the European Union summit in Rome in October, she declared that, if necessary, she would veto Jacques Delors' plan to establish a single European currency. She followed that with a hard-hitting anti-European speech in the House of Commons. In November, Howe replied with a stinging attack on her leadership, which had a great effect on the Conservative MPs and the public. Howe, with whom Thatcher had once worked so closely and effectively, resigned his post as leader of the Conservative Party in the House.

John Major and Douglas Hurd attempted to rally the Conservative MPs, but Howe had unleashed a powerful feeling that could not be stopped. Finally a prominent Conservative had openly challenged Mrs. Thatcher.

The next day, with the Conservatives' annual leadership election approaching, Michael Heseltine declared himself a candidate, citing the unpopularity of Mrs. Thatcher and promising to replace the poll tax. The *Times*, the leading Conservative newspaper, reluctantly supported Mrs. Thatcher, but the *Sunday Times* declared that she had become an "electoral liability."

Margaret Thatcher realized that Heseltine and his supporters were using the same method that she had used to displace Sir Edward Heath—the annual party vote on the leadership. But her situation was different.

When she had gained the leadership, Heath had been defeated in two elections, and the Conservative Party was out of office. In November 1990, she had won three consecutive elections, the Conservatives had been in power for eleven years, and the next election was two years off. The victor in the Falklands was preparing Britain for war in the Gulf. Rejection seemed unthinkable.

Confidently she went off to Paris to a summit meeting and was out of the country when the first ballot took place. Her absence meant that those who voted against her did not have to look her in the eye while doing it. On the first ballot she defeated Heseltine by 204 to 152 with 16 abstentions, but she had fallen two votes short of the required 15 percent margin and a second ballot would be required.

She hurried back from Paris in a desperate effort to stem the tide, but it had become clear that she could not unite a divided and shaken party. When she met individually with members of her Cabinet, one by one they made lukewarm pledges of support but added that she could not win. They saw Heseltine as a disruptive figure. They argued that the only way to stop him was for her to step down and allow other candidates to come forward. Mrs. Thatcher knew that she was finished.

She announced her intention to resign the leadership of the Conservative Party on 22 November 1990, commenting: "It's a funny old world." Six days later she went to Buckingham Palace and tendered her resignation as prime minister to the Queen.

Margaret Thatcher's resignation shocked the House of Commons and led to a party crisis. Sir Geoffrey Howe declared that it was time for a "team approach" to Cabinet decisions. Michael Heseltine announced that he would regard it as a "huge honor" to lead the Conservative Party. Douglas Hurd was also a candidate.

Mrs. Thatcher insisted that the Conservatives choose John Major to replace her as party leader and prime minister. Major was seen as a noncontroversial figure who would provide time for the divisions in the party to heal. The Thatcherites favored Major as one who would continue the Thatcher agenda. The pro-Europeans were pleased with Major's acceptance of the ERM. The backbenchers knew and liked him. Although not well known to the public, Major was popular among party workers in the constituencies.

When the ballot was taken on 27 November, John Major was two votes short of a majority. Hurd and Heseltine withdrew and Major became the new Conservative leader and prime minister. Heseltine realized that his opportunity to become prime minister had vanished. However, by challenging Mrs. Thatcher he had given the Conservative Party an opportunity to make a fresh start. "He who wields the knife never wears the crown," he remarked.

The fall of Margaret Thatcher was as astonishing as her rise to the highest office in 1979. During those eleven years she had dominated the British political scene and made herself a world figure. What had happened to bring her to such a sudden and bitter end?

Perhaps she had stayed in office too long. When she resigned, not one member of her original Cabinet remained. The leadership and confidence that were welcome in 1979 had become an imperious manner that led her to ignore or defy political advice, of which the poll tax was the most damaging example. Her frequent trips abroad weakened her grasp of public opinion at home. Hers was an executive mentality: apart from the mandatory "Prime Minister's Questions," she seldom participated in parliamentary debates. Her visits to the House of Commons tea room, which had been frequent early in her ministry, became a rare event in her later years.

She had outlasted and, to some extent, resolved the issues that had brought her to office. For one reason or another, she had worn out her welcome.

5

Thatcherite Reform

The Civil Service

The British civil service was world famous for its impartiality, competence, and devotion to good government. At the top of the civil service were approximately one hundred permanent secretaries ("mandarins"), almost all of them urbane gentlemen educated at Oxford and Cambridge in liberal studies. Their responsibility was to assist the minister in running his department by providing information and advice, while helping him to avoid mistakes that would be politically or personally embarrassing. They were the top of a civil service pyramid of 720,000 employees.

Margaret Thatcher was not impressed. She was convinced that the civil service was riddled with poorly defined responsibilities and without cost-benefit accountability. In the upper levels she suspected a genteel "old-boy" network that encouraged log-rolling and buck-passing. She believed that the structures and routines of the civil service were inefficient and unresponsive to the needs of a dynamic nation.

Thatcher was a great admirer of successful businessmen, and she sought to introduce into the civil service the practices of large businesses. She asked Sir Derek Rayner of Marks & Spencer, a highly regarded middle-class retail chain, to serve as her adviser on efficiency in government.

Rayner established an "Efficiency Unit" at No. 10 to conduct in-depth investigations of departments, looking for ways to achieve better performance and save money. He discovered that the Ministry of Agriculture was breeding its own rats for research at a cost of £30 per rat when they could be bought commercially for £2. Rayner pushed for a reduction of paperwork. The claim was made that twenty-seven thousand forms were

101

eliminated and another forty thousand were redesigned. Some savings were made, although the civil service complained that many of the supposed savings were illusory.

Coming from a large retail chain with many stores, Rayner began decentralizing administration, establishing semi-autonomous "cost centers" managed by administrators with minimal supervision by the responsible department. A new system of financial management was introduced to define objectives, measure results, and assess costs.

Sir Robin Ibbs, who succeeded Rayner as head of the Efficiency Office, proposed to dismantle the hierarchical, bureaucratic, departmental structure of the civil service, replacing it with semi-autonomous agencies. At the top would be a core group of 50,000 civil servants with policy-making responsibilities. The remaining 550,000, who performed administrative or routine functions, would be organized into agencies largely independent of ministerial control. They would be managed by responsible executives as "businesses." People who dealt with these agencies would be "customers."

Change began slowly with rather distinct agencies, such as the Stationery Office, which issued official publications and ran a chain of bookstores scattered throughout the country. By the end of Mrs. Thatcher's ministry in 1990 there were thirty-four agencies employing eighty-thousand people.

The National Health Service

Britain was the only major industrial state to maintain a national, publicly funded health service, including medical care, prescriptions, and hospital care for all its people. The mission of the NHS was greater than it could possibly fulfill. People could go to the doctor as often as they wished at no cost to them, and some abused that privilege. The NHS also owned and operated the hospitals, managing a huge workforce carrying out a wide variety of duties in thousands of buildings of varying size, age, and suitability.

Despite constant complaints about its shortcomings, the National Health Service (NHS) was the most cherished institution of the welfare state. A major problem was the growing demand for health care due to advances in medicine and the aging of the population. Although the demand for health care is virtually limitless, by any standard the NHS was underfunded. At a time when other major industrialized nations were spending up to 10 percent of the Gross National Product on health care, the NHS struggled with 6 percent.

Every year the funding of the NHS increased, but never fast enough to keep up with medical costs and the increase of health needs. The approach of the Thatcher ministry to the NHS, as with all other activities of government, was to insist on strict adherence to spending limits, with new needs financed out of savings from greater efficiency. Mrs. Thatcher's view was that the NHS was badly administered. When she was criticized for failing to support the NHS she replied: "the NHS is safe only with us, because we will see that it is prudently managed and financed."

As with the civil service, Thatcher turned to a businessman to recommend efficiencies. In 1983, she appointed Sir Roy Griffiths, managing director of the Sainsbury supermarket chain, to review the administrative structure of the NHS and make recommendations for improvement. Sir Roy was aghast at what he found. "If Florence Nightingale were carrying her lamp through the corridors of the NHS today," he said, "she would almost certainly be searching for the people in charge."

The Ministry of Health and Social Security had general responsibility for the NHS, which was exercised through a cumbersome structure of regional and district health authorities. The NHS was the biggest employer of labor in Europe but had no clear lines of authority and scarcely knew how many people were on its payroll.

Griffiths recommended establishing a central management board and professional management staffs for the regional and district health and hospital authorities. Although additional staff would add to the administrative costs of the NHS, he believed that they would more than pay for themselves by improved efficiency. In 1984 the government established general managers in all the health authorities, a step that infuriated physicians and employee unions, who been pretty much running the NHS to suit themselves.

In an institution as large as the NHS, things inevitably went wrong. Waiting lists lengthened; districts ran out of money before the end of the fiscal year. In 1986–1987 the media were filled with medical horror stories, inevitably attributed to lack of adequate funding. In the House of

Commons, the semiweekly "Prime Minister's Questions" became a nightmare of accusations and pathetic anecdotes.

The British Medical Association complained that the Health Service was "under-funded, under-mined, and under threat." The nurses made well-justified claims for pay increases that were backed up by one-day stoppages and other disruptions. It was pointed out that large numbers of doctors and nurses were leaving the Health Service for the private sector or other countries, especially the United States.

In 1987, the Thatcher ministry proposed to impose charges for periodic dental and eye checkups. The result was a row with the medical profession that brought the festering problems of the NHS back into the public eye. The proposal was seen as a violation of the principle of preventive medicine that might be further extended in the future. A revolt of Conservative backbenchers took place, in which the Labour Party joined enthusiastically. The British Medical Association declared its opposition. The nurses again resorted to a strike to protest their low pay.

In January 1988, Mrs. Thatcher established a committee of ministers, chaired by herself, to make a comprehensive review of the National Health Service. The report of the committee, published in July, was entitled *The Future of the National Health Service*. One result of the report was the separation of the Department of Health and Social Security into two separate departments. The ambitious Kenneth Clarke was appointed Minister for Health with a mandate for reform. Additional funds were provided to give a substantial pay raise to the nurses and catch up on unmet needs.

Investigations were undertaken to find places where savings could be made. One proposal was to sell off unessential NHS property, including residences for nurses. Another was to put many NHS activities out to contract, such as cleaning, laundry, and food services. Opportunities for savings in the cost of medicine were found in the use of generic drugs or contracting with pharmaceutical companies for reduced prices on drugs. Useful as such reforms might be, they did not change the problems of a national health service in an age of rapidly growing medical costs and needs.

The Thatcher ministry's reform proposals were introduced in 1989 and passed in 1990 as the ministry was coming to a close. The legislation changed fundamentally the role of the district health authorities. Instead of operating a health service they would contract with providers of medical care.

Hospitals were authorized to organize themselves as trusts (free-standing corporations) within the NHS. These hospitals would hire their own employees on their own terms, and contract for food services, janitorial services, laundry, and other hospital needs. Eventually most hospitals became trusts.

The district health authorities received government funding based on a formula that included population, age of the population, and other factors affecting health needs. With those funds they would contract with the hospitals to provide services. The hospitals would compete with each other to get the contracts upon which their continued existence depended. If the district authorities were dissatisfied, they could take their business elsewhere (if an alternative provider existed) and the hospital would suffer the consequences.

A similar principle was introduced in regard to the doctors. Groups of doctors with more than seven thousand patients could separate from the district management. Instead, they would receive funds directly from the NHS that they would use to support their own practice or to purchase the services of specialists and hospitals in meeting the needs of their patients. Under this system, specialists and hospitals would compete to obtain referrals from the fund-holding doctors, who held the money bags.

As was to be expected with an institution as popular as the NHS, proposals for change provoked a furious debate. The Labour Party objected to introducing market considerations into an institution that had been established as a public service. The British Medical Association complained strenuously at introducing "the competition culture" into the practice of medicine. The bishop of Birmingham described the reforms as "unChristian" because they treated patients as consumers, in contrast to the example of Jesus.

Schools

In her second ministry, Mrs. Thatcher acted aggressively in dealing with schools. Although it was generally recognized that education in Britain's best schools was excellent, there was reason to believe that in many less prestigious schools the level of student accomplishment fell short of what was needed in an advanced society.

Politics and ideology also played a part in the movement for school reform. Many Conservatives felt that schools had been taken over by radical teachers, whose views were anticapitalist and antibusiness, and whose teaching methods did not require mastery of subject matter. Furthermore, the National Union of Teachers (NUT) was closely allied with the Labour Party.

Having served as education minister under Heath, Margaret Thatcher claimed special knowledge about education. She was much influenced by Sir Keith Joseph, who saw education as crucial in modernizing the economy and breaking "the cycle of deprivation" found in much of industrial Britain. When Mrs. Thatcher became prime minister, Sir Keith became minister of industry, where he helped formulate her policies toward the nationalized industries. In 1981, he moved to the Ministry of Education & Science.

Conservative critics declared that the existing school curriculum did not give enough attention to fundamental subjects such as mathematics and science, geography, history, and writing. Teachers were criticized for emphasizing the personal development of the student rather than verifiable gains in knowledge and skills. To this was joined the complaint that schooling did not adequately prepare young people for employment in business and industry.

Choice and competition were fundamental principles with Mrs. Thatcher, and she believed they applied to schools as well as the economy. As minister of education under Heath, she had tried to stop the advance of comprehensive schools, but without success. Now, as prime minister, she succeeded in repealing Labour Party legislation requiring all local education authorities to go comprehensive. Some of the effects of this policy were offset by providing an additional thirty-five thousand scholarships (the Assisted Places Scheme) for students whose parents could not afford the fees of the independent schools.

In 1985 Sir Keith Joseph attempted to use the teachers' pay claim to achieve one of his objectives: evaluation of teachers. He promised more money in the future if the teachers would agree to a system of regular evaluation as the basis for individual pay raises. The NUT replied that evaluation was an insult to the teachers' professional training, competence, and commitment. The union urged the teachers to resist, and for the next several years sporadic strikes and other forms of resistance disrupted the schools.

The ministry's plans for school reform were embodied in legislation in 1988, but not until after long and heated debates. The legislation prescribed a national curriculum of core subjects giving more emphasis to English, mathematics, and science. Assurances were given that the new curriculum would include sufficient time for religious education. Welsh nationalism was satisfied by an agreement that the Welsh language would be a major subject in Welsh schools.

An important part of the reform was the provision for national achievement tests at ages seven, eleven, fourteen, and sixteen. The results of the tests would be published, which would make possible a national evaluation and ranking of schools. Teachers were opposed to "league tables" (like American baseball standings) that might reflect unfavorably on them. This dispute remained unsettled under Mrs. Thatcher.

Margaret Thatcher believed that local authorities, especially in Labour-controlled metropolitan areas, were dominated by NUT, which had consistently opposed her reforms. To outflank the NUT, management of the schools was transferred from the local education authorities to the governing boards of the schools. Parents were given the right to choose the school that their children would attend.

Parents were also authorized to decide by a vote whether the school would "opt out" of local control and receive its funding directly from the Treasury. The governors of the "grant-maintained" schools would choose their own headmaster and teachers, select the students that they would admit, shape their own curriculum (in accord with the national curriculum), and manage their budget as they thought best.

Opposition to the proposal came from a variety of directions. Some feared that opting-out would be most attractive to the better schools, leaving the poorer schools and less able students to the local authorities. The Department of Education was concerned that lack of supervision would permit eccentricity and irresponsibility; the Treasury was uneasy about lack of control of spending. The National Union of Teachers saw that its power would be undermined.

Local educational authorities resented the challenge of grant-maintained schools and often did all they could to keep schools from opting out. Many parents and children wished to continue the schools as they were. Ultimately, opting-out proved to be less popular than expected.

Universities

Although an Oxford graduate herself (or perhaps because of it), Margaret Thatcher had little sympathy for the universities. She was inclined to think that the universities were bastions of privilege and dilettantism, generally radical in politics, and producing graduates unprepared to enter into the real world of work. She felt that universities needed drastic reform to bring them to modern standards of productivity and efficiency.

Her views were partially a matter of cost. She insisted that university expansion could no longer continue. In 1981, a 15 percent cut over three years was imposed. The total number of students that could be admitted to British universities was reduced, and many programs and research activities were eliminated. Building projects were curtailed and early retirement programs were introduced to reduce the number of faculty. Oxford University retaliated by refusing to confer an honorary degree on the university's most famous alumna, but then Oxford had been around for eight hundred years and could afford to annoy the prime minister.

The universities lost their cherished independence when a fundamental change was made in the operations of the University Grants Committee (UGC), which allocated government funds to the universities. Instead of lump-sum grants to be used by each university at its own discretion, grants were earmarked for specific purposes. Funding for teaching was separated from funding for research. Reviews of departmental strengths and weaknesses were undertaken in a variety of subjects. In short, the UGC exercised greater control in pursuit of the Thatcherite principle of accountability.

In her third ministry, Mrs. Thatcher kept up the pressure on the universities to limit growth and costs. The University Grants Committee was replaced by a Universities Funding Council that provided funds to the universities with specific performance guidelines. At least half the members of the council were to be drawn from outside the field of education, presumably to keep the universities relevant to societal needs. The council also had a full-time staff to exercise close supervision and keep the paperwork flowing.

Financial support of the universities was curtailed, and universities were warned that increased enrollments would not bring additional funding. The principle was announced that programs should be determined, not by student demand, but by the needs of the competitive economy that the Thatcher ministry was building. To promote the new Thatcherite economy, grants were skewed toward science and engineering, for which there was small student demand while popular subjects, like the humanities and the social sciences, were starved. Inspectors given the Orwellian title "academic quality assessors" were sent to evaluate university-sponsored research. Tenure was abolished for future university appointments.

In 1984, Sir Keith Joseph, as education minister, proposed abolition of free tuition, with parents contributing to the tuition costs of their offspring according to their means. The result was a mass revolt by Conservative backbenchers, representing themselves and the middle-class voters who were the backbone of the Conservative Party. Sir Keith had to back down, taking the expected savings out of the science budget instead. Overseas students, however, were required to pay the full cost of their education, a step that made minuscule savings but carried a heavy cost in British prestige and influence in the Commonwealth countries.

British university students still received grants from local authorities for their living costs, but the Thatcherite restrictions on local spending meant that these were not increased and students had to cover rising costs for subsistence in other ways. Some of them began taking part-time jobs, a common American practice but virtually unheard of in Britain.

The polytechnics and colleges, with their career oriented programs, were favored by the Thatcher ministry as more in accord with the needs of the national economy. Their lower costs per student and their ability to absorb increasing numbers made them attractive to the cost conscious Thatcher ministry. They continued to grow rapidly, until by 1987 their enrollments surpassed the universities'. In 1988, the polytechnics were removed from local management and funding and put under the Polytechnics Funding Council.

The Environment

With her emphasis on economic growth, Margaret Thatcher gave low priority to protection and improvement of the environment. She wanted to encourage industrial development, not introduce environmental controls that might be an added burden on industry. Privatization was another

consideration: the sale of the electric power industry would be jeopardized by introducing strict controls on coal-burning generators; the sale of
nuclear plants would be made difficult by tight environmental restrictions
on their operations and wastes. Strict controls on water quality would
affect the salability and price of the water companies.

One factor that increased the involvement of Thatcher government in
the environment was the need to implement policies required by the European Community. Another was the growth of the environmental
("green") movement, which drew most of its strength from middle-class,
small-town, and rural people. Elections for the European Parliament provided a way for people to make a statement, and in the European election
of 1989, the Green Party received up to 20 percent of the vote in some
areas.

In 1987, the Inspectorate of Pollution was established within the Department of the Environment. However, this office was given modest resources and its mandate was limited to industrial pollution. The next year
the government signed the international agreement to reduce the emission
of substances that injured the ozone layer, but environmentalists were not
pleased when more use of nuclear power was recommended as one way
to do it.

In the 1980s, a small dark cloud appeared on the horizon in the form
of "mad cow disease" (bovine spongiform encephapathology), a fatal disease that destroyed the brains of cattle. It was found that the disease was
spread by adding the offal of infected sheep to cattle feed as a protein
supplement. This practice was prohibited in 1988, and the only solution
appeared to be to destroy all cattle born before that date.

Such a drastic action could not be undertaken hastily, and a Tory government was inclined to take the time needed to obtain scientific verifica-
tion before inflicting such a blow upon one of its important constituencies.
In 1990, a frightened public insisted that British beef be banned from
schools and hospitals. A year earlier the United States had banned the
importation of British beef.

Law and Order

Margaret Thatcher was a forceful advocate of the "law and order" strand
in British conservatism, with its emphasis on maintaining private prop-

erty, social order, and the authority of government. In 1979 and 1980 racial tensions in major cities led to riots that Mrs. Thatcher and her Conservative constituencies were determined to control.

In 1981, riots broke out in a run-down, racially mixed part of south London named Brixton. They began with a major police operation to arrest burglars and muggers who infested the area. Over a hundred police officers were involved and hundreds of youths (mainly black males) were arrested or stopped and searched. The riot that followed lasted for three days and hundreds of people were injured, including 150 policemen. Although most of the rioters were black, they were joined by white youths, and all races participated in the looting that followed.

The next day there were clashes in another part of London between white skinheads and Asian immigrants. When the police attempted to restore order, the mob turned against them. During the summer similar riots broke out in Liverpool (Toxteth), Manchester (Moss Side), and other cities. In every case the police were the initial target of the rioters, and looting followed.

In 1981, Lord Scarman, a highly respected judge, was named to conduct an inquiry into the Brixton riot. The *Scarman Report*, which was presented later that year, pointed out the problems created by unemployment, poor housing, ethnic conflict, and low educational achievement. Scarman noted that there was a high level of street crime in these neighborhoods. When the police cracked down, black youths felt they were victims of racial prejudice. Scarman concluded that the immediate cause of the Brixton riot was the anger of young black males toward the police.

The police defended themselves by saying that most crimes were committed by blacks and no racial prejudice was involved. While faulting the police for not maintaining better relations with the community, Scarman in general commended the conduct of the police in dealing with the riot.

In his report, Scarman advocated strengthening police forces to deal quickly with riots while urging special training to make the police sensitive to racial resentments. He urged "positive discrimination" to overcome the sense of negative discrimination felt by the black population. The report also called for an independent body to investigate complaints of racism in the police.

Although she agreed with much of the analysis of the *Scarman Report*, Mrs. Thatcher insisted that inner city problems did not justify rioting, looting, and crime, especially if they were carried out in the guise of social protest. She was convinced that one reason for disorders was the belief among young hooligans of all races that they could get away with it. She was willing to support sensitivity training for police, but she was also determined to back them up with improved riot control equipment and increased powers to make arrests. The police were one of the few aspects of the civil government where spending was significantly increased.

Despite the prime minister's hard line, the ministry did undertake some steps to deal with the economic and social disadvantages of the people living in the riot areas. Michael Heseltine was given responsibility for a task force charged with finding ways to improve living conditions in the Liverpool area. Despite tight budgets, funding for urban development programs in depressed areas was substantially increased.

In 1985, riots between black youths and the police took place in London, Birmingham, Liverpool, and elsewhere. The London riot was precipitated by a police attempt to make an arrest in Brixton in which shots were fired. A crowd attacked the local police station with Molotov cocktails, and an orgy of burning and looting followed. The police reported 724 crimes and 53 people injured (including 10 police officers). Two white women were raped, and 230 arrests were made.

Shortly thereafter another police raid led to riots in an impoverished housing estate in north London, where guns were used against police and reporters. One police officer was hacked to death with a knife and a machete while defending firemen trying to control a blazing building. In Birmingham, the arrest of a black youth for drug offenses led to attacks by skinheads and black toughs on Asian shopkeepers, two of whom were burned to death defending a sub-post office.

This time the ministry made a harsh response. The riots were treated, not as race-relations issues but as "law and order" issues. Douglas Hurd, home secretary, remarked that the riot "was not a cry for help but a cry for loot." The chairman of the Conservative Party declared that unemployment could not explain "a hundred people falling on a single policeman and murdering him." Labour joined in the hue and cry. Roy Hattersly, a mature and moderate Labour MP, condemned the riot as criminal, and different from the riots of 1981, which grew out of deprivation and despair. Labour accused the Conservatives of not being tough enough on crime. Others blamed the government for neglecting the inner city and the police for "insensitivity."

Mrs. Thatcher's first response was that there was "no excuse, no justification whatever for the riots." At the party conference that autumn she stated angrily: "Those who take to the streets on the first available pretext, to fire, loot and plunder, will be subject to the full rigors of the criminal law." Hurd made it clear that there would not be another *Scarman Report*. He armed airport policemen with submachine guns and other counterterrorist gear, and the London Metropolitan Police were equipped with water cannon and other instruments for riot control.

The Criminal Justice Bill (1986) demonstrated the Thatcher ministry's commitment to "law and order." It provided for longer sentences, compensation to victims of crime, limitation on defense challenges to jurors, and privacy for children called to testify in child abuse cases. The Public Order Act of the same year gave the police new powers and resources for riot control. It reflected the view of many Conservatives that a strong hand was necessary to deal with the volatile populations of the central cities.

By itself, more legislation could not reduce crime, and the number of reported offenses increased from 3.1 million in 1980 to 4.4 million in 1990. More offenders were being caught, but the rate of detection declined. Prisons were jammed, and in 1990 Strangeways Prison in Manchester erupted in violence and destruction that lasted for twenty-five days. By that time the British public was less offended by police in riot gear and more interested in police protection on the streets.

Margaret Thatcher's tough "law and order" views met a surprising defeat in 1979, when a bill to restore the death penalty was defeated. The death penalty had long been a part of Tory political rhetoric and Mrs. Thatcher favored it. When a free vote was taken in the House of Commons, opposition surfaced in both parties and the bill failed by a large margin. A similar proposal was made annually for the next few years, but the death penalty was always defeated. Parliament also ended corporal punishment in schools by one vote, Mrs. Thatcher voting against the proposal.

There was much discussion of a breakdown of personal morality attributed to a variety of causes, including Thatcherism, which one bishop described as "insufficiently Christian." Mrs. Thatcher struck back by quoting St. Paul: "If a man will not work, he shall not eat."

Another kind of rioting belied the reputation of he British people as polite and orderly. British football crowds were notoriously rowdy, and in 1985 ugly crowd behavior became a national embarrassment. In May, British fans at the European Cup final in Belgium attacked Italian supporters, leading to a stampede in which more than thirty spectators were killed. When the governing body of European football barred British clubs from European competition, most Britons agreed that firm action was long overdue. Shortly thereafter hooliganism broke out among British soccer fans at a match in Germany. Mrs. Thatcher was furious, and legislation was passed requiring identity cards for admission to matches.

One of the problems of British soccer was old stadiums with large standing-room areas bordering the field where the hooligans gathered. The worst disaster in British football history took place at Sheffield in 1989: ninety-five people were killed when a stampede took place in the standing-room area and spectators were trapped against the fence. The answer to that problem was to have numbered seats and require every person attending to have a ticket for a specific seat, thus ending the standing-room area where disorders usually took place.

Northern Ireland

In 1921 the island of Ireland was divided between the independent Republic of Ireland and the six northern counties (Ulster), which chose to remain with the United Kingdom. Northern Ireland received Home Rule, which meant that it had its own ministry, civil service, police (the Royal Irish Constabulary), and parliament. It also sent MPs to the Parliament in Westminster. Its people participated fully in the benefits of the British welfare state.

Life in Northern Ireland was dominated by powerful communal attachments and antagonisms. The Protestants, who were in the majority, thought of themselves as British, and relied on their membership in the United Kingdom to guarantee that they would never be absorbed into the Republic. Among the Catholic minority, the sense of Irish nationalism was strong. They maintained ties with the Republic and thought of themselves as Irish.

In 1968, long-simmering conflicts led to Catholic civil rights marches demanding reform of the electoral system, which was rigged to favor the Protestants. The Catholics complained of discrimination in education, housing, and other public services. When a conciliatory prime minister of Northern Ireland proposed reforms, the Protestants reacted in force and violent clashes broke out between the two communities. A paramilitary group calling itself the Irish Republican Army (IRA) was formed to protect the neighborhoods of West Belfast from Protestant assaults. It soon became a terrorist organization seeking to end British authority in Northern Ireland.

In 1969, seeking a quick military solution to what was really a political and communal problem, Harold Wilson sent in units of the British army to restore order. When Heath became prime minister he strengthened the military presence, but strikes and violence continued. In 1971, the first British soldier was killed by the IRA, and the government of Northern Ireland began interning suspected terrorists without trial. By 1972, more than twenty-thousand British troops were stationed in Northern Ireland, supported by much-expanded police forces.

In January 1972 ("Bloody Sunday"), British paratroops trying to preserve order during a demonstration panicked and killed thirteen Catholics at Londonderry. The IRA responded with "Bloody Friday" in July, when nine people were killed and one hundred and thirty injured by nineteen IRA bombs that went off in Belfast. Heath reacted firmly. He suspended the Protestant-controlled government of Ulster and imposed direct rule from London.

The IRA declared that British troops were an army of occupation and legitimate targets for terrorist bombings. The worst year was 1972, when there were almost fourteen hundred explosions and many more bomb scares. In that year, one hundred and forty-six security officers (army and police) were killed. The IRA preferred to use car bombs, but when innocent civilians were also injured, the IRA lost support, even among its most devoted protectors in the Catholic neighborhoods.

Instead the IRA extended the terror into Britain. Seven died and one hundred and twenty were injured when two Birmingham pubs were bombed in 1974. In 1975 London was struck by a series of bombings at the Tower of London, Harrod's department store, the Hilton Hotel, and several underground stations.

When the Thatcher government came to power, it had no declared policy concerning Northern Ireland apart from the promise in the election

manifesto to "maintain the union." Unionism continued to be Mrs.
Thatcher's policy throughout her eleven years in No. 10. To some extent
her unionism put her on the side of the Protestants, but she saw it also
as maintaining the sovereign integrity of the British state. Within that
framework she was willing to work to resolve the grievances of the Catholics.

Shortly after taking office, Mrs. Thatcher received news that Lord
Mountbatten, a member of the royal family and a man of distinguished
public service, had been killed, along with three others, when the IRA
planted a bomb on his boat. The same day eighteen British soldiers were
killed by two IRA landmines detonated by remote control. The first mine
killed a group of soldiers, and when other soldiers arrived to care for their
injured comrades a second mine exploded.

Mrs. Thatcher met the president of Ireland at Lord Mountbatten's funeral where she initiated efforts to obtain cooperation in law enforcement
between the British and the Irish authorities, an approach abhorrent to
the unionists. She was convinced that defeating terrorism would require
close cooperation between Britain and the Republic of Ireland in policing
the border, where the IRA stored smuggled weapons or could avoid cap-
ture when pursued.

The problem of public order was aggravated in October, 1980, when a
group of IRA prisoners in the Maze Prison led by Bobby Sands went on a
hunger strike to assert their demand to be treated as "political prisoners."
Mrs. Thatcher firmly refused political status for men whom she regarded
as common criminals.

During the hunger strike the prisoners were offered meals three times
a day, which they refused, although they drank water. Mrs. Thatcher refused to impose force-feeding, but when a prisoner lost consciousness
members of the family were authorized to use intravenous feeding. As fate
would have it, during the strike the member of Parliament for a Catholic
constituency died and Sands registered as a candidate for the seat. Sands
was elected by a narrow margin over the unionist candidate.

In the meantime the hunger strike had gained extensive media coverage, which is always responsive to human drama and usually sympathetic
to underdogs. Sands died after sixty-six days of fasting and others followed until ten IRA hunger strikers had died. At this point the families
of the remaining strikers agreed to intravenous feeding to prevent further
deaths, and the IRA called off the strike.

Despite additional troops flown in from Britain, violent clashes broke out and seventy-three people were killed. Particularly outrageous was a random shooting into a small Protestant church during the service, killing three worshipers and wounding seven. The IRA also assassinated a Catholic judge as he was leaving church, on the grounds that by holding judicial office he was supporting British oppression. The effect of these events was to polarize further the unionist and nationalist populations of Northern Ireland. British treatment of the prisoners also inflamed public opinion in the Republic and brought an end to Mrs. Thatcher's early efforts at cooperation.

After the failure of the hunger strikes of 1981, the IRA decided to take its war of terrorism to the British mainland. In October 1981, a bomb filled with six-inch nails was exploded outside Chelsea Barracks in London, killing one bystander and injuring many soldiers. In July 1982, the IRA set off two bombs in London: one in Hyde Park directed at the Horse Guards, and the second under the bandstand in Regent's Park while a military band was playing. Eight people, soldiers and civilians, were killed and fifty-three people were injured. During the Christmas shopping period of 1983, an IRA bomb in a car parked at Harrod's department store in London killed five people, one of them an American, and injured ninety-one others, some of them seriously.

In 1984, terrorism almost brought the Thatcher ministry to a fatal end. In October of that year the Conservative Party Conference met in Brighton. At 3:00 A.M. an IRA bomb exploded in the Grand Hotel, where Mrs. Thatcher and many leading Conservative politicians were staying. Five floors of the hotel, including Thatcher's suite, were wrecked and five people were killed, including a Conservative member of Parliament. Thatcher was unhurt. She appeared at the conference that morning as scheduled and received a great ovation.

Despite discouragements and IRA threats, Margaret Thatcher continued her efforts at cooperation with the Republic of Ireland as a way to control terrorism. The Thatcher ministry did not flinch in its commitment that Northern Ireland should remain part of the United Kingdom as long as the majority wished it, but it was also ready to concede that the Republic of Ireland had "a legitimate interest in Northern Ireland, and a special part to play in the politics of the minority there."

The result was the Anglo-Irish Agreement, which was signed in November 1985. To reassure the unionists, the Irish government recognized British sovereignty over Northern Ireland and agreed that no change would be made without the consent of the majority of the people of Northern Ireland. To satisfy the nationalists, the Republic was authorized to represent them in intergovernmental meetings. A permanent secretariat was to be established in Belfast to administer the agreement.

The agreement was rejected by the unionists as giving the Republic a voice in the affairs of Northern Ireland. They suspected that once the camel got its nose in the tent it would not stop there. An opinion poll found 49 percent of the unionists opposed, and only 14 percent in favor. The leader of the Ulster Unionist Party declared that Northern Ireland, "bound and trussed like a turkey for the oven," was going to be turned over to the Republic.

The Social Democratic and Labour Party (SDLP), the main nationalist party in Northern Ireland, hailed the agreement. The agreement was rejected by Sinn Fein, the political wing of the IRA, as recognizing the separation of Northern Ireland from the rest of the island.

The British House of Commons ratified the agreement overwhelmingly, as did the Irish Dail, although the vote was closer. In Britain, the contentions of Northern Ireland were regarded as a nuisance and a bore. In general, the British public welcomed any agreement that would fob these problems off on the Irish people themselves.

Behind these institutional arrangements lay Margaret Thatcher's fierce determination to stop terrorism, and in that she did not succeed. The violence of the IRA had given risen to a counter force, swaggering bands of loyalist paramilitaries, who used intimidation to drive Catholics from their homes. On the first anniversary of the agreement, Protestant demonstrations took place in Belfast in which two people died, seventy were injured, and seventy shops in the center of the city were damaged and some looted.

It soon became clear that the IRA was still in business. In November 1987, the IRA exploded a bomb in Enniskillen, Northern Ireland, during an observance honoring war dead. Part of the building in which the service was being held collapsed, killing eleven people and injuring more than sixty.

An incident in 1988 inflamed the situation. Three Irish terrorists preparing a bombing in Gibraltar were discovered by British troops and shot dead. Their funeral outside of Belfast drew a huge crowd of sympathizers, who regarded them as martyrs. At the funeral, a gunman fired on the mourners and three were killed. At the funeral of one of the mourners, the infuriated crowd turned on two young soldiers in civilian clothes, pulled them from their car, and lynched them on the spot. When Mrs. Thatcher went to console the relatives of the slain soldiers, Gerry Adams, leader of Sinn Fein, told her to expect many more.

The Commonwealth

For more than two decades, British politics had been disturbed by the Rhodesian issue. The white minority government, led by the wily and tenacious Ian Smith, had declared independence and was holding out against giving political power to the black African majority. The white settlers realized that little sympathy could be expected from Britain, and they were ostracized by the rest of the world. Their only active support came from the *apartheid* regime of the Union of South Africa. In 1976, South Africa, pressed by the United States, withdrew its support for the Smith regime. It was evident that the isolated position of the settlers could not be indefinitely sustained.

Rhodesia was a divisive issue within the Conservative Party, where "kith and kin" sentiments toward the settlers were strong. Mrs. Thatcher was determined to remove this festering sore. Shortly after taking office she stepped forward and called a constitutional conference in London. The contending leaders were presented with a constitution that gave power to the black majority but guaranteed the rights of the white minority for ten years. The document was presented on a "take it or leave it" basis. After the predictable protestations, the constitution was accepted.

In December 1979, British authority over Rhodesia was temporarily restored and a governor was sent to oversee the transition to the new constitution. Shortly thereafter the independent state of Zimbabwe came into existence. Margaret Thatcher was credited with a triumph that had removed an embarrassment for Britain, and that was her main concern.

South Africa had been part of the British Empire and Commonwealth for a century and a half until it left the Commonwealth in 1961. The white population was divided between the Afrikaners, descendants of the original Dutch settlers, and people of British background. The ruling Nationalist Party was primarily a party of the Afrikaners. South Africa also had a substantial population of mixed race and of Indian descent. The great majority of the people consisted of black Africans, who were denied political and civil rights and, under the policy of *apartheid*, were required to live in separate areas.

Margaret Thatcher's toughness was conspicuously displayed in the continuing dispute over the Union of South Africa, for the South African policy of *apartheid* aroused worldwide condemnation and demands for economic sanctions. While stating her own disapproval of *apartheid*, Mrs. Thatcher wished to preserve constructive relations with that country.

At the Commonwealth conference in 1985, her refusal to impose sanctions infuriated the other members. Angry scenes took place at the Commonwealth Conference in 1986. Mrs. Thatcher continued to hold out against the denunciations of other Commonwealth members and the pressures of world opinion. The European Community, Canada, and the United States imposed economic sanctions on South Africa, leaving Britain isolated on this issue.

Eventually external and internal political pressures brought the South African economy to its knees. Within the ruling Nationalist Party there was growing recognition that it had become necessary to bring the black majority into the political process. In 1989, F. W. de Klerk became president. The next year Nelson Mandela and other prominent black leaders were released from prison and the African National Congress, led by Mandela, was permitted to engage in political activity.

Despite bitter opposition from the Afrikaners and considerable apprehension by other whites, the South African government began preparations for a new constitution in which blacks would participate. Working together, De Klerk and Mandela kept a volatile situation under control until the work was complete.

By the time Margaret Thatcher left office, the process of establishing a nonracial South Africa was well on its way. In 1993 the Nobel Peace Prize was awarded jointly to President De Klerk and Nelson Mandela, and in 1994 Mandela was inaugurated as president of the new Union of South Africa.

In the Far East, it was essential to settle the status of Hong Kong, for Communist China was determined to take over the colony when the British lease ran out in 1997. Under British rule Hong Kong had become a world center of finance, trade, and industry, and any workable settlement would have to preserve the distinctive characteristics of the colony.

In 1982 Mrs. Thatcher visited China in an attempt to resolve disputes about Hong Kong. Although the people of Hong Kong wanted British rule to continue, the Chinese were determined to obtain sovereignty. Britain had no choice but to attempt to get the best deal possible for the colony. The Chinese recognized the economic value of Hong Kong to the their economy, which needed commercial ties with the industrialized world. Thatcher attempted to persuade them to continue the existing system of government and the capitalistic economy.

Despite their ideological objections to capitalism, the Chinese recognized the value of Hong Kong as a gateway to the outside world. The main concern of the Chinese was that their sovereignty be recognized. Deng Xiaoping, the Chinese premier, proposed the formula "one country, two systems," that would allow Hong Kong to continue unchanged while becoming part of the Peoples Republic of China.

After long negotiations, Thatcher faced the inevitable. In December 1984, she traveled to China to sign a joint agreement by which Britain agreed to cede Hong Kong to China in 1997. She also made it clear that, in the interim, Britain intended to move the government of Hong Kong toward greater democracy. The Chinese, in turn, agreed to give Hong Kong special status for fifty years as a financial center and free port, with civil liberties and an elected legislature. The agreement was the focal point when Queen Elizabeth II visited the colony in 1986.

The Hong Kong agreement raised again the issue of immigration. The non-British residents of Hong Kong were not entitled to settle in the United Kingdom. Despite widespread sympathy with their plight, both parties agreed that it would be impossible to accept the number of Hong Kong people that wanted to come. Eventually the decision was reached to grant British citizenship to some two hundred thousand administrators and officials, to encourage them to remain until the transition to Chinese rule was complete.

6

John Major and the Thatcher Inheritance, 1990 to 1996

John Who?

John Major was relatively unknown when he became prime minister. His career exemplified the democratic Britain that had emerged from World War II. His father was a former entertainer; his mother was a dancer in his father's traveling show. He grew up in Brixton, a poor and racially mixed part of London. He did not attend a university, leaving school at age sixteen. He held a variety of jobs before taking a job in a bank. He became councillor for the low-income borough of Lambeth, where his rapport with working-class people enabled him to get elected to the House of Commons in 1979.

Major was intelligent, articulate, hard working, and personable. As a party whip in the House of Commons, he had become well acquainted with the Conservative members. Under Nigel Lawson, he was chief secretary to the Treasury, where he developed a detailed knowledge of where the money went, the key consideration in all government.

His surprising move to the Foreign Office in July 1989, replacing Sir Geoffrey Howe, was followed rapidly by a move to the Exchequer, where he replaced Nigel Lawson. In November 1990, Major was probably as amazed as anyone to find that he was the prime minister. At age forty-seven, he was the youngest prime minister of the twentieth century until Tony Blair (age forty-three) succeeded him.

John Major moved into No. 10 Downing Street with his usual earnestness and good nature. As prime minister, he continued to advance the substance of Thatcherism while altering its style. Lacking Margaret

Thatcher's prestige and dominating ways, he consulted regularly with his Cabinet and worked to repair the cracks in the Conservative Party. The Cabinet was based on the "new men" who had risen under Thatcher, including some who had turned against her at the end. Continuity with the older generation was maintained by Douglas Hurd, who remained as Foreign Secretary. Norman Lamont, with whom Major had worked closely at the Exchequer, succeeded Major as chancellor of the Exchequer.

Major showed his desire for reconciliation by bringing Michael Heseltine into the Cabinet as minister for the environment. In this office (which also dealt with local government), Heseltine was given responsibility for finding an alternative to the hated poll tax.

In his first New Year message, Major, alluding to his own personal background, stated that his goal was to make Britain an "opportunity society" where individuals would receive the education and other support needed to make their own way rather than becoming dependent on government.

The Poll Tax

Margaret Thatcher's stubborn insistence on the poll tax had been an important reason for her downfall, and the Major ministry knew that the tax had to go. The first step was to increase the subsidies to local governments in order to reduce the level of poll tax, and, it was hoped, the level of public outrage. To fund the transition, the new chancellor of the Exchequer proposed increasing VAT (a kind of sales tax) from 15 percent to 17.5 percent, an unpopular step in itself. The pill was sweetened by increases in funding for health and education.

The problem with repealing the poll tax was to find a suitable replacement. Heseltine proposed a new basis for local government finance, the council tax, which combined a tax per person similar to the poll tax with a tax based on the market value of one's residence. The rate of tax was graduated into eight bands (brackets), with the higher bands paying more. The business rates would remain unchanged. To provide time for transition, replacement of the poll tax by the council tax did not take place for two years, a situation that left masses of poll taxes uncollectable and angered those who paid.

To keep the council tax under control, caps were placed on both the taxing and spending powers of local authorities. The government determined the amount needed to provide a standard level of service, with local government providing 20 percent of the cost and the central government the remainder. The authorized expenditure of each local authority was determined by the government, and borrowing to evade these limits was prohibited. The centralizing thrust of Thatcherism in relation to local government had been taken about as far as possible.

The Gulf War

When he took office, John Major was confronted with the Gulf War, to which Britain was already committed. He came out firmly on the need to reverse Iraqi aggression, and polls showed strong public support (60 percent) for the war. The Conservative members in the House of Commons supported the war, although Sir Edward Heath thought that negotiation could bring a satisfactory settlement. The Liberal Democrats and about three-fourths of the Labour members supported the United Nations' action. The large Moslem community in Britain was divided on the war.

In January 1991, after a massive buildup, Allied forces attacked Iraq by air and on the ground. The war was conducted in the full glare of television, which provided exciting viewing. The result was a stunning victory, and John Major was able to share in the plaudits that rained down upon the victorious Allied leaders. The ratings of President George Bush in the political polls soared to 90 percent, and polls showed that John Major had the highest rating of any prime minister since Winston Churchill. Bush and Major soon discovered how ephemeral such TV-based ratings were.

Major and his foreign secretary, Douglas Hurd, continued the foreign policies of Margaret Thatcher. Shortly after becoming prime minister, John Major visited President Bush in Washington and established a personal relationship that was cemented by their common involvement in the Gulf War. In May 1991, Queen Elizabeth II visited the United States to strengthen relations, take advantage of the improved rapport with the Bush administration, and reduce fears that the United States and Britain were going their separate ways. It seemed that the Gulf War had renewed "the special relationship" that Mrs. Thatcher had tended so assiduously.

In the meantime, foreign policy was dramatically changed by the collapse of the Soviet Union. While Mikhail Gorbachev struggled to maintain control, Boris Yeltsin was elected president of the Russian Federation and emerged as a rival to Gorbachev. In December 1991, the Ukraine declared its independence, followed by Belorussia and other provinces. Later that month, Gorbachev resigned. The Soviet Union had ceased to exist.

The Movement for European Unity

John Major wanted to reverse the often contentious relationship with the European Community that had resulted from Margaret Thatcher's abrasive personality. When he took office in November 1990, he faced an intergovernmental conference on Jacques Delors' plan for closer European union. In preparing for the conference, he adopted a conciliatory tone. Meeting with Chancellor Kohl in March 1991, he stated effusively that for his generation "Europe was a cause of political inspiration." He added that his goal for Britain was to be "at the very heart of Europe."

Nevertheless, it was clear that in Britain and the Conservative Party deep differences existed concerning the movement toward European unity. The immediate issue was a single European currency. Major attempted to balance conflicting views by accepting the idea "in principle" while insisting on convergence of the various national economies before implementing it. "We could say no," he declared. "If we cannot find common ground we may have to say no. And if necessary, we will."

In December 1991, the Council of Ministers met at Maastricht in the Netherlands to approve a treaty that would strengthen the political and economic unity of the Community. At Maastricht, Jacques Delors brought forth his proposals for a federal Europe with a common foreign policy and defense, a common currency, and uniform social policies and costs.

John Major declared that Britain could accept the treaty only if she could "opt out" of the single currency and the common social policy. Without its own currency, Britain could not control the money supply, interest rates, and other elements crucial to the British economy. The social policy of the European Community involved high labor costs that, Major insisted, Britain could not afford.

The Maastricht conference was John Major's first great foreign policy test, and he succeeded to the satisfaction of most of his countrymen. With the assistance of Chancellor Kohl, Major was given his "opt outs," to the dismay of Jacques Delors. He also succeeded in removing the word "federal" from the clause calling for a closer union.

The ambitions of Jacques Delors had generated a growing reaction among many of the Conservative backbenchers, who dug in their heels in defense of British sovereignty. To the ever present tug-of-war between the global and European views of Britain's future, was added the centuries-old antagonism between the English and the French, spiced with more than a dash of anti-Germanism.

Major supported the treaty with his "opt outs," and he pleaded for support of the balance he had struck between Britain's independence and her economic interests in Europe. Out of office, Margaret Thatcher stated her opposition, resting her case on the importance of preserving British sovereignty. Sir Edward Heath replied by arguing that "we have a European culture as well as individual national aspects" and urged immediate implementation of a common currency.

The Labour Party, like the Conservatives, was divided. Labour had become more sympathetic to the European Community because the common social policy would give unions and workers benefits that the Thatcher administration had taken away. On the other hand, ordinary working people, the bedrock of the Labour Party, were strongly patriotic and typically dubious about getting too close to Europe.

Business leaders were determined to maintain access to the European market, but they did not want the flexibility that Mrs. Thatcher had brought to the British economy to be lost in the rigidities and regulations of the European Community. Polls showed that more than half the British people opposed closer union with Europe and fewer than 40 percent favored the treaty.

Economic Crisis

In the industrial world, the cheers of victory in the Gulf War were soon muted by the onset of a world recession. The British economy contracted by 2.5 percent and investment fell from £80 million in 1990 to £72 million in 1992. At the end of 1991, the recession hit bottom: business failures reached a record number, car sales were down, and more than seventy thousand mortgages had been foreclosed.

This time the recession hit the south of England hardest. In 1990, unemployment in the south of England had been 4.5 percent when in the north it was 8 percent. By 1993, unemployment had reached three million (the highest since 1986). Regionally, the misery index had been almost equalized: unemployment in the north was 10.4 percent and in the south it was 9.5 percent. Job losses fell mainly on managerial and clerical workers as businesses cut employees in an effort to stay afloat.

One beneficial effect of the recession was a decline in inflation from 9.3 percent in 1990 to 4 percent early in 1992, but interest rates did not fall proportionately. British membership in the Exchange Rate Mechanism (ERM) meant that interest rates remained above 10 percent to support the pound. Faced with the enormous costs of rebuilding the former East Germany, German interest rates were high to control inflation. The Major ministry, trapped in the ERM, kept pace, which foreclosed other steps that might have been taken to stimulate the economy.

Unemployment and high interest rates forced many homeowners to default on their mortgages and house prices plummeted. In 1992, house prices fell 7.8 percent on average and 11.4 percent in London. More than 1.5 million homeowners were faced with negative equity—their house was worth less than the mortgage. In 1992, Canary Wharf, a huge property development in the former London dockyards, went bankrupt. Banks were left holding loans that could not be repaid. The building trades were devastated.

Britain's manufacturing base declined dramatically as inefficient firms went to the wall. British Steel announced a 20 percent cut in production and put workers on short time. Other large firms in the auto industry and aerospace announced job cuts, especially in middle-management and white-collar positions.

To soften the effects of the recession, John Major loosened the purse strings, leaving a deficit that would eventually have to be closed. He made generous pay settlements with public employees, expanded government programs for training unemployed workers, offered financial support to local governments to ease the transition from the poll tax to the council tax, and in other ways showed a willingness to spend that was uncharacteristic of Thatcherism. In so doing, he sowed the seeds of a financial crisis yet to come.

The Election of 1992

In a party democracy like Britain's, the ultimate test of a leader is the ability to win votes for the party in an election. Much of Mrs. Thatcher's support in the Conservative Party rested upon the fact that she had won three elections. Her leadership was overthrown when it was believed that she could not win the fourth. Unknown and unproven, many Conservatives saw John Major as the sacrificial lamb who would lead the party in an election it was expected to lose.

They were wrong. With the departure of Margaret Thatcher, the fortunes of the Conservative Party rapidly improved. Before Thatcher's resignation, polls showed 34 percent favoring the Conservatives and 46 percent Labour. A few weeks after John Major's accession, the numbers were reversed: Conservatives 45 percent, Labour 39 percent. The reason was not John Major, who was virtually unknown; it was the absence of Margaret Thatcher.

John Major enjoyed a surprisingly long honeymoon. He was most popular during his first two years, when Britain was wracked by inflation and recession. His main asset was his ability to unite the party and minimize public squabbling. He was a consolidator, keeping Mrs. Thatcher's agenda moving along, but giving Conservatives a breather from her relentless activism. As time passed voters came to like John Major and his low-keyed style. By installing a new prime minister and other fresh faces in the Cabinet, it seemed as if a change had taken place, although the essentials of the Conservative government remained as before.

The election took place in April 1992. The Conservative Party's manifesto promised a continuation of Thatcherism by privatizing British Coal and British Rail. Emphasis was placed on improving the quality of the public services. Polls showed the Conservatives with one great advantage: despite the recession, more of the voters (40 percent) trusted them on the management of the economy than Labour (under 30 percent). The Maastricht Treaty was not an important issue.

Labour approached the election with a sense of optimism, and the polls gave Labour a slight edge over the Conservatives throughout the campaign. After years of struggle with the left wing and his own earlier ideas, Neil Kinnock had given the Labour Party a set of policies that would appeal to the changing electorate. Economic growth was touted as the answer to poverty and unemployment and the basis for better and more comprehensive social services. The strongest plank in Labour's platform was its commitment to the National Health Service. Labour claimed that the internal market introduced under Margaret Thatcher was the first step toward privatization of health care.

Labour also came out in favor of Britain's membership in the European Economic Community. Labour intellectuals had concluded that the growth of international trade and multinational corporations made it impossible to maintain socialism on a national basis. The trade unions had also changed their views; they saw in the social policies of the European Community a way to recoup the losses of power and benefits that they had suffered under Thatcherism. From resistance to Europe, the Labour Party became a supporter.

This was an election where the campaign probably made the difference. The tabloids conducted a relentless campaign against Kinnock. The *Sun*, topped them all with the headline: "IF KINNOCK WINS TODAY WILL THE LAST PERSON TO LEAVE BRITAIN PLEASE TURN OUT THE LIGHTS."

Television was an important factor in the campaign. On TV, John Major conveyed the image of an earnest, decent, well-meaning leader who understood ordinary people and their needs. On several occasions he displayed his ability to talk to the voters while standing on a soapbox. He stressed his humble origins and his desire to provide opportunities through education and training. At times the flamboyant, verbose Kinnock appeared bombastic and overconfident. Kinnock's triumphalism at a rally in Sheffield was perhaps a turnoff for some voters.

The election of 1992 was the most embarrassing ever for the polls. A week before the election they gave Labour a slim lead, with the possibility of a hung Parliament. They missed a late swing to the Conservatives, as many uncommitted voters made up their minds in the last week or two. Ladbroke's, a chain of betting parlors, got it right. They had money at stake, and perhaps they were closer to the real world.

When the votes were counted, it was found that the electorate had decided to stay with the Conservatives. The Conservatives got their usual 42 percent of the votes and scraped by with a narrow margin of twenty-one seats in Parliament. The next day the feisty tabloid with the huge circulation boasted: "IT'S *THE SUN* WOT WON IT." Mrs. Thatcher, who did not seek reelection, received a peerage and entered the House of

Lords. Betty Boothroyd was chosen speaker of the House of Commons, the first woman to hold this office.

Labour improved its share of the vote to 34 percent, mainly at the expense of the Liberal Democrats, and did unexpectedly well in marginal seats. With only 18 percent of the votes, the Liberal Democrats had declined from 25 percent in 1983 and 23 percent in 1987. It was evident that the voters were sorting themselves out into two main groups without much room for a third party.

The Conservative victory confirmed that a political realignment had taken place that could withstand a lackluster leader and a bad economy. The Conservatives dominated the south of England, where population and affluence were growing. Most Labour votes were cast in the declining industrial areas of northern England, Scotland, and Wales. Labour drew 52 percent of the votes of people in manual occupations, at a time when such jobs were declining. People in nonmanual occupations were mainly Conservative (55 percent) or Liberal (23 percent). It was evident that Labour had not yet overcome the legacy of the past, especially among women.

The election again displayed the disadvantages of third parties, which won 24 percent of the vote but only 7 percent of the seats. The Liberal Democrats had twenty seats with 18 percent of the votes, the Scottish Nationalists three seats, and the Welsh Nationalists (Plaid Cymru) four. Northern Ireland has its own political parties: the Ulster Unionists won nine seats, the Democratic Unionists three, the Social Democratic and Labour Party (SLDP) four, and the Ulster Popular Unionist Party one.

Neil Kinnock retired as leader of the Labour Party and John Smith, a sturdy, shrewd Scottish lawyer, was chosen as his successor. Smith's tough questioning in the House of Commons hammered home the ego conflicts and policy differences of the ministry. He undertook what he called "the long game," a long-term effort to rebuild the party. Most important were his successful efforts to reduce the union block vote at the party conference, and give more weight in the constituency organizations to individual members. Henceforth, the Labour Party was mainly a party of individuals, not an association of organizations and special interests.

John Major had led his party in a successful election, but his slim majority left him on shaky ground. Seldom had a prime minister been so weak in his own party after an electoral victory. His slim margin left him vulnerable to pressures from dissident Conservatives or from the Ulster Unionists. For the moment, those in the Conservative Party who considered him to be an ineffective leader had no likely alternative, but his support within the party was soft. At best, he had proven to be a survivor.

"Black Wednesday"

As chancellor of the Exchequer, John Major had recommended membership in the Exchange Rate Mechanism (ERM) of the European Economic Community, and as prime minister he stuck doggedly to that decision, despite the stifling interest rates required to keep the pound at the required price in relation to the German mark. Major's successor at the Exchequer, Norman Lamont, declared his determination to remain within the ERM, raising interest rates to 12 percent and then 15 percent to keep the pound attractive to foreign investors. Vast British reserves were dissipated to support the value of sterling on the international money markets.

Eventually the pound collapsed. On "Black Wednesday," 16 September 1992, the British public was shocked when a precipitous drop in the international value of the pound made it necessary to leave the ERM. Other countries were in similar straits. Italy withdrew after the German Bundesbank had spent large sums to support the lira, and France was able to remain in only after the Bank of France had spent half its reserves. Spain, Portugal, and Ireland also devalued their currencies. The debacle strengthened the arguments of those who held that efforts to remain in step with Europe would only be damaging to Britain.

John Major had persuaded Margaret Thatcher to enter the ERM. Now it was Major who took Britain out. Ministers clearly were dazed by the debacle. The public was outraged. "NOW WE'VE ALL BEEN SCREWED BY THE CABINET," screamed *The Sun*.

In actuality, an event that seemed to be a disaster proved to be a benefit. Leaving the ERM turned the economic situation around for Britain. Instantly imported goods became more expensive and British exports became proportionately cheaper. By December, inflation had fallen to 2.6 percent. No longer required to keep interest rates high, Norman Lamont was able to reduce rates to 7 percent. He promised a budget designed to stimulate industry, housing, and investment. If not exactly a "U-Turn," it certainly was more than a modest course correction.

"Black Wednesday," which followed the election by five months, shattered the Tory reputation for economic competence, and was a shock from which John Major never recovered. Public borrowing doubled over the previous year, as did the balance of payments deficit. People wondered why Britain had joined the ERM and had paid such a high price to continue the pain for two years. The fiasco intensified the growing division within the Conservative Party concerning relations with the European Community. John Major's long honeymoon with the British public eroded as the recession dragged on. In 1993, a poll showed that only 16 percent of the people had confidence in Major and 77 percent were dissatisfied.

The Budget Crisis.

The Conservatives had won the election of 1992 on the grounds that they were the party of responsible public finance: holding the line on taxes and tight control of public spending. Immediately after the election, however, the Major ministry faced a financial crisis partially of its own making.

John Major lacked Margaret Thatcher's authority and toughness. When he became prime minister, he had agreed to spending increases that would be popular with the public and would establish a favorable climate for the approaching election. Unlike his predecessor, John Major believed in an important role for government. He was willing to spend for education, training for the unemployed, the National Health Service, and social security.

The recession added to fiscal problems of the Major ministry. The revenue held fairly steady, but from 1990 to 1994 spending increased by 36 percent. The number of people claiming unemployment benefits climbed by 45 percent, a huge drain on the Treasury. The deficit for 1993 was 6.4 percent of the Gross Domestic Product: more than double that of 1992 and nine times greater than in 1991. Spending and borrowing had gotten out of hand.

It was time to pay the piper. In March 1993, Norman Lamont proposed sharp increases in taxes, including a phased-in extension of VAT to domestic fuel and electric power, and increased national insurance contributions. These were increases that prosperous people could handle comfortably, but VAT on home heating would hit hard the poor, the unemployed, pensioners, and struggling young families.

These tax increases violated election promises and seemed to confirm the widespread idea that the Conservatives were the party of the well-to-do, lacking an understanding of those who were less well off. A tax on home heating threatened the comfort and safety of millions. It was almost as insensitive as the poll tax. Parliamentary and public outrage was so intense that two days later John Major announced that funds would be provided to help ten million poor people pay the VAT on fuel.

John Major was well aware of the political effects of increased taxation. The resulting disputes in the Cabinet led to the resignation of Lamont, who was replaced by the energetic Kenneth Clarke. Lamont, once Major's close friend, did not accept his dismissal gracefully. In his resignation speech, he criticized the short-term approach of the government. "We give the impression of being in office but not in power," he charged.

Lamont was not alone in this view. Polls in April 1993, showed declining support for the Conservative Party, even in its strongholds in the south and west. Gallup polls in early 1993 showed public support for Conservatives at 31 percent, Labour at 48 percent, and the Liberal Democrats at 16 percent. By summer these numbers were 25 percent for the Conservatives, Labour 45 percent, and the Liberal Democrats 26 percent.

In the county elections of 1993, the Conservative vote plummeted to 31 percent, the party's lowest level in any twentieth-century election. Formerly impregnable Tory shires were lost, mainly to the Liberal Democrats. It was evident that the Tory political base was crumbling. When he was asked if he intended to resign, Major declared: "I'm fit, I'm well, I'm here, and I'm staying."

The Maastricht Treaty

The Maastricht Treaty was not an issue in the election of April 1992. Everyone assumed that it would pass during the summer. Signs of trouble appeared in May when twenty-six Tory rebels voted against the treaty and another four abstained. A few weeks later eighty-four Conservative MPs signed a motion asking for a "fresh start" on relations with the European Community. Lady Thatcher declared her intention to vote against the treaty in the House of Lords. A poll showed that the British were the least favorable toward the European Union (52 percent) of any member country. The *Sun* expressed its opinion in a striking headline: "UP YOURS, DELORS."

In 1992, the first votes on Maastricht had gone John Major's way, but since then the dissidents in the Conservative Party had been gaining strength. "Black Wednesday" added fuel to the fire. Rejection of the treaty in a Danish referendum (a decision reversed in a second referendum) delayed the legislative process and enabled the "Euro-skeptics," as they were called, to rally their forces. The French approved the treaty by the narrowest of margins.

The Conservative Party conference in October was dominated by hostility to the treaty. John Major believed that the British veto in the Council of Ministers, plus his "opt outs," gave Britain all the security she needed. He sounded like Margaret Thatcher when he exclaimed: "I will never, come hell or high water, let our distinctive British identity be lost in a federal Europe."

When the treaty came before Parliament in November, 1992, John Smith seized the opportunity to embarrass the government and widen the fissure in the Conservative Party. Although Labour favored the treaty, opposition at crucial points in the ratification process would give Tory rebels a chance to show their colors. The Paving Motion, which began the ratification process, aroused a fierce debate, won by the government 319 to 313 only after intense pressure on Conservative MPs and with the support of the Liberal Democrats. On a follow-up motion by the ministry, twenty-six Tories voted with Labour against the government. With the support of the Liberal Democrats, the government motion passed by only three votes.

The debate over Maastricht continued into 1993. When Labour proposed that the treaty be submitted to the voters in a referendum, the government defeated the proposal by a comfortable margin, but fifty-one Tory rebels voted for it and another thirteen abstained. It was commonly believed that in a referendum the treaty would lose. When the referendum was proposed in the House of Lords, Lady Thatcher voted for it—the first time that she had ever voted against a Conservative government.

Within the Conservative Party the antagonisms spawned by Europe took on the features of a cultural conflict. Ever since the days of Lord Chesterfield and William Hogarth, two interwoven strands had coexisted in British culture: cosmopolitanism and insularity. Disputes about the European Union brought them out into the open.

Finally John Major showed that he could crack the whip. In July 1993, the Maastricht Treaty had been before the House of Commons for a year and a half. Labour moved an amendment that the Social Chapter must be included in the treaty. The amendment was supported by Conservative Euro-skeptics because it would insure defeat of the entire treaty. The amendment failed due to the tiebreaker vote of the Speaker, Betty Booth-royd. On the main motion the government was defeated, 324 to 316, with twenty-four Conservatives voting against and one abstaining.

At this point, John Major decided to call a halt to the wrangling. He demanded a vote of confidence, and the Conservative rebels, faced by the prospect of an election if the government was defeated, gave in. The nine Unionist members from Northern Ireland agreed to give their support in exchange for a pledge that the government would lend a sympathetic ear to their special concerns.

The Treaty with the "opt outs" was approved with a majority of forty. John Major had shown that he could be tough when necessary, but he had not healed the rift in his own party concerning Britain's relations with the European Community.

John Major Under Siege

When the Conservative Party conference met in October 1993, John Major was still prime minister despite his low standing in the polls. Given his failing support, Major looked for a formula that would serve as a rallying cry. At the conference he used the slogan "back to basics," which he defined as "self-discipline and respect for law; consideration for others; accepting responsibility for yourself and your family."

"Back to basics" rested on increasing public concern with the moral character of the young. In February 1993, two ten-year-old boys in a shopping mall lured a toddler away from his mother and killed him. Teenage crime was widespread, especially in the large public housing estates inhabited by low-income people. Data showed that one-third of births were to unwed mothers, most of them young and living in poverty. The new slogan resonated with Conservatives, because it implied tightening the welfare system and restraining the idle and disorderly lives that many

Conservatives assumed were characteristic of those who depended on public aid.

The opening months of 1994 were a comedy of mishaps. "Back to basics" became a source of mocking humor when it was discovered that a married Conservative minister had fathered a child out of wedlock; another promising young Conservative member of Parliament died as a result of a strange autoerotic practice; the wife of a Conservative peer and junior minister committed suicide in reaction to her husband's philandering; and the chief of the defence staff decided to retire when a young woman with whom he was romantically involved sold her story to the tabloid press.

Under the circumstances, the best John Major could do was to claim that "back to basics" referred to public policy, not personal morality. Nevertheless, the flap contributed to the view—assiduously promoted by the up-scale newspapers—that he was a political lightweight who did not belong at No. 10 Downing Street.

The financial crisis continued to plague the Major ministry. Kenneth Clarke, the new chancellor of the Exchequer, faced a mountain of debt. He began a rigorous review of spending, looking for cuts. Public sector salaries were frozen, and the universities were further squeezed.

In 1994, Clarke imposed the second installment of Lamont's VAT increase on fuel. At this point, the Tory backbenchers erupted and the government was defeated, 319 to 311. Once again John Major's slim majority had given the backbenchers an influence out of proportion to their numbers. Clarke hastily withdrew the VAT increase and replaced it with increased taxes on gasoline, tobacco, and alcohol.

Collectively, the Lamont-Clarke budgets were the largest peacetime tax increases in British history. The public reaction was predictable. Even friendly newspapers like the *Times* were outraged. One prominent Tory called the tax increases "a long walk to the scaffold." Clarke's last-minute efforts to cut spending were too little, too late. The Conservative reputation for sound public finance had been irreparably damaged, and public confidence in the election promises of political leaders reached a new low.

Proposed privatizations aroused additional controversy within the Conservative Party. As minister for trade and industry, Michael Heseltine announced plans for the privatization of the coal industry, including closing thirty-one pits and laying off 60 percent of the workforce. Entire communities would be devastated. After loud protests from Conservative and Labour members, Heseltine promised to delay the closures and provide £165 million in aid to the affected areas. The next year he agreed to keep thirteen of the condemned pits open, and the privatization went forward.

Equally controversial was the government's plan to privatize British Rail by franchising rail services to independent operators. Like coal, the railroads had been the foundation of industrial Britain, and it was hard to accept that their time was passing. In small town and rural England, the Tory heartland, fears were expressed that small branch lines and stations would be closed and discount fares ended. After some concessions, the bill passed. Plans to privatize the Post Office had to be withdrawn due to backbench fears that small post offices would be closed.

Despite these discouragements, the prime minister himself did not lose his verve and cheerful demeanor. The papers were filled with columns declaring that a leadership change was imperative. A *Times* poll in March 1994 gave John Major ratings of 20 percent for honesty, 17 percent for understanding the problems facing Britain, 11 percent for leadership, 51 percent on "out of touch with ordinary people," and 5 percent on "has a lot of personality." Only 20 percent of the voters thought he was doing a good job. By midsummer Major's ratings were the lowest of any prime minister since 1940, when polling began.

The Conservative Party's political base was melting away. In the polls, Labour was at 48 percent and making striking advances in the middle class, where support for Labour and the Conservatives was equally divided. Conservative support was 28 percent and the Liberal Democrats were at 20 percent, their bedrock figure. In May of 1994 the Conservatives received only 27 percent of the vote in the local elections.

Michael Heseltine, who had asserted his independence under Mrs. Thatcher but meekly accepted office under John Major, was widely touted as Major's successor. His nickname was "Tarzan": it was said that he could "fill a room" with his powerful presence, in contrast to the modest overachiever who had become prime minister by mistake. Kenneth Clarke also stated his desire to be prime minister when John Major left. Faced with the prospect of a leadership contest, Heseltine did not pursue his chances further.

The Major ministry was further embarrassed when news leaked out about the Matrix Churchill arms deal with Iraq prior to the Gulf War, when John Major was foreign secretary. At their trial in 1992, the Matrix

Churchill executives claimed that the government had known what they were doing and had given its tacit consent.

At this point the ministers concerned panicked. On the basis of protecting the national security, they attempted to cover up their role by obtaining gag orders that denied the defense access to the relevant documents. Left twisting in the wind by the government, the Matrix Churchill executives pleaded guilty. They were fined and received suspended sentences.

The challenge to the ministers then became to cover up the coverup. On appeal, a judge refused to agree to the gag orders and the sentences were quashed. When the ministers were accused of letting innocent men be convicted to avoid political embarrassment, John Major appointed Lord Justice Richard Scott, an esteemed judge, to investigate.

The Scott report was published in February 1996. Mrs. Thatcher and John Major received light taps on the back of the hand on the grounds that they had been inadequately briefed. The ministers involved were severely censured. Later in the year, the House of Commons laid down guidelines requiring ministers and heads of agencies to answer parliamentary questions fully and completely.

Additional embarrassments resulted from an investigation of the Pergau Dam affair, where it became quite clear that Mrs. Thatcher had improperly used foreign aid to grease the skids for large sales of weaponry. John Major found that some of Mrs. Thatcher's less attractive chickens were coming home to roost.

As if his other problems were not enough, in 1993 John Major faced another crisis in public opinion, when long-simmering anxieties about "mad cow disease" (BSE) were intensified. Each week three hundred new cases of BSE appeared, although the offal that carries the disease had been banned since 1989. Scientists learned that BSE could pass to humans by eating infected beef, leading to a disease in humans that was invariably fatal. Although human instances were few, there was widespread public uneasiness in Britain and in other countries.

Standing up for British farmers, at first John Major temporized. He reacted angrily when the European Union banned the export of British beef. The farmers complained that the ministry had caved in to pressure from the European Union, and the reputation of the ministry was damaged by its hesitations and delays. In Europe, as well as in Britain, the BSE problem left Major looking weak and ineffective.

The "sleaze factor" continued to dog the ministry. In 1995, questions were raised concerning the outside income of MPs, based upon reports that some members had been paid by special interests to raise questions in the House of Commons. Although this was certainly petty sleaze, and demeaning to the members who did it, there was a strong sense that MPs should not have outside employment that might influence their judgment, such as an association with an important law firm or a directorship of a large corporation.

John Major, whose personal integrity was not in question, responded by establishing a committee led by Lord Nolan, a respected peer, to set standards of conduct in public life. When the Nolan committee reported in 1995, it stated that there was no evidence of "systematic corruption," but proposed a new code of conduct for MPs, self-regulation through a Standards and Privileges Committee, and curtailment of opportunities for MPs to earn outside income. Some MPs felt that their salaries were too low to support their family obligations and decided to return to the private sector.

Maastricht Again

Continuing disputes within the Conservative Party concerning the European Union were damaging to the Major ministry, for they indicated a lack of leadership and discipline in an aspect of government where the public expects its leaders to speak with one voice.

John Major believed that the Maastricht Treaty, with his hard-won "opt outs," was a sufficient settlement of the question. In September 1993, he published an article in *The Economist* in which he stated that he sought "a different kind of Europe," which would be a "loose union of sovereign national states" including as many democracies as possible. Maastricht and no further became the theme of the Major government.

Labour took a strong stand in favor of active involvement in the European Union. They portrayed the Conservatives as the misfits of Europe. Although Labour too had its Euro-skeptics, they were not prominent in its leadership. The Liberal Democratic Party continued its support for British participation in the movement for European unity.

In March 1994, John Major contrasted the Conservatives and Labour by stating that he was "fighting Britain's corner hard." He charged that Labour would "sign away our votes, sign away our competitiveness, and sign away our money." He referred to John Smith as "Monsieur Oui, the poodle of Brussels." Polls showed that the majority of the British public regarded the Tories as the "patriotic party" in contrast to the pro-European views of Labour and the Liberal Democrats.

Within the Conservative Party, however, John Major's moderate view was challenged from both sides. Advocates of European unity, like Sir Edward Heath and Kenneth Clarke, defended the movement for European unity. The Euro-skeptics, who were strong on the Conservative back benches, demanded assurances that the government would not accept further integration with Europe. They insisted that the prime minister challenge the authority in Britain of the European Commission and the European Court of Justice.

The official Conservative statement on the European Union (April 1994) stood fast on the Maastricht Treaty and Britain's precious "opt outs." It favored a "decentralized Europe" and accused the opposition parties of favoring a "centralized superstate in Europe." NATO should remain the basis of European defense.

These divisions within the Conservative Party came to a head at the end of 1994 on a bill to increase Britain's financial contribution to the European Union. To forestall expected opposition from the Euro-skeptics, Major staked the future of his government on passage of the bill. Unwilling to face the prospect of an election under unfavorable circumstances, the Conservatives supported the bill, which passed by a close vote.

The Euro-skeptics took advantage of the opportunity to express their dissatisfaction with the European Union and Britain's place in it. Despite Major's threat, eight Conservative rebels abstained. The rebels were "denied the whip," that is, excluded from the Conservative parliamentary party.

Responding to pressures within his own party and the country, John Major increasingly took a Euro-skeptic line. In a TV interview with David Frost in January 1995, he said that he was opposed to constitutional changes in the European Union that would limit British sovereignty or weaken the British veto, and that he would resist additional powers for the European Parliament. As to the single European currency, he continued to finesse the issue by refusing to make any commitment, adopting a "wait and see" policy. In February, Major stated that "unless economic conditions were right, a single currency would tear the European Union apart."

In March the government survived another crucial vote on Europe by a narrow 319 to 314, with Norman Lamont voting against and eight Tories abstaining. Given his slim majority, Major had no choice but to offer an olive branch to the eight rebels who had defied the party leadership. In April the "whipless" Tories returned to the fold, unrepentant and unchanging in their views.

By 1995, the Euro-skeptics had won the battle within the Conservative Party. The main "Euro-enthusiasts" were found among the older generation, including Sir Edward Heath and Douglas Hurd; their only strong ally within the ministry was Kenneth Clarke. The rising new formula was "Euro-realism," which recognized the importance of Britain's membership in the European Union, but advocated a looser community open to the Atlantic world and Eastern Europe.

In June 1995, John Major, tired of constant harassment from his own party, resigned as leader and called for a new leadership election. He told the Conservatives to "put up or shut up." Major was fully supported by Michael Heseltine, thus depriving his opponents of the most credible alternative. He won the leadership election handily, which momentarily strengthened his position, but the sniping soon resumed. Heseltine was rewarded and his ambitions were satisfied by appointment as Deputy Prime Minister, serving as a trouble-shooter, undertaking special projects, and replacing the prime minister at meetings of Cabinet committees.

Preserving the United Kingdom

In April 1992, John Major described England as "the country of long shadows on county (cricket) grounds, warm beer, invincible green suburbs, and dog lovers." Although this romantic picture was far removed from the crumbling buildings and hard streets of his native Brixton, it reflected his essential Englishness. When he was able, Major moved to the rural county of Huntingdon, which corresponded more closely to his English dream.

Proud as he was of his Englishness, John Major was prime minister of a country with several other nationalities. Their differences have been accommodated by considerable administrative devolution: the secretaries of state for Scotland and Wales have minicapitals in Edinburgh and Cardiff, which exercise extensive responsibilities. Scottish and Welsh

MPs form committees of the House of Commons that deal with legislation concerning those parts of the United Kingdom. Northern Ireland is a case unto itself.

Most of the population and wealth of the United Kingdom are concentrated in England, which is the stronghold of the Conservative Party. Scotland is another matter. The Conservative Party has not gained a majority in Scotland since 1955; in the election of 1992, the Conservatives won only 25 percent of the Scottish vote.

The Conservative grip on power led some in Scotland to return to the idea of devolution, presumably buried in the referendum of 1979. The Labour Party was dominant in Scotland, but its inability to win a majority in the United Kingdom left Scotland on the outside looking in. Scots had the sense that they were ruled by the English, with little or no chance of asserting their own concerns.

The policies of Margaret Thatcher had been devastating to Scotland, with its large public sector, unionized and overmanned industries, and extensive welfare dependency. Mrs. Thatcher's closures of nationalized industrial plants, restrictions on local governments, and financial squeeze on the public services left the old industrial cities of Scotland prostrate. One benefit of Thatcherism to Scotland was the sale of council houses, leading to 58 percent home ownership by 1996.

Scottish nationalism gained confidence in the 1980s with the revival of the Scottish economy. The Scots had a fine school system and a strong work ethic. Foreign investors began building high-tech factories in parts of Scotland with cheap land, good workers, and easy access to Europe. Electronics was an important new industry, and "silicon glen" produced 30 percent of all computers manufactured in the European Union.

A major factor in the revival of Scottish nationalism was North Sea oil, which came ashore in Scotland although the revenues went to London. Scots had the feeling that the English were benefiting from "their oil." Another influence was the European Economic Community. When Britain had an empire and was the acknowledged economic leader of the world, there were great advantages to Scotland in being part of the United Kingdom. Those advantages disappeared when the empire faded away and British membership in the European Community gave Scotland the economic outlets it needed.

In the 1980s the Scottish National Convention was formed, a nonpartisan group comprised of representatives of the Labour and Liberal Demo-

cratic parties, the trade unions, and the churches. The Convention
advocated a Scottish assembly elected under proportional representation
with powers to tax. It appeared that a majority of the Scottish population
agreed. The Scottish Nationalist Party did not join, preferring full independence within the European Community.

Like Margaret Thatcher, John Major was a strong unionist. In 1995, he
warned that devolution could lead to the breakup of the United Kingdom.
He charged that the proposed assembly would be a needless expense and
would impose a "tartan" tax on Scotland. He expressed concern that
devolution would encourage proposals for devolved regional governments
in other parts of the United Kingdom.

Labour, seeking to hold the Scottish vote, supported the concept of a
Scottish assembly. Without that pledge, Scottish voters would have bolted
in large numbers from Labour to the Scottish National Party. Labour proposed a two-part referendum. The first would determine whether the people of Scotland wanted an assembly, and the second whether they wanted
it to have limited taxing powers. Many Labour MPs preferred to accomplish Scottish devolution by act of Parliament. They recalled the referendum of (1979), when not enough Scots turned out to pass it. Polls showed
that 80 percent of Scots wanted a referendum.

Wales was always included in discussions of devolution, but there
seemed to be little public interest. Wales did not have the strong and
distinctive cultural heritage of Scotland, and the industrial areas of southern Wales identified more closely with England. The Welsh nationalist
party (Plaid Cymru) was weak and regarded by some as a party of eccen-
trics. Labour also promised a referendum on devolution for Wales.

Northern Ireland

The most troublesome part of the United Kingdom was Northern Ireland.
Despite his unionism, John Major decided that it was necessary to achieve
a constitutional resolution that recognized the force of Irish nationalism
and the desire among nationalists, in the Republic and in Northern Ireland, to bring some form of political unity to the entire island. While
keeping Northern Ireland within the United Kingdom, he was open to
some form of power-sharing with the Republic of Ireland.

Meanwhile, he had to deal with the IRA, which continued its bombing attacks in Britain. The most daring took place in February 1991 during the Gulf War, when the War Cabinet was meeting. Mortar shells were lobbed onto the roof of No. 10 Downing Street from a parked van with an opening cut in the top.

In April 1992, a powerful IRA bomb went off in the City of London killing three people, injuring ninety-one, and causing damage estimated at £1 billion. A year later, another IRA bomb was exploded in the City, wreaking great damage and leaving one person dead and forty injured. The little stone church, St. Ethelburga, which had stood in the City for six hundred years, surviving both the Fire of London (1666) and the Blitz of World War II, was another victim. The church will be rebuilt as part of a Centre for Reconciliation and Peace that offers assistance to victims of terrorism.

Violence north of the border was potentially threatening to the Republic of Ireland, and the Irish prime minister, Albert Reynolds, proved willing to help. In 1993, the Major ministry began discussions with the Irish government and other groups concerned with the affairs of Northern Ireland, including secret talks with Sinn Fein, the political wing of the IRA. In December 1993, Major and Reynolds met at No. 10 and issued the Downing Street Declaration, which began a new series of negotiations intended to bring Sinn Fein into the process.

The declaration called for an end to terrorism and violence, and stated that political talks with all parties concerned, including Sinn Fein, could begin after three months of peace. The people of the Republic and of Northern Ireland were assured that no changes would take place without popular support as shown in a referendum.

In general, the declaration was welcome to the British people, who were tired of the unending turmoil of Northern Ireland and worried by the extension of IRA terrorism to Britain. The IRA intensified this concern by setting off bombs in Oxford Street (a major shopping street in London) during the Christmas shopping season and dropping mortar shells on Heathrow Airport.

The unionist (mainly Protestant) population of Northern Ireland was outraged. They feared that someday Britain would abandon them to the Irish Republic. They were opposed to any steps that would involve the Republic in the affairs of Northern Ireland. They wanted no political involvement with Sinn Fein, and they were determined to fight IRA terrorism tooth and nail.

The nine Ulster Unionist members of the Commons, who normally supported the Major ministry, were upset at the idea of talking with IRA terrorists about anything, especially Northern Ireland. They resented seeing Gerry Adams, spokesman for Sinn Fein, the political wing of the IRA, making statements on television. They were appalled when President Bill Clinton permitted Adams, a front man for terrorists, to visit the United States and raise money for the cause. John Major endeavored to reassure them by reaffirming his promise that any settlement would be subject to a referendum of the people of Northern Ireland. With his slim majority, John Major could not afford to lose their support.

Despite heated and tedious debates in the media, some progress was being made. Perhaps Gerry Adams enjoyed being vaulted into prominence and wanted to continue his role as a world statesman. In August 1994, the IRA declared a cease-fire, and the Ulster loyalists followed with a similar declaration in October.

In February 1995, the British and Irish governments published the *Framework Document* for negotiations intended to lead to peace and reconciliation in Northern Ireland. The main thrust of the *Framework Document* was that of Margaret Thatcher in 1985: increased cooperation between London and Dublin, a cross-border assembly of representatives from both parts of the island, Irish abandonment of a claim to Northern Ireland, and a referendum in Northern Ireland to approve any changes. The government also began reducing the number of troops in Northern Ireland, which was expected to continue as long as the cease-fire lasted.

Gerry Adams was rewarded with a trip to Washington, meeting with President Clinton in the White House on St. Patrick's Day, 1995. The White House announced that the Adams visit was in recognition of his willingness to discuss with the British government the reduction of IRA weaponry. The British government reminded the Americans that Adams was the spokesman for a terrorist group that was still heavily armed and dangerous, but American domestic politics prevailed.

As his paper-thin majority in the House of Commons crumbled, John Major was increasingly dependent on the Ulster Unionists for support. To satisfy them, he insisted that the IRA begin decommissioning its weapons, a condition not included in the *Framework Document* and rejected by the IRA. In the next several months, Major made several trips to Northern Ireland, where he announced the lifting of restrictions and promised a referendum on any final settlement. In November President Clinton was enthusiastically received when he made a visit to Northern Ireland to congratulate the people on the steps that had been taken to end the violence.

In January 1996, American involvement continued when former Senator George Mitchell went to Northern Ireland as leader of a three-man commission (the others were a Canadian and a Finn) sent to provide impartial mediators. Encouraged by the American role, Sinn Fein declared that the IRA would not give up its weapons until a full agreement had been reached. The Ulster Unionists refused to accept any settlement extracted at the point of a gun; they insisted that the IRA give up their weapons before they would begin any negotiations. Dependent on Unionist support in the House of Commons, John Major had no choice but to go along with them.

Patiently, John Major played this tedious game, inching the contentious politicians of Northern Ireland forward. Departing from the *Framework Document*, he proposed a special election in Northern Ireland to choose a conference body of eighty-two members that might possibly break the impasse. The IRA showed what it thought of this idea by setting off a huge bomb in the London docklands, close to the new financial and newspaper offices. Gerry Adams seemed to be isolated, even in the Clinton White House. He said he was "saddened" by the blast, and his standing dwindled.

Despite bombings in Britain, the cease-fire continued in Northern Ireland, which justified continuing the peace process. In the elections for the all-party conference held in June 1996, the voters showed their approval of the cease-fire by giving Sinn Fein 15 percent of the vote. The IRA showed its colors by setting off a huge bomb that devastated central Manchester and injured more than two hundred people.

The all-party peace talks for Northern Ireland went ahead without Sinn Fein, which refused to disavow the return to violence by the IRA and in particular the bomb in Manchester. In July, a march of angry Protestants through a Catholic neighborhood of Belfast led to new disorders. In September, London police raided an IRA center in London, where they seized a large quantity of weapons and explosives. The next month the IRA exploded a bomb in the British Army headquarters near Belfast.

In Northern Ireland, killings and bombings declined, but beatings and church burnings continue to be everyday occurrences.

Shaping a Post–Cold War Foreign Policy

With the Cold War consigned to the historians, John Major had to define
a new foreign policy for Britain. He handled his role smoothly and there
were few partisan differences on foreign policy, apart from the endless
wrangles about the European Union. The Major ministry was firmly committed to NATO, which institutionalized a security role for the United
States in Europe. American involvement was especially important to Britain. Although "the special relationship" of the postwar period had disappeared, close political, economic, and cultural ties continued.

Relations between the Major ministry and the Clinton administration
were at first cool. During the presidential campaign of 1992, the Bush
people had asked the Conservative Party Central Office to search the
public records for evidence of any antiwar activities by Bill Clinton while
he was a student in Britain during the Vietnam War. Nothing damaging
was found. Bill Clinton won the election, and the Conservative Party was
duly embarrassed.

Britain's relationship with Russia under Boris Yeltsin was problematical, due to the lack of a stable Russian government, the floundering of
the reform program, and concerns that Russian nationalism and militarism might return. The reelection of Yeltsin in 1996 was reassuring, but
much depended on the precarious state of Yeltsin's health.

John Major's credentials as a free trader were unquestioned. He participated constructively in the negotiations that led eventually to acceptance
of the General Agreement on Tariffs and Trade (GATT), which was intended to reduce barriers to trade throughout the world. In these discussions, Major displayed his negotiating skills and mastery of detail, and he
played an important part in surmounting many of the difficulties inherent
in such a huge undertaking. The final signing of the GATT took place in
Marrakech, Morocco, in April 1994.

Bosnia

The main foreign policy issue of the Major ministry was the breakdown of
Yugoslavia in 1991. The Serbs took over the Yugoslav government and

army, and undertook to create a "greater Serbia." The European Union, led by Germany, recognized the independence of Croatia. War broke out between the Serbs and Croats for disputed territories, including Bosnia-Herzegovina, which the European powers recognized as an independent state.

Serbia and Croatia each laid claim to parts of Bosnia, and they supported Bosnian Serbs and Croats who rose up against the Moslem-dominated government in the capital city of Sarajevo. Horrifying accounts of concentration camps, atrocities, and "ethnic cleansing" were published in newspapers and broadcast on television. The United Nations launched an effort to alleviate the suffering by bringing humanitarian aid to the Bosnians. When aid workers and convoys were threatened by the warring parties, the United Nations called upon its members to provide troops to protect the humanitarian effort.

Britain and France agreed to contribute troops and other resources for humanitarian purposes, although it was recognized that peacekeeping could not take place where there was no peace. Lacking power to impose a settlement, the United Nations involvement was ineffectual and the atrocities continued. Since British troops were an important part of the United Nations force, and a British general was in command, the daily diet of unfavorable news from the former Bosnia was politically unsettling in Britain.

By 1995, the view had taken hold that only NATO, with American ground forces and military infrastructure, had sufficient power to bring the war to an end. Responding to urgent British appeals, in December 1995 the Clinton administration summoned the leaders of the warring parties to an Air Force base in Dayton, Ohio, where they were sequestered and subjected to unremitting negotiations that eventually produced an agreement. NATO forces, including thirteen thousand British troops, entered Bosnia to maintain the lines of demarcation between the various parts and prevent further atrocities. Open warfare ended, but life in Bosnia was still disrupted and the NATO mission continued into 1997, although the size and role of the forces was reduced.

The Challenge of "New Labour"

The weakening of the Major ministry and the Conservative Party was due, in part, to the emergence of a Labour Party and leader with a credible claim to being an alternative government. By 1993, the excesses of the unions under Labour and the troubles of "the winter of discontent" had become a fading memory. The unions had been tamed, and in that respect Mrs. Thatcher's legislation had made possible the rebirth of the Labour Party.

Although John Smith was recognized as a man of strong character and reasonable policies, his age and Scottishness made him seem like a relic of the Labour Party past. Labour's future lay in building on the steady undercurrent of resistance to Thatcherism. The British people retained a strong sense of community and collective responsibility for the common good. Smith saw that the way to make the Labour Party appealing to the voters was to respond to this point of view. He was steadily gaining public respect when the "long game" ended with his sudden death from a heart attack in 1994.

As his successor the party chose Tony Blair, age forty-one. Unlike his two predecessors, Blair was English, but with close ties to Scotland. His father was a successful barrister whose plans to run for Parliament were cut short by a stroke in 1963. Tony Blair was born in Edinburgh and lived for a time in Glasgow and Australia before his family settled in Durham, in the north of England. He was educated in a prestigious private school in Edinburgh, followed by Oxford. He studied law with a prominent London barrister, where his future wife, Cherie Booth, was also a student. He was elected to Parliament in 1983. He became a protege of Neil Kinnock and active in Kinnock's efforts to modernize the Labour Party.

As leader of the Labour Party, Blair displayed an intensity and single-ness of purpose that gave Labour new energy. He realized that victory was possible if he could reverse the negative public image of the Labour Party that had led to defeat in four previous elections. Labour had come to be seen as the party of the disadvantaged and downwardly mobile: the unions, the unemployed and unemployable, social security recipients, ethnic minorities, and the dismal lost cities of the industrial north and Scotland.

Blair aimed his policies at the Thatcherite constituency: middle-income Britain comprised of people with steady jobs and good prospects for the future. These people did not want to pay high taxes to support a welfare state that had little for them. They were worried by problems of education, health care, crime, and the breakdown of the family.

At the Labour Party conference in October 1994, Blair proclaimed that he intended to create a "new Labour Party," including revising its constitution. The great symbol of "Old Labour" was Clause IV of the party constitution, which advocated nationalization of industry. Although there was no prospect of new nationalizations or undoing the privatizations of the Thatcher and Major ministries, Labour's left wing was unwilling to abandon its most cherished shibboleth. After an intensive campaign, in April 1995 Blair succeeded in persuading a special party conference to accept a new Clause IV that advocated market enterprise and competition leading to "a thriving private sector and high quality public services."

Under Blair's leadership, the Labour Party abandoned virtually all that it had once stood for. His principles for "New Labour" proved to be much like those of the Conservatives: acceptance of a capitalist economy within a free market, tight control of taxation and expenditure, low inflation, commitment to improvements in education, law enforcement, and health care, containment of welfare costs, and a vigorous attack on unemployment, crime, and other social ills.

Even his view of government was Thatcherite. He agreed that "there was too much collective power, too much bureaucracy, too much state intervention, and too many vested interests around it." He assured the voters that "New Labour" was no longer the party of high taxes and spending. He declared that his policy toward the unions would be "fairness, not favours." He adopted the Thatcherite "law and order" agenda: "Tough on crime, tough on the causes of crime."

With an election close at hand, Tony Blair knew that strong leadership and party unity were essential. He proposed reforms of the Labour Party's National Executive Council (NEC) that would strengthen his grip and keep it from providing a forum for dissident views. He changed the annual conference from a meeting where issues were debated, sometimes heatedly, to a showplace where the ideas of the party leadership were presented in a controlled format. Apart from a few grumbles about his "presidential style" and domineering ways, "Old Labour" collapsed while "New Labour," the fruits of office in sight, fell into line.

As public support for John Major faded and the Conservative Party crumbled, Tony Blair seemed to have found the formula for success. A *Times* poll in September 1996, showed how the electoral landscape had changed in the previous two years. Labour was at 52 percent, the Tories at 29 percent, and the Liberal Democrats at 14 percent. Labour held the lead on the standard poll questions: most likely to keep promises, understanding Britain's problems, advocacy of sensible policies, concerned about people, not out-of-touch, and party unity. The approaching election was Tony Blair's to lose, and he was determined not to make the mistakes that had doomed Labour in the past.

7

The Completion of Thatcherism, 1990 to 1997

The Queen and Royal Family

During the Major ministry, the role and dignity of the monarchy were threatened as a result of the personal problems of the royal family. The duke of York and his uninhibited duchess decided to end their marriage after months of lurid coverage in the tabloids. Even more sensational was the breakdown of the marriage of the Prince of Wales and his wife, whose chilly relationship had long been known. They were divorced in 1996.

These embarrassments led to Thatcherite questions about the functionality and cost of the monarchy. Part of this cost is paid out of the Civil List, the public funds that support the royal family. Additional public funding is provided within departmental budgets, which pick up the cost of the royal palaces, yacht, train, and planes. The queen's private wealth is estimated at £7 billion and growing.

Polls showed that most people thought that too many members of the royal family were being supported at public expense. They also thought that the queen should pay tax on her private income. To add to the queen's troubles, in 1992 a disastrous fire inflicted much damage on Windsor Castle, bringing demands that she pay for repairs from her own private fortune. To help pay the cost of restoration, Buckingham Palace is now open to the public for part of the year.

The Civil List Act of 1992 provided public support only for the queen, the duke of Edinburgh, and the queen mother. Prince Charles receives the income of the Duchy of Cornwall, properties located mainly in the west of England, which was considered sufficient. Other members of the royal family are supported by the queen out of her private income. Queen Elizabeth II agreed to begin paying income taxes on her private income, as did Prince Charles on his income from the Duchy of Cornwall.

In 1991 Thatcherism reached the monarchy, when the queen was given a block grant to manage the royal palaces. She cut costs by 25 percent over five years. In 1996, it was decided to apply the same principle to royal travel other than the yacht, and block grants were provided for the royal air squadron and the royal train.

In 1997, it was announced that the last voyage of the royal yacht *Britannia* will be to Hong Kong for ceremonies accompanying the turnover of the colony to the People's Republic of China. When the ceremonies are finished, Prince Charles and the royal governor will come aboard and sail away into the imperial sunset.

Seeking support from "the patriotic vote," the Major ministry proposed that *Britannia* be replaced by a new yacht built in a British shipyard, a project that was well received by Tory nationalists. The ministry soon found that it had stepped on another banana skin. Labour had not been consulted and withheld its approval. Prince Charles was annoyed because he did not think a yacht was a good idea, given the sensitive state of the monarchy. The queen was upset at finding herself the object of political controversy. Whether the yacht will ever be built is now questionable.

Reforming Government

Margaret Thatcher introduced fundamental reforms in British public administration, and the principles of Thatcherism were widely extended under her successor. John Major was genuinely devoted to good government, and he put his personal influence behind efforts to make government work better. The goals of the Major ministry were unveiled in a document entitled *The Citizen's Charter*. The key principle was to make government more responsive to ordinary citizens. Government departments and agencies were expected to deal promptly and openly with the citizens whom they served. Each agency was required to post a statement of the standards of service it intended to maintain. Penalties would be imposed if those standards were not met, and individuals who experienced delays or poor service were entitled to compensation. It seems that the *Charter*, by putting agencies and public servants on the spot, raised the level of service.

The principles of the *Charter* were extended beyond government agencies. In the National Health Service, doctors were required to provide information about the kinds of medical care they offered and make reasonable efforts to meet appointments on time. Hospitals were ranked on the facilities and care they provided, and the maximum waiting times for patients were posted. British Rail was required to post its standards of cleanliness and on-time performance; passengers would be entitled to financial compensation if the posted standards were not met. Every year British Rail paid out a considerable sum in compensation to passengers for late trains.

During the Major ministry, the *Next Steps* principle separating the policy role of departments from the delivery of services was widely extended by the creation of new executive agencies. In 1991 and 1992, the large revenue departments were organized into agencies, Customs and Excise being decentralized into thirty "executive units" and the Inland Revenue into thirty-four. In the huge Department of Social Security, 98 percent of employees were in agencies, although it was discovered that some of them were transferred nominally while continuing to work in the department. By 1995, there were 102 agencies employing more than 60 percent of the Civil Service.

An important feature of Thatcherism was "contracting out" or "market testing," which meant contracting with private firms to perform services formerly performed by public employees. In 1991 the Treasury published a document entitled *Competing for Quality* which proposed competitive bidding by private enterprise for professional, specialist, and clerical services. It was believed that private firms in a competitive situation would give better service, and it was expected that substantial savings would be achieved by eliminating the salaries, pensions, perks, and other overhead expenses of civil servants.

By January 1995, more than £1 billion of government work had been transferred to private contractors, and twenty-six thousand civil service jobs had disappeared. These contracts included everything from keeping up the royal parks to data processing for government departments. Many of the redundant civil servants were employed by the private contractors who displaced them. Some civil servants formed private firms and bid for their own jobs. In 1995 Thatcherism reached the mightiest department of them all, when it was announced that the Treasury would lose one-third of its personnel.

Despite eighteen years of effort to restrain the size of government, the public sector is still 20 percent of the British workforce and takes more than 40 percent of a much-enlarged Gross Domestic Product. Government may or may not work better, but it is not cheaper.

Local Government

Given Mrs. Thatcher's respect for her councillor father, the upheaval that she introduced into local government is startling. The counties (shires) and incorporated towns (boroughs), supplemented by the parish, had been the basis of English local government for centuries. In 1888 the shires were given elected councils, and some of the larger shires were divided into several parts, making a total of sixty-two county councils. The metropolitan area of London was given unified government under the London County Council, which was later expanded to the Greater London Council.

This system remained until an extensive reorganization undertaken by the Heath ministry in 1974. By that time, urban sprawl had made the old system obsolete. The Greater London Council was continued, although many of the responsibilities of local government remained with the boroughs. The counties were reorganized into six metropolitan counties (the largest concentrations of urban sprawl) and thirty typical counties. The counties were divided into districts. The counties and districts shared responsibility for roads, public transport, police, fire protection, education, and the environment. The boroughs disappeared into the districts, but some urban districts continued the name "borough" and the district chairperson was sometimes given the courtesy title of "mayor."

With her determination to achieve efficiency and accountability, Margaret Thatcher extended her reforming zeal to local government. Her immediate goal was to fight inflation by bringing public spending under control, and that goal had to include limiting the expenditures of local government. In so doing, she centralized authority and weakened local initiative and responsibility.

Her attack on local government also had a political dimension. Local government, especially in the industrial areas, was a major power base of the Labour Party and the public employee unions. Mrs. Thatcher charged that local spending was abused for political purposes, and she would have none of that. The ill-conceived poll tax was the result.

Under the Conservatives local government, once an important element in the British constitution and in Conservative thought, has been emasculated. Centralization has included supervision and control of local government spending, centralized administrative requirements such as the contracting out of public services, and national standards in formerly local responsibilities such as education and community care of the elderly.

As with so many things, it left to John Major to complete what Margaret Thatcher had begun. The Major ministry decided that Britain was too small to need two separate layers of local government (counties, districts), and committed itself to the principle of unitary local government. The shires would disappear and rural England would be divided into tidy units of moderate size. Towns would become distinct units independent of their rural surroundings. All would be supervised by the Department for the Environment and given well-ordered functions and budgets.

The Local Government Commission under Sir John Banham was appointed, and was expected to recommend a unitary structure. As he traveled about taking testimony, Sir John discovered that people were attached to their counties and districts, and that most people wanted to maintain a two-level system. He was impressed by the variety of arrangements that had developed between towns and suburbs, counties and districts to meet local needs.

When the commission finally reported in 1995, the government was dismayed to find that Sir John recommended that thirty-two of the thirty-nine shires should remain and that many large towns should continue under their county councils. Other towns, the commission agreed, should be independent local government units.

Neither political party was pleased with the report. The Conservatives were relieved that most shires were preserved, but were unhappy with the proposal to remove some large towns from shire control. Labour welcomed Sir John's proposal to give some towns greater independence, but they objected to preserving the role of the shires and much of the two-level system.

It turned out that John Major wanted to preserve his county of Huntingdonshire, whose council was controlled by Conservatives. Kenneth Clarke

advocated a unitary system to preserve his urban constituency from inter-
ference by a Labour-dominated county council. The report was criticized
by the minister for the environment because it failed to recommend the
unitary system that the government preferred. He accepted the proposals
for twelve of the shires, but rejected the rest.

Sir John and most members of the commission resigned, and the project
remained unfinished. During the investigation, the existing local government units had made fervent promises of cooperation, "one-stop shops"
for citizens, decentralization of services, and the like. In 1996, in its
closing report, the commission stated that these promises, "obtained in
the sight of the gallows," had not been kept.

In its quest for an example of unitary government, the Commission
noted the bucolic minicounty of Rutland (pop. 34,000), which had been
joined to Leicestershire in 1974. There was a great deal of local loyalty
in Rutland, and the people had never accepted the change. In 1997,
presumably with the election in view, Rutland was restored, although still
dependent on Leicestershire for police, fire protection, and other services
which it could not provide for itself. Thus ended John Major's reform of
local government.

One relic of Thatcherism in local government is the disjointed condition of that great metropolitan area commonly called London. To restore
some degree of coordination, in 1993 the Department of the Environment
established a high level group of civil servants called the Office for London to supervise the affairs of the metropolis. Most of the responsibility
for London local government rests with the boroughs. The London Metropolitan Police report to the Home Secretary. London Transport continues,
contracting with various bus companies to operate London's famous red
buses. London Underground remains a publicly operated service, receiving financial support from the Treasury. In 1997 the possibility of privatization was raised, but consideration of that project was deferred until
after the election.

London is one of the world's great cities and is thriving in its present
form. Nevertheless, London's continuing growth, congestion, and problems of crime and dilapidation seem to require some form of metropolitan
government. Tony Blair has committed Labour to unified government for
the London metropolitan area, possibly with a popularly elected mayor.

Privatization

When Margaret Thatcher left office, privatization had gained a momentum of its own and powerful interests had gathered to support it: managers who wanted private-sector salaries and perks, workers who thought that privatization was the key to their future, investors who wanted to buy shares, and the Treasury, which needed the money.

By 1994 most of Mrs. Thatcher's privatized firms were doing well. British Steel has become the only profitable steelmaker in Europe. British Airways has become the world's largest and most profitable airline and is acquiring airlines abroad to extend its reach, while most of the world's airlines are losing money. In 1996 British Airways and American Airlines announced an alliance to establish a worldwide service of unparalled resources and range, including a large number of precious landing slots at Heathrow Airport. The British Airports Authority has doubled its profits since privatization in 1987 and is extending its management services to other parts of the world. British Aerospace is doing well selling fighter planes abroad.

British Telecom (BT) has become a world leader in telecommunications. In 1991 and 1993 the final batches of Telecom stock were sold. Those who had purchased and held British Telecom stock from the beginning had a capital gain of 300 percent. An international agreement in 1997 to open up telecommunications in sixty-eight countries is expected to give Telecom important new opportunities to extend its global reach.

Mrs. Thatcher's failed attempt to sell Rover was reversed in 1994, when Rover was sold to BMW, a German automaker. With that, the last British auto manufacturer had fallen to foreigners. In 1996 Britain celebrated a century of cars and carmaking. Britain still had a thriving auto industry, but it was no longer British.

John Major followed through on the privatizations that had been planned under Margaret Thatcher. In 1991, the Ports Bill was passed to sell off the Port of London Authority and Associated British Ports, and government-owned ports in Southampton, Hull, and elsewhere. By this time the London docks were derelict, but the land had great value for property development.

The privatization of the electricity industry continued in 1991 when 60 percent of the two generating companies was sold. The privatization was a success even before the shares were offered, with applications for shares almost twice the number of shares available. Most of the remaining shares were sold in 1995.

The most difficult problem was disposal of the nuclear plants, which were unattractive investments and carried with them potentially heavy losses for environmental pollution. In 1995 they were organized as British Energy, and the next year they were privatized, although the sale did not go well. In order to sell British Energy, the government had to agree to pick up the cost of decommissioning obsolete nuclear plants. The government was glad to be rid of them.

The twelve separate electricity distribution companies are disappearing rapidly, as mergers and takeovers reshape the electricity distribution industry. American firms began buying into the electric companies. They believed that the profits of these companies could be substantially improved by the use of American technology.

Despite some successes, privatization of public utilities was widely unpopular. A poll in September 1996, showed that the privatized utilities ranked high on the public hate list, and British Gas was the most despised of all. One reason was the disproportionate remuneration given to its officers and directors. Another was a chaotic billing system, where people had their gas cut off for nonpayment when they had never received a bill. In a search for immediate profits, British Gas had engaged in an excess of downsizing, and was unable to fulfill service contracts in the cold of winter or even answer the phone in a reasonable period of time.

A major problem of British Gas was the twenty-five year, high-cost contracts that it had made with gas producers when it was privatized. When worldwide gas prices fell sharply, the government ended British Gas's monopoly and permitted low-cost producers to enter the British market. The effects were devastating to the profits of British Gas. British Gas has since been divided and reorganized to prevent the gas contracts from dragging down the entire company.

The British public was never pleased with privatization of the water companies, and experience since then has made them deeply dissatisfied. Since privatization, water bills have risen approximately 40 percent, primarily to fund capital improvements and environmental cleanup, but some of the additional revenue went into high executive salaries. During the dry summer of 1996, Yorkshire Water, one of the most criticized, lost one-third of its water through leakage. Watering of lawns and washing of cars were prohibited. Nevertheless, Yorkshire Water proposed a special dividend to its shareholders (already well rewarded) instead of spending more on improvement of its leaky waterpipes.

Another major step in privatization was British Coal. The privatization plan divided the assets of British Coal among five regional packages that were to be put up for sale. British Coal held a great deal of land and property not used for mining. Some of this property was well located for industrial development. An informed estimate was that British Coal was worth about £135 million with property valued at £300 million.

In 1994, British Coal began selling off its collieries to private buyers. The miners union had no choice but to accept these changes, conceding that the number of miners would decline but those that remained would have steady jobs. In 1995 the remaining property, mainly large areas of wasteland, was sold. The last employee turned out the lights, left the office, and British Coal was no more.

A curious bit of media nostalgia was renewed attention to Arthur Scargill, who was feted as the last fighting hero of the British labor movement and as a relic of a way of life, once so important to Britain, that had passed from the scene.

More controversial was the plan to privatize the Post Office. The Post Office was eager for privatization, confident that it could operate a high-technology mail and parcel service that would be competitive throughout the world. Post Office executives knew that only private industry would make the kind of investment necessary to be competitive. As in other privatizations, they expected to receive private-sector salaries and bonuses.

The plan developed by the government separated Post Office Counters, which dealt with the public, from Royal Mail, which processed and delivered mail. Privatization met clamorous resistance due to the possibility that convenient but unprofitable small post offices would be closed. The plan was abandoned in 1994 due to backbench opposition. With its slim majority and mounting political difficulties, the Major ministry was unwilling at that time to tackle the politically dangerous task of postal privatization.

In July 1992, the last of the great privatizations began when the ministry announced plans to privatize British Rail. There was need for new management, new capital, new technology, new equipment, new tracks, and new labor relations. Entire communities would be threatened and hundreds of thousands of jobs were at stake.

Privatizing British Rail meant splitting it up into more than sixty companies that would be sold separately. The tracks and stations were put under a public corporation called Railtrack, which would manage ten thousand miles of track, four thousand stations, and numerous other railroad assets. The transportation services of British Rail would be franchised to twenty-five separate rail lines that would operate the trains and pay fees to Railtrack for the use of the tracks and stations. A third privatized corporation would take over rolling stock and lease it to the franchised rail lines. Other pieces of the complex puzzle would also be sold off.

The proposed privatization of British Rail aroused considerable resistance. Predictably, the Labour Party opposed it. It was evident to the railroad unions that there would be heavy job losses as new methods and technology replaced the obsolete practices of the past. In 1996, as privatization approached, Labour conceded that, if it gained power, it would not have the money to renationalize.

Another source of resistance to the privatization of British Rail was public anxiety that the operating franchises would close down unprofitable small stations and feeder lines. Tory backbenchers from rural areas were sensitive to such concerns. The government stated that the new companies would be required to run a specified number of trains, and the minister of transport expressed hope that they would offer new and better services.

The main concern of the government was to avoid unpopular increases in fares—"a poll tax on wheels." The principle was adopted that fares would not be permitted to rise faster than inflation. The government promised substantial subsidies to the privatized companies, to get them off to a good start and help them begin the process of modernizing. The privatized companies now have a predictable stream of capital for the next ten years.

As the privatization plan unfolded, executives of British Rail began incorporating to make bids for the operating franchises, bringing in capital from banks and other investors. Banks set up special accounts where workers could make weekly deposits that would be converted into shares if the bid was successful.

In 1996 the first privatized trains began running. The new operators were eager to modernize their lines. Well defined standards of performance were written into the contracts that they made with Railtrack, the privatized support companies, and the unions. Clear accounting systems were put in place, for the first time since the railroads were nationalized. The last operating franchise was awarded in February 1997. At the end of March the remaining BR trains made their final runs, and publicly-owned rail service in Britain came to an end.

The privatization of British Rail did not go smoothly. Some franchise operators were inexperienced, and it was difficult to coordinate schedules for twenty-five different franchises. Feather-bedding had been rampant on British Rail, and the franchised operators sometimes downsized hastily and without allowing for the complexity of the railroad network. Turbulent scenes took place at railway stations as trains were cancelled or delayed. One operator faced heavy fines from the regulator for failing to provide reliable service. A national system established by twenty of the twenty-six operators to answer questions about schedules and fares broke down and had to be entirely reorganized. By March 1997, shares in the railroad operating companies had fallen 23 percent.

The key to the privatization of British Rail was the disposal of Railtrack, which possessed enormous assets of land and buildings, including huge stations at city centers. To make Railtrack marketable, the government invested substantial amounts in the improvement of the stations, tracks, and signalling, and wrote off Railtrack's debt. In May 1996, John Major announced the successful sale of Railtrack.

The privatization of British Rail provided large profits for entrepreneurs. British Rail sold its engines and cars to three companies that leased them to the franchised operators. The management and staff of one of the leasing companies put up 20 percent of the money themselves and borrowed the rest from a merchant bank. They introduced innovative methods for managing rolling stock, and six months later they sold out at a profit of 600 percent As a result of the sale, some fifty secretaries, clerks, and other administrative staff will receive £500,000 each, and the directors are dividing a pie of £34 million. As one secretary said: "This is better than winning the lottery."

Proposals to privatize the London Underground face enormous obstacles, but the system needs a massive infusion of capital that the government cannot provide. A public corporation that will float shares and use the money to rebuild the system is one possibility. In March, 1997 one small part of the system was privatized, when the Docklands Light Railway, which serves the new enterprises in the docklands, was turned over to a management-employee group which signed a seven-year lease.

One privately owned public project that floundered was the Channel Tunnel, which opened for regular service in November 1994. Delays in planning the link with London meant that travelers still had to ride on the old, slow railroad tracks from Waterloo Station to the tunnel. Although early losses were expected, Euro-Tunnel reported that losses in 1995 had more than doubled from 1994. Operating revenue equaled operating costs, but the corporation could not pay its interest and amortization costs to investors. The Eurostar trains were carrying far fewer than the expected load of passengers. In October 1996 the Euro-Tunnel was bankrupt. Foreclosure was prevented by a deal in which additional shares were sold in an amount almost equivalent to the original shares. In short, purchasers of the original shares lost almost half their equity.

In November 1996, a bad fire broke out in the tunnel when a heavy truck carrying a load of plastic caught fire and filled the tunnel with poisonous smoke. Other trucks also caught fire, and the evacuation procedures did not function well. It appeared that the tunnel would be closed for several months, or perhaps longer. It would take much longer than that to restore public confidence.

A privatization that brought with it nostalgia for the ideals of former times was the sale of the new towns that had begun with Letchworth (north of London) in the early twentieth century. More new towns had been founded by the Labour government after World War II. These planned communities were based on ideas of that time concerning desirable features for urban living, including ownership of the property by a corporation responsible to the residents.

Over time the sense of community that the new towns were intended to inspire waned. These planned communities had proven to be attractive places to live, but their corporate structure had become unwelcome. People wanted to own their own houses and be the masters of their own small domains.

Under Mrs. Thatcher, the process began of selling off the land, buildings, houses and factories of the new-town corporations. In 1995, it was reported that the Commission for New Towns had nearly completed selling off the assets of those communities.

It was agreed that deregulation of the bus lines in 1986 had led to excessive competition. Many "cowboy" bus lines with low capitalization, ill-trained drivers, and old, poorly maintained buses had sprung into existence, clogging up town centers and spewing pollution. Liverpool, for example, had three bus lines in 1986, and in 1995 it had fifty-seven. Some towns planned to make their city center a pedestrian walkway to keep the buses out.

In 1996 the transport minister announced a return to a modest regulation of buses, including engine emission standards, safety standards, and correlation of bus timetables. The largest bus companies welcomed the opportunity to eliminate the small, one-horse lines that had driven down fares but also had created chaos in the business.

The privatization frenzy brought suggestions to sell off the government buildings in Whitehall and elsewhere. Many of these properties are no longer needed in the era of downsizing and contracting out. Others can be replaced by smaller or more economical buildings. With modern communications, agencies can be moved out of high rent areas like London or other major cities to efficient, purpose-built facilities elsewhere. The Private Finance Initiative, introduced in 1994, can be used to reduce the capital budget by having private enterprise put up buildings to be leased to government agencies.

The properties called the Crown Estate include office buildings, residential, agricultural, and seafront lands. These are of enormous value. Proposals have even been made to sell some of the royal palaces. Harold Macmillan's remark about selling the family silver did not seem so farfetched after all.

The Workforce

The Major ministry continued the Thatcherite commitment to a flexible labor force adaptable to the needs of a changing economy. Mrs. Thatcher had destroyed one obstacle to labor flexibility: the political power and economic leverage of the unions. Unemployment had finished the job, leaving workers with little recourse but to adjust to the vagaries of the labor market.

The Major ministry drove a stake into the heart of British trade unionism in 1992 and 1993 with legislation that gave workers the right to join the union of their choice or none at all. Employers were authorized to offer workers inducements to decertify their union, an additional blow to union membership. The legislation included some worthwhile provisions concerning pregnancy, maternal leave, and health and safety.

It was thought that this legislation would mark the end of the unions, but in many places they continued because they were a convenience to employers and employees as a medium for communication. In some cases shop-stewards were taken into management and became middlemen rather than exclusively spokesmen for the workers. In 1990, the proportion of workers covered by collective bargaining agreements was still 41 percent in the private sector and 78 percent in the public sector.

Long strikes have become a thing of the past, the last being the engineering strike in 1990. The nationalized industries, where strikes were most devastating, are now privatized, and workers know that if they strike for more than a few days they may lose their jobs. The one-day strike repeated frequently has become labor's weapon of choice.

Almost all strikes take place in the public sector—the heart of trade unionism—where workers feel that they have a monopoly of an essential service. Even there the tide may be turning, as seen in the tough line taken by John Major in 1996 toward one-day strikes in the Royal Mail and London Underground. Tony Blair maintained a hands-off stance toward strikes—no help there, either.

An example of the Major ministry's commitment to a free labor market was the abolition of the Wages Councils, which established minimum wages for workers in nonunionized sectors of the economy. The measure was strongly supported by hotels, restaurants, retailers, janitorial services, and other employers of low-paid workers, many of them women or immigrants. Thus ended an institution that had begun with the trade boards instituted by Winston Churchill under the Liberal government in 1908. Labour is committed to a minimum wage.

The changing job market altered the employment of men and women. Since 1979 the number of employed women has increased by 700,000 but the number of employed men has decreased by 2.7 million. The deindustrialization of Britain has destroyed many well-paid jobs for men while creating many low-paid jobs for women. Such was the price paid as Britain changed to a postindustrial economy.

The number of part-time jobs has increased notably, especially among women. Although these are often regarded as an inferior kind of employment, investigation has shown that most of these jobs have considerable permanence and that many people holding part-time jobs want them that way. These jobs, especially when held by women, are not seen as sustaining the household but as adding welcome additional income.

A hopeful sign is that economic productivity per worker in Britain has notably improved. There is general agreement that Britain's offices and factories are better operated than before, and that British workers have a more positive attitude toward work. This gain, however, is to some extent a result of shunting the less efficient workers into unemployment.

The Welfare State and Social Security

One of the consequences of Thatcherism was to increase significantly the disparity between the wealthiest and the poor. A study by the Rowntree Foundation showed that between 1979 and 1992 the real incomes of the richest 10 percent had risen by 55 percent, while the real incomes of the poorest 10 percent stayed the same. In the United Kingdom the top 1 percent of the population owns 18 percent of the wealth, and the top 10 percent owns 49 percent. The bottom 50 percent of the population own only 8 percent of the wealth. For these people, their job or pension is almost all they have, and when unemployed they have nothing to fall back upon but the benefits of the welfare state.

The problem of the British welfare state is that it promises benefits that Britain cannot afford, or is unwilling to pay for. The total cost of the welfare state has increased in relation to the Gross Domestic Product, from 23 percent of GDP in 1979 to 26 percent of a much larger GDP in 1995. The Thatcherites attempted to control welfare costs by improving efficiency through contracting out, internal markets, and similar devices, but that was not enough. As the state services decline, people who can afford it send their children to private schools, take out loans for university education, and purchase private health insurance, pension funds, and elderly care. As that process proceeds, support for the public system declines even further. The individualism of Thatcherism is the result of a welfare state that has promised more than it can perform.

Social Security payments are approximately one-third of all government expenditures, and 30 percent greater than health and education combined. According to the *Economist* (11 May 1996), expenditures are distributed as follows: pensions and community care for the elderly (45 percent), long-term invalids and disabled (23 percent), family benefits including housing and child benefit (19 percent), and unemployment benefits (11 percent).

The largest single component of the welfare state is pensions. The elderly population has increased and will continue to increase, for demographic reasons and due to longer lifespans. The basic state pension is a flat-rate pension, indexed to prices and funded by national insurance contributions. This state pension is low, and pensioners without other resources normally require public assistance benefits to survive. The Thatcher ministry encouraged people to "top up" the state pension with private pension and savings plans. In the past Labour has proposed increasing the basic state pension. Tony Blair dropped that idea as unaffordable. Labour proposed instead to give improved welfare benefits to the 700,000 poorest pensioners. The Conservatives have proposed replacing the state pension with private pension plans.

Child benefit goes to all mothers with children up to sixteen years of age regardless of need. It is also paid for children from sixteen to eighteen who are in school, a benefit paid disproportionately to the middle class, since many working-class young people leave school at sixteen to enter the workforce. Labour proposed dropping child benefit for students over sixteen, replacing it with means-tested training programs for over-sixteens from poor families. The Conservatives, seeing that this proposal would deprive middle-class families of a benefit they had come to expect, jumped on it as a tax on students.

Thatcherism contributed to changes in the British economy that left many people unemployed indefinitely. The price paid has been increased expenditure for the means-tested benefits, such as income support and housing benefit, which go mainly to unemployed adults. In 1993, the Department of Social Security began a determined effort to control costs, and incurred much hostility for rigorously enforcing the requirements. In January 1996, a report from the National Audit Office stated that almost 10 percent of welfare recipients had presented fraudulent claims and had received £1.4 billion in improper benefit payments.

Since the status of recipients often changes, it was difficult for the Department of Social Security to monitor all claims. Some payments, such as family support and disability benefits depended almost entirely on information supplied by the recipients. It was found that ten thousand public employees of Lambeth, a Labour-controlled low-income part of London, were also receiving welfare payments, most of them unjustified.

The Conservatives have long maintained, and are supported by re-spected Labour MPs such as Frank Field, that many benefits provided by the state encourage attitudes and behaviors that are socially damaging, such as dishonesty, irresponsibility, dependence, and family breakdown. "Benefit lifers" and "the yob culture" are seen as the inevitable result of a welfare system where people can live on public benefits and make no effort to work. People can be simultaneously collecting income support, child benefit, housing benefit, and public payment of their council tax.

In December 1996, the *Sunday Times* reported that one-fifth of house-holds (many headed by single mothers) have no working adult and no incentive to find work because they would gain little over the benefits that they receive. It was found that 31 percent of British children live in such households, usually headed by a single parent.

There is general agreement that reform of the welfare system requires insistence that able-bodied people of working age find employment or undergo training likely to lead to employment. The Major ministry intro-duced the "Job Seeker's Allowance," which requires a systematic, moni-tored, thirteen-week search for a job. During that time job seekers would get a "top-up" benefit of £10 per week in addition to their welfare bene-fits. Another program, "Project Work," requires thirteen weeks of job search or training, followed, if necessary, by thirteen weeks working on community projects. Labour has taken a similar approach, proposing compulsory work or vocational training as a requirement for receiving benefits.

A report in November 1996, showed that "the poverty trap" was some-what porous. Between 1991 and 1994, more than half of the people whose income was in the lowest 10 percent rose out of poverty. Although others were slipping into that category, there was movement within the poor that provided hope for borderline cases.

The National Health Service

When the National Health Service was established in 1948 it was over-whelmed, due to lack of resources and a vast backlog of unmet needs. Since then it has been seen that there is no limit to the demand for health care. The complexity and cost of modern medicine, and the extension of the average life span, have confronted the National Health Service with problems that seem insoluble.

Statistics for 1994 showed that Britain spent less per capita for health care (£808 per year) than any other advanced country. Britain spends approximately 6 percent of GNP on health care (15 percent of the total is private medicine) while most industrialized countries spend approximately 10 percent. Mrs. Thatcher attempted to control Health Service costs with better administration. The Thatcher reforms in health care were introduced late in her ministry and implementation was left to her successor. In the early 1990s, John Major sweetened the pill with substantially increased appropriations, which were cut back in the budget crisis of 1993.

In accord with the Thatcherite "contracting out" principle, the National Health and Community Care Act (1990) relieved the district health authorities from management of the National Health Service. Instead, they became purchasing agencies, contracting with doctors and hospitals for health care.

To further break down the bureaucratic structure of the National Health Service, family doctors in large practices were eligible to receive funds directly from the NHS ("fund-holding"), which they used to purchase services from medical specialists or hospitals. Hospitals were given the option of becoming free-standing corporations (trusts), receiving payment for their services either from fund-holding doctors or the district health authorities.

Out of thirty thousand doctors in the NHS, sixteen thousand are fund-holders. The "internal market" based on fund-holding doctors and trust hospitals was intended to bring competition into health care. Since doctors and hospitals were paid partly according to the number of patients they served, they had an inducement to take on more patients. An Audit Commission report stated that fund-holding had been beneficial in establishing better communications between doctors and specialists, and in encouraging restraint in prescribing. The Commission added that the majority of doctors "do not appear to be especially good at management."

More than 90 percent of hospitals are free-standing trusts. It is likely that trust hospitals keep tighter control of their costs, and they may have become more "user friendly" to keep the doctors and patients satisfied. There is a temptation for them to add to their income by increasing the number of private beds. In 1997, the realities of the internal market began to intrude, as some hospitals closed because they were losing money.

Adopting Thatcherite principles, doctors and hospitals have begun contracting out clinical and maintenance needs to private firms, thus creating potentially large opportunities for private enterprise within the NHS. Some moonlighting NHS doctors have organized specialized groups that will provide extra medical services as needed, thus enabling hospitals to maintain a smaller permanent staff. One hospital has invited bids to provide up to six hundred heart operations per year.

The Prescription Processing Agency, a department of the NHS, has been put out to contract with private computer firms. Boots, the chain of chemists (drug stores), has contracted with some hospitals to provide prescription drugs at a discount. Other firms are contracted to provide laboratory services. Labour has criticized these practices as steps toward privatization of health care.

With tight budgets and growing medical needs, it seems likely that the NHS will have to impose user charges on people who can afford them for many of its services. Dissatisfied with the NHS, more than 12 percent of the population have voluntarily taken out private health insurance, and the number is expected to increase to 16 percent by the year 2000.

Schools

The highly competitive world of the late twentieth century made education an important national interest, for the routine industrial jobs that required a strong back have declined, and a well-educated, flexible workforce has become essential.

Apart from the distinguished and expensive private schools such as Eton and Harrow (oddly called public schools), Britain has a variety of schools, primary and secondary, many of them founded and still maintained by churches. Others are operated by local education authorities. All of them are subject to control and inspection by the Department of Education and Employment.

Characteristically, Margaret Thatcher's educational reforms began by reducing the powers of local authorities, which were often controlled by Labour and responsive to the National Union of Teachers. During her ministry, parents were given a voice on the governing bodies of schools, and schools were given control of their budgets.

The centralizing thrust of Thatcherism was continued by John Major. In 1994, the Funding Agency for Schools was launched. Its function was to provide funding for those schools that chose to opt out of the local education authority and receive direct grants from the government. The agency would also provide funds for the building of new schools, which were expected to be grant maintained. The intention of the Major ministry was that an increasing number of schools would opt out of the local education authority and receive their funding from the Funding Agency for Schools.

This agency would become the base for Conservative efforts to strengthen school selection of pupils and parental selection of schools. Opt-out schools are allowed to select 50 percent of their pupils by test scores and interviews. Most of the schools that opted out were prestigious schools with high academic standards, and by opting out they were able to maintain selectivity in admissions and maintain their quality. Although presented as "parental choice," in many instances it was the school that did the choosing. Thus the central government, through the Funding Agency for Schools, will be supporting the best state schools instead of aiding those schools most in need of help.

To increase the number of places available, the grant-maintained schools have been encouraged to expand, although many prefer to retain their present size, fearing dilution of quality. The schools that do not opt out are permitted to select only 20 percent of their pupils, so they are at a competitive disadvantage for bright students. One result of school choice has been "sink schools," which collect children unwanted by other schools.

To answer the charge of elitism, the Assisted Places Scheme was established by Margaret Thatcher in 1980 to enable low-income students to attend private schools. The program takes in ten thousand students per year, or a total of forty thousand. As with most Conservative proposals for schools, it turned out to be another middle-class benefit. Most recipients came from families with middle-class values and lifestyles although the family income was low, such as middle-class divorcees with children. Labour has promised to abolish the scheme and use the money saved to reduce class sizes on the primary school level.

Despite enthusiastic predictions, the opportunity to opt out of the local education authority was not popular. Polling has shown that most parents do not want selective schools; they want a selective stream within truly comprehensive schools. Out of twenty-four thousand schools, it appeared that no more than one thousand would become grant-maintained, despite the attractive inducements offered by the government.

One reason was the collapse of the Conservative Party on the local level, where Liberal and Labour councils have discouraged opt outs. Another was local loyalties, as the general public rallied in support of their schools. In some places it was thought that local authorities would be more reliable than opting out, where funding might be threatened by a budget crisis or by a Labour government.

Part of the Thatcherite education reform was to establish a national curriculum that would standardize instructional content throughout the nation, making possible national examinations that would provide league tables (comparative data) on schools. Information would also be published on levels of truancy and the number of hours of instruction, where wide variations existed. Schools that ranked low would be put on the spot to improve attendance and performance.

John Patten, who became minister of education and employment in 1992, had the task of implementing the national curriculum and the examinations based on it. In the struggle for space, history was a loser. The time allocated to history was cut by more than 20 percent to leave more time for English, mathematics, and science. Among the casualties of curriculum reform was British history, which was not required for the General Certificate of Secondary Education (GCSE). The effect of curricular change was seen in 1996, when the number of students taking history for the GCSE was down 5.3 percent, although the number of sixteen-year olds was up by 3 percent.

In 1993, Patten attempted to implement national testing, but he met determined resistance from the teachers. Apart from the extra work involved, the teachers were reluctant to have the performance of their students (and themselves) made a matter of public attention and compared with the examination results of other schools. The National Union of Teachers advised its members to boycott the tests. Patten announced that if the boycott continued, he would contract out the grading. When agreement was finally reached with the teachers on the national curriculum, national testing with league tables began.

The next year an office for the supervision of schools (Ofsted) was established to maintain academic standards and take over schools that failed to pass muster. Chris Woodhead became the chief inspector of schools. Woodhead blamed theories of progressive education for the decline in student performance and urged more emphasis on discipline and subject matter instead of "child-centred education," "discovery learning," "inter-active instruction," "problem-solving," and education "relevant" to the interests of the child. Children, he said, needed to learn the kinds of things that they would need when they became adults, not whatever interested them at the moment.

In 1996 the results of the first tests were revealed. The nation was shocked to find that roughly 40 percent of pupils who took the eleven-plus fell below the standard in English and math. Although full league table ratings of schools were not published, Woodhead cited thirty outstanding state-supported schools and another one hundred that had improved their test results significantly. He promised a rigorous attack on poor teaching, including naming the best and worst teachers at each school. He stated that at least fifteen thousand teachers should be summarily dismissed.

Critics claim that league tables have distorted the educational mission of schools, which seek to attract the best pupils and get rid of poor students. Excessive efforts are made to prepare students for quantifiable tests rather than assisting them to develop their individual potentials. Sports, music, and other desirable extracurricular activities have been sacrificed in the effort to raise league table rankings.

Independent schools believe they must gain high rankings to attract superior students. State schools strive to maintain respectability and avoid losing the better pupils to the independent schools. In the league tables for 1996 an independent girls' school topped the list. Winchester College and other leading boys' schools were high. The leading state school was twenty-fifth.

Ofsted was concerned at the large number of expulsions, which have soared since league tables began. Expulsions are up 300 percent from 1992–1993 and suspensions or other disciplinary exclusions are up 800 percent. Of those expelled or suspended, 90 percent were boys from troubled homes. Ofsted reported that Afro-Caribbean boys were falling behind in school and that "colour-blind" policies did not work with them. Expulsions of black pupils were six times those of white students. Ofsted believes that schools are expelling problem students to keep their ratings up, rather than working with them.

In 1997, Woodhead declared that his next step was improved teacher training. He advocated getting away from "child-centred" teaching where children worked in groups. He wanted "whole class" teaching, where the teacher stands in front of the class as an authority figure. This method will be introduced into teacher-training programs in September 1997. The new teacher-training curriculum will define what students should learn at each level of instruction.

People were shocked when the headmaster of a school in London was stabbed as he tried to stop a fight between boys of his school and another school. The incident drew attention to unruliness in schools, which teachers complain makes it impossible to teach. Teachers at a school in Yorkshire, where a woman teacher was assaulted by a male pupil, voted to strike unless sixty disruptive pupils in an enrollment of six hundred and twenty were expelled.

Education secretary Gillian Shephard advocated a return to corporal punishment, which has been banned by the European Union. Although she was rebuked by John Major, when her proposal came before the House of Commons ninety Tory backbenchers defied the ministry and voted for it. They argued that caning was preferable to expulsion, and more effective.

A persistent cause of dispute was religious education, mandated as part of the national curriculum by the Education Act of 1988. The Act stated that the national curriculum should "reflect the fact that the religious traditions of Great Britain are, in the main, Christian while taking account of the other principal religions represented." The study of Christianity was defended as important for strengthening moral values and understanding the national culture. It was taken for granted that religion would be taught in a neutral but favorable manner, without efforts to promote or debunk it. A brief period of daily worship was also included in the religious education requirement.

When Patten insisted that local school authorities maintain the required programs of religious education and daily worship, one head teacher remarked: "Religious education is becoming a political football booted around the back-to-basics park. The Government should clean up its own act before expecting schools to promote religious and moral values that the Cabinet conspicuously lack."

The first draft of the religious education syllabus stated that, in addition to Christianity, students by age sixteen should have covered Buddhism, Hinduism, Islam, Judaism, and Sikhism. The Church of England and other Christian denominations argued that Britain was a Christian country and for that reason most of the time for religious education should be devoted to Christianity, even for non-Christian students. Furthermore, it would be difficult for religious education teachers to be knowledgeable about all these religions.

Large immigrant populations from India, Pakistan, Bangladesh, the Middle East, and Africa meant that in some cities other religions had strong claims to attention in the schools. Eventually it was decided that half the time would be given to Christianity and half to the other great world religions, with some freedom for teachers to make adjustments in schools with large numbers of immigrant children.

This solution did not satisfy Britain's large Moslem community. In 1996 a state school in Birmingham agreed to establish separate classes for Moslem students taught by a qualified Moslem teacher. This step led to pressure from Moslem groups elsewhere for separate religious education, a principle that they were quite willing to extend to Christians, Hindus, and other denominations.

Labour still prefers comprehensive schools, but realistically has accepted most of the Thatcherite reforms. Tony Blair sent his own son to a grant-maintained school, despite criticism from within the Labour Party and cries of "hypocrisy" from the Conservatives. Labour also will accept selection on the basis of academic ability or special talents, leaving that to local bodies to decide. When Labour-controlled councils proposed to abolish the remaining one hundred and sixty-one grammar schools, Blair stated emphatically that he would resist that idea.

Labour also does not oppose league tables based on standardized national tests. Responding to the insistence of the teachers, Labour wants league tables to show "value-added," not just results. They want Ofsted to help failing schools, rather than go about the country pointing out faults.

The long-established A-Level examinations in special subjects have continued to be requirements for admission to a university. A-Levels can also be a valuable qualification for employment, although John Major left school with none. As increasing numbers sought admission to a university, sixth-form colleges have proliferated to prepare students for the A-

Level examinations. The centralizing tendency of Thatcherism came into play in 1993, when these colleges were freed from the local education authorities. Now they receive their funding directly from the Treasury.

Universities

In 1979 one person in eight attended a university; now it is one in three. The number of part-time students is almost equal to full-time. A notable feature of the 1970s and 1980s was the great increase in the number of women in higher education. From 1971 to 1993 the number of women enrolled increased by 250 percent. In 1971 male students outnumbered women 2 to 1; by 1993 men and women were approximately equal. Science courses attract twice as many men as women; the ratio is almost exactly reversed in literature and arts courses. In the social sciences, the enrollments of men and women are about the same.

When John Major took office, Kenneth Clarke became minister of education and employment. With characteristic Thatcherite disdain for local government, Clarke removed the polytechnics from local funding and control. The Polytechnics and Colleges Funding Council was established to provide grants from the Treasury and to establish standards of expenditure and performance to which the polytechnics were required to adhere.

Next Clarke decided that the polytechnics, which previously had emphasized career-oriented programs, would become universities. In 1960, Britain had twenty-four universities; in 1996, with the transformation of the polytechnics, there were one hundred and five. This rapid expansion raised questions, not only of cost, but of academic standards and the employability of graduates.

By 1996 Clarke was chancellor of the Exchequer, and viewing universities from a different perspective. He announced that enrollments would be frozen, grants for operating funds would remain roughly the same, and capital expenditures would be slashed to the bone. In 1995, public funding for the universities and colleges was cut 2.5 percent. In 1996 Clarke called for a 7 percent cut in public funding and a 31 percent cut in capital spending. Another "efficiency gain" of 10 percent is anticipated for 1997.

The universities had no choice but to begin charging "top-up" fees to the students and their parents. Early in 1997 the university vice-chancellors warned students preparing for admission in 1998 to prepare to pay entrance fees up to £1,000, with abatements based on ability to pay. They proposed loans to students for tuition, with twenty years to repay. The government established a public agency to make loans to students for their living costs, since local authority grants for student living expenses have been declining. Thatcherism had struck again: the "free lunch" was coming to an end.

The Police, Crime, and Prisons

Margaret Thatcher was a strong and uncompromising advocate of "law and order," a theme that resonated among the Conservative rank and file. John Major continued the Thatcher approach, and tough policies against crime, drugs, and public disorder continued.

In recent years, the police have been challenged by crime that is more than local bad behavior, including organized crime on the national and international level, the drug trade, gangs, political terrorism, collections of hooligans from all over the country at sporting events, and violent demonstrations at military bases, nuclear plants, and construction sites.

Police efforts to deal with the new problems they face, sometimes heavy-handed or blundering, have brought a decline in public confidence. A study of Londoners in 1975 found that 90 percent of the adults and 80 percent of the teenagers trusted and liked the police. In 1989 a poll showed that only 43 percent of the public had "a great deal of respect for the police" while almost as many had "mixed feelings" and 14 percent had "little respect."

In 1992 Kenneth Clarke moved to the Home Office. He took up the Thatcherite cry of "law and order" in response to growing public concern about crime and social breakdown. Recorded crimes had more than doubled since 1979, and summer riots in run-down metropolitan housing estates had become the norm.

Clarke announced an extensive reorganization of the police on Thatcherite principles: centralized authority, forces streamlined for efficiency and economy, tight control over costs, fixed-term contracts with regular evaluations, and performance-based pay.

Like the teachers, the police were indignant at this effort to change their ways of doing things. Approximately twenty thousand police officers assembled in Wembley Arena to protest, and half of the chief constables stated their support of the officers.

In 1993 Clarke moved to the Exchequer, and was succeeded at the Home Office by Michael Howard. At the Conservative conference in October, Howard announced an ambitious attack on crime and criminals. He followed up this promise with proposed legislation that would strengthen local law enforcement bodies, but would also bring them under closer central control. He proposed using MI5, the agency established to deal with spying and terrorism within the country, to help police deal with large-scale organized crime, much like the American FBI.

The police and local magistrates were offended by the criticism implied by the Police and Magistrates Bill, about which they had not been consulted. They resented the new role for MI5; they wanted a clear statement that the agency could act only "in support of law enforcement" and not undertake independent "crime-busting" activities. They complained that the home secretary wanted to destroy the independence of the police and create a continental style ministry of the interior.

Howard was quite taken aback at the resistance that his "law and order" bill had aroused. He agreed to changes proposed by the House of Lords which, he said, "would put the independence of police authorities beyond doubt." In a modified version, the bill gave MI5 powers to fight crime within Britain, but they could act only in cooperation with the local police. The Thatcherite principle of centralizing authority in the interest of efficiency had given way to local pressures.

In 1996, a shocking killing of schoolchildren in Scotland brought a powerful public reaction against private ownership of handguns. Swept by emotion stimulated by the families of the slain children, Parliament responded with legislation outlawing handguns except .22 caliber kept securely in gun clubs. Conservative backbenchers, responding to gun dealers and owners, claimed that the legislation went too far. The Major ministry had offended another of its special interest constituencies.

As Parliament opened in November 1996, it appeared that Howard would be the principal ballcarrier in the run-up to the election. Howard came forward with thirteen crime bills, some presented by the government itself and some to be introduced by private members with the blessing of the government. These included empowering the police to confiscate alcoholic beverages from underage drinkers, close nightclubs where drugs were found, test prisoners for alcohol, and make DNA profiles of prisoners. Other bills would increase sentences for "yob" drivers who recklessly caused accidents, and outlaw incitement to terrorism abroad.

Howard's new Police Bill proposed granting the police and customs officials power to search or bug premises secretly in the quest for evidence of serious crime. At first Labour supported the measure, since it did not want to seem soft on crime. When the Liberal Democrats, the press, and the House of Lords raised objections on grounds of civil liberties, Howard was forced to accept an amendment requiring prior authorization by a chief constable and approval by a judge. The legislation established a national crime squad to work with the regional police forces in dealing with organized crime.

Howard offended the judges with legislation which stipulated a mandatory life sentence for anyone convicted of two violent or sexual crimes and minimum prison sentences for persistent burglars and drug dealers. The judges opposed mandatory sentences, claiming that they needed discretionary powers to make the punishment fit the criminal. Eventually the legislation was passed, along with prohibitions of stalking and racial abuse.

The increase in crime and the problems of dealing with new kinds of criminals have placed a heavy burden on the British prison system, with its antiquated facilities, old-fashioned methods, and inadequate funding. Conditions in prisons were revealed dramatically in 1990 when a violent riot broke out at Strangeways Prison in Manchester. The riot lasted for twenty-four days, resulting in the death of one prisoner and inflicting injuries that probably contributed to the death of a prison officer. Riots also broke out at seven other prisons, some of them resulting in injuries.

The next year Lord Woolf (now Master of the Rolls, the highest civil judge) presented a report resulting from the riot at Strangeways. He argued for a more positive approach to prisons: education, rehabilitation efforts, maintaining family ties. It was evident that the *Woolf Report* would require extensive reform of prisons and a substantial increase in funding.

When he came to the Home Office in 1992, Kenneth Clarke introduced reforms based on the *Woolf Report*. In 1993 the Prison Service became an independent agency responsible to the Home Office. Derek Lewis, a respected businessman, was brought to head the agency and introduce the new principles. Lewis implemented many of the recommendations of the *Woolf Report* with the goal of preparing prisoners for their return to society. Prisoners spent their time productively in working, education, and active sports. Telephones were installed so they could keep in touch with their families.

In 1993 Clarke went to the Exchequer, where he faced a financial crisis. From that perspective, his prison reforms were too costly and funding was cut. Michael Howard, who replaced Clarke, advocated a regime that would be both tough and economical, with emphasis on punishment rather than rehabilitation. Howard interfered repeatedly in Prison Service matters, and in October 1995 he dismissed Lewis, calling for an agency head who would introduce the kind of tough regime called for by financial stringency and Thatcherite ideology.

In 1995 some spectacular escapes brought an emphasis on security. Prisoner contacts with the outside world, including families, were tightly curtailed. To make prison even less comfortable, Howard proposed removing television sets from prison cells, an idea opposed by the Prison Service as likely to provoke riots. The Prison Service now faces a 13 percent cut over three years, although the number of prisoners is rising rapidly and Britain's aging prisons must be remodelled, replaced, and expanded. Education, job training, and other positive activities have been reduced and improved buildings postponed indefinitely. Privatization of prisons under the Private Finance Initiative is a possibility.

The Church of England

One of the historic institutions of authority and respect in England is the Church of England. Church attendance has declined greatly in recent years and the pronouncements of the clergy on current issues are often dismissed as irrelevant, but a segment of the British public, especially in small towns and rural areas, is deeply attached to the Church. The recent suggestion by Prince Charles that the monarch be called "Defender of Faith" instead of "*the* Faith" was not well received by Church leaders.

Attendance at Sunday morning worship continues to fall, and in 1995 was slightly over one million. Promotional efforts to persuade people to come to church on Easter Sunday have not been successful. However, one-fourth of all British babies are baptized in the Church of England.

The clergy are getting older, mainly as a result of the unusually large intake of clergy in the 1950s and the sharp fall-off in ordinations since then. Another factor in the aging of the clergy is the considerable number

of successful business and professional people (also of the 1950s generation) who wish to pursue a new career of service in the Church. Most of
the parishioners who attend regularly are also of the older generation.
These days very few young people are being ordained and attendance
among that age group is low.

In addition to an aging clergy, the Church is the custodian of thirteen
thousand aged buildings classified as grade-one, 40 percent of all grade-
one buildings in the United Kingdom. Many of them are parish churches
in small villages that have difficulty maintaining them. Others are splendid Victorian churches in decaying urban centers. The Church claims
that these buildings cannot be maintained with its own resources or the
support of private organizations, and has requested £50 million from the
government for repair and rehabilitation of these buildings.

In the City of London, the magnificent churches designed by Sir Chris-
topher Wren are poorly attended on Sundays, but they are used during
the week for lunch-time lectures and concerts attended by the people who
work in the shops and offices. In 1994 the Bishop of London recommended that twenty-four of the City's thirty-six churches be desanctified
and put to other uses, such as libraries or meeting rooms. The National
Trust for Cathedrals, similar to the National Trust that has preserved so
many of Britain's stately homes and other important historical remains,
has been formed to do the same for the cathedrals.

Thatcherism had little influence on the Church, but then the Church
had little influence on Margaret Thatcher, apart from annoying her by
criticizing her "uncaring" attitude. In one respect, the Church yielded to
the mentality of the Thatcher age. In the 1980s the Church, ignoring the
recommendation of its founder to serve God rather than Mammon, was
swept up in the property boom, losing £800,000 from property investments that went sour.

In the 1990s the Church recovered almost all its losses by selling its
non-performing shopping centers and other real estate and investing in
the stock market. However, this manna from Heaven was not enough. In
1994, the archbishops of Canterbury and York announced a sweeping
review of the structure of the Church, including consolidation of its ten
thousand parishes. They announced that the income of the clergy could
be kept at a decent level only by reducing the number of clergymen.

In 1994, after years of debate, the Church of England ordained its first women priests, although women had been filling lesser posts in the Church for some time. The step was opposed mainly by Anglo-Catholics, both for theological reasons and because it put another barrier in the way of reunion with the Church of Rome.

The main force behind the change was the women's movement, but there was broad agreement among lay members of both genders that the step was overdue. Women's role as caretakers has rapidly expanded from motherhood, teaching, and nursing into professional roles as doctors, lawyers, and accountants. Serving as priests in the Church seemed to be a logical extension of that process. When the first ordained women took up their duties, there was almost universal agreement among parishioners that they wondered what all the fuss was about.

The National Lottery

The lottery was established in 1994, and, given the British penchant for gambling, has been enormously successful, taking in more than £1 billion in its first year. The lottery is under the supervision of the National Heritage Department and is operated by Camelot, a company that bid for the rights and gets 5 percent of the proceeds. The Treasury takes 12 percent, and the rest is used for prizes, payments to sellers of tickets, and worthy causes. An agency (Oflot) was created to regulate the lottery.

The lottery gave the British people some relief from the emphasis on fiscal responsibility and administrative efficiency typical of Thatcherism. The uses of the lottery money are as diverse as the British people themselves. Lottery money goes to the National Heritage Fund, established in 1980 to buy land, buildings, works of art, and historic items that are seen as important relics of the British past. In 1997 the Department of Heritage gave handsome grants of lottery money to art galleries and museums in London, Manchester, and elsewhere. The Arts Council will use some lottery money to revive the British film industry. There was much criticism of the poor performance of British athletes at the 1996 Olympic Games in Atlanta. Aided by lottery money, the Sports Council intends to establish a

National Academy of Sport to train Olympic athletes and a state-of-the-art stadium at Wembley.

Lottery money appears to the public as a windfall that can be used for luxuries, even when necessities are lacking. For ministers, it has proven to be a golden apple of discord. Some people complain that the money is spent disproportionately for the interests of elites, as in the costly rebuilding of Covent Garden Opera. Others complain that lottery money goes to programs for undeserving persons, such as alcoholics, HIV victims, and prisoners. After wagering its assets (unsuccessfully) in the property boom, and (successfully) in the stock market, the Church of England condemned the lottery on moral grounds.

The Millennium Celebration

As the year 2000 approached the British people prepared to celebrate the coming of a new millennium. The Millenium Fund was established using lottery money (to be supplemented by private funding) to undertake projects memorializing the occasion. It is intended that the Millenium Fund will have completed its work by the year 2000 and will go out of existence.

The major project is the Millenium Exhibit at Greenwich, located on a deserted industrial site contributed by British Gas. A new Underground station has been built (Jubilee Line), and people will also be able to arrive by riverboat. Plans have been approved for an enormous dome, constructed of steel girders in an intricate pattern, and covered by a plastic roof. It will hold fifty thousand people and will be the setting for large scale millenium programs. However, estimated costs were higher than expected, and sufficient private matching money has not been forthcoming. Labour says it will review the entire project when it comes to office.

Most of the activities of the millenium celebration are aimed at making life in Britain more informative or enjoyable. British Airways will pay the cost of building the world's largest ferris wheel, to be located on the south bank of the Thames across from the houses of Parliament. Among the projects approved by the Millenium Commission are a seed bank in Sussex, a stadium for Cardiff (an opera house was rejected), an environmental center in Doncaster, restoring Portsmouth harbor, an extension of the Tate Gallery in the abandoned Bankside power station, a stadium for Glasgow, an arts center for Salford, a science and arts center in Bristol, a bioscience center in Newcastle, and a science and technology park in Birmingham.

The Prince of Wales decried the lack of a spiritual dimension in the millenium observances, which he thought should include some attention to Christianity. He proposed a thirteen-segment TV series on the history of Christianity, but it did not win the approval of the Millenium Commission. The Heritage Secretary pointed to the floodlighting of churches as evidence that the contributions of Christianity to Britain had not been overlooked.

Undiscouraged, the leaders of the various faiths proposed to the Millenium Commission to build a Christian Centre in Battersea that will hold ten thousand people. They announced that they would use it for religious observances of the millenium, and after that it would be available for all kinds of large gatherings. The structure would also provide twenty-five hundred low cost beds for young people visiting London.

The Millenium Commission has agreed to fund the renovation of two hundred village halls that have become dilapidated. Numerous proposals have been approved to improve parks, bicycle paths, and recreational areas. In these projects, the British people stated their priorities: to build or restore facilities that would make Britain more livable for everyone.

Expressing her individualist philosophy, Margaret Thatcher once said: "There is no such thing as society." The millenium celebration proved her wrong.

8

The Age of Thatcherism Closes, 1996 to 1 May 1997

John Major Hanging On

By 1996, John Major was locked into a political situation that gave him virtually no freedom of action. His slim majority exaggerated the influence of dissidents within his own party, especially the Euro-skeptics. The nine votes of the Ulster Unionists became essential and limited his efforts to bring peace to Northern Ireland. The growing popularity of Tony Blair and New Labour eliminated the possibility of a snap election. All John Major could do was to try to keep his ministry afloat until something good turned up, which seemed unlikely.

In January 1996, a *Times* poll showed that Labour still held a commanding lead. Labour was at 55 percent, the Conservatives at 29 percent, and the Liberal Democrats at 13 percent. The poll revealed that 76 percent of those interviewed were dissatisfied with the government. The popularity of Tony Blair was an important factor: 54 percent of those interviewed thought that Blair was ready to be prime minister. In another poll, 62 percent thought that Blair had changed the Labour Party for the better, while only 21 percent thought that Labour "has not changed very much, despite what Blair says."

The poll also demonstrated the importance of John Major to the Conservative Party. Although 35 percent of the public liked John Major, only 16 percent liked his policies, suggesting a public view that he was a good man trapped in an unpopular party. With Tony Blair riding high, Conservative chances depended upon drawing a distinction between Blair and

187

his party, suggesting that "Old Labour," repudiated by the voters in every election since 1979, would prevail over the new Labour Party that Tony Blair was building.

In December, 1996 John Major fought back with a strong TV interview in which the best qualities of "Honest John" were evident: forthrightness, knowledgeability, and experience. He stated that he would stand by his "wait and see" policy on the single currency, even if it led to an early election. He would oppose further unification of the European Union.

The *Sunday Times* poll in December, 1996 showed that the views of the voters had not changed appreciably since January: Labour was at 50 percent, the Conservatives were at 31 percent, and the Liberal Democrats at 14 percent. Approval of John Major as prime minister, from mild to strong was 68 percent, with 31 percent giving him a "poor" rating. In an amazing reversal, on economic competence Labour had a fifteen point advantage.

In any case, the coming election would not be a referendum on Thatcherism. The principles of Margaret Thatcher had become part of a new consensus, and the main policies of Thatcherism had been implemented. The state had been reformed and its frontiers rolled back. It still took 42 percent of the Gross Domestic Product and hopes to reduce that below 40 percent seemed unlikely to be fulfilled. The economy had been through two recessions and a wrenching restructuring, but it had revived in a new and modern form. Thatcherism and the dragons that it had slain were no longer a party advantage to the Conservatives.

Economically Britain was doing reasonably well. Thatcherism had worked: Britain was no longer declining in relation to her European peers, and since 1993 had been doing somewhat better. A study of international competitiveness put Britain behind only the U. S. and Japan among the large advanced nations, and ahead of Germany and France. The study rated Britain highly in financial services and in attractiveness for inward investment.

The economy was growing at a 2.5 percent rate, interest rates were 6 percent, and inflation was low at 3 percent. Exports had risen 42 percent since leaving the ERM. The deficit for 1996 was 4.4 percent of Gross Domestic Product, too high to meet the Maastricht standard for monetary union, but going down. Financial and service industries enjoyed strong growth, and manufacturing was picking up. Solid prospects for the future were underpinned by strong savings. Led by invisible exports such as financial services, the balance of payments was virtually balanced for the first time since 1985.

Total employment had changed very little since 1992. Jobs held by men had declined, and jobs held by women had increased. Part-time jobs were up by 8 percent; full-time jobs down by 2 percent. Since 1992 employment in London and the Home Counties had been strong. Manufacturing jobs continued to fall, while service jobs were increasing. Reflecting Britain's growing role as a financial and commercial center, service employment in business was up 19 percent since 1992, and hotel and restaurant jobs were up 8 percent. In 1996, unemployment at 6.7 percent was lower than any other European country and gradually falling. By March, 1997 unemployment was at 6.2 percent, well below two million but still higher than when Margaret Thatcher took office in 1979.

One sign of economic improvement was a rise in house prices, which in 1996 rose by 10 percent in greater London and the southeast, and somewhat less elsewhere. The result was a decline in negative equity, which was cut in half, falling from 1.7 million in 1993 to 800,000 at the end of 1996, a bit of good news for the Conservatives in an election year.

Britain had become the most attractive advanced country in the world (with the exception of the United States) for investment from other countries. The United States was the largest investor in Britain, while Britain returned the favor by investing almost as much in the United States. After the United States, the largest outside investors in the United Kingdom were Germany, France, and Sweden.

Britain's economic revival had resulted in a strong pound, a point of national pride but actually a mixed blessing. The strong pound gave a strong signal to the rest of the world that Britain is back, but it was a burden on exports and made Britain more expensive for tourism (a major industry). It was beneficial to financial services but damaging to manufacturing, which needs all the help it can get. It makes imports cheaper, and thereby helps keep inflation down.

Despite the economic recovery noticeable in many parts of Britain, the "feel-good factor" was absent. As one Conservative put it, it was "a voteless recovery."

The European Union

In 1996 the main thrust of the European Union was toward a single currency, a goal strongly supported by Chancellor Kohl of Germany, the crucial player in the process. The plan was for the member countries (or some of them) to qualify financially for the single currency in 1999, then enter a three-year transition period and fully adopt the euro in 2002. Leaving the Exchange Rate Mechanism (ERM) in 1992 and the growing influence of the Euro-skeptics left Britain looking on from the sidelines.

The intergovernmental conference called to advance European unity began in Florence in June 1996. It was concerned primarily with the strict guidelines required for introduction of the single currency. The process of bringing the finances of member states into line was called "convergence." The main convergence requirements for participation in the single currency were that the annual national deficit be 3 percent or less of Gross Domestic Product, and that the country's total debt be no more than 60 percent of its GDP.

Britain qualified in terms of its public debt (54 percent of GDP), but did not meet the deficit criterion with a 1996 deficit of 4.4 percent of GDP. The British deficit in 1997 was predicted to be 3.7 percent, a considerable improvement. Countries far from meeting the debt requirement in 1995 were Belgium (134 percent of GDP), Italy (125 percent of GDP), Greece (112 percent of GDP), and Ireland (82 percent of GDP). Even Germany with a deficit of 3.5 percent and France (4.8 percent) did not meet the convergence requirements, but they imposed strict financial discipline to achieve the goal and were expected to "fudge" the rest of the requirements.

British business held mixed views on the common currency. Trade with the European Union would be simplified, but the euro might complicate the 40 percent of British trade conducted with other countries. London has five hundred and twenty foreign banks from seventy-six countries, and conducts more foreign exchange transactions than any city in the world. Some analysts believe that this position would continue outside the single currency; some worried that it might not. The single currency was expected to encourage inward investment, because it would continue Britain's status as the best place for access to Europe.

A negative consequence would be linking Britain to the high taxes and huge borrowing that will be needed to pay Europe's unfunded pensions. Thanks to Mrs. Thatcher's tax-advantaged savings programs, Britain's private pension funds are greater than those of all the other countries of the European Union combined. Britain's prudent savers would not wish to experience the economic effects of supporting people who rely entirely on their governments for a comfortable old age.

The dispute with the European Union concerning BSE was especially disturbing to the Conservative Party, the party of agriculture. In March 1996, the European Union banned exports of British beef until the BSE issue was resolved. The ban included gelatin and even semen, which clearly could not transmit BSE. John Major fought back by declaring that he would veto every EU decision that required agreement by Britain. At the Florence summit in June he changed his tune, and agreed to a selective cull of 120,000 beef cattle. In turn, the EU stated that it would consider lifting the embargo when British beef was believed to be safe.

Under great pressure from the Euro-skeptics, supported by the farmers, Major reversed himself in September. He announced that the plan to slaughter great numbers of beef cattle would be dropped. He claimed that the latest scientific evidence showed that BSE would die out naturally in five years. Furthermore, mass slaughter would be politically unacceptable. Brussels was unmoved, and eventually Britain gave in. In December 1996, Douglas Hogg, the minister for agriculture, admitted that the EU would not lift the ban on British exports of beef until the culling resumed, as agreed at Florence. Beaten, the department prepared to resume culling.

John Major's handling of the "beef war" injured him in a variety of ways. It strengthened the public judgment of the Major ministry as incompetent; it deepened the fissure in his party concerning Europe; and it diminished his support among the most loyal constituency of the Conservative Party—agriculture and related industries. The fuss over beef disturbed British businesspeople, who saw constructive participation within the European Community as a vital interest. And the ministry's meek climbdown was in striking contrast to Margaret Thatcher's forceful "handbagging."

In the meantime, the European Union moved forward toward monetary unity. In December, the Council of Ministers agreed to abandon the rigid convergence guidelines proposed by Germany for the single currency, which included fines on countries that exceeded the limit on deficits. The French insisted that such decisions be "political" rather than automatic, which made it more likely that the common currency would be established according to schedule.

John Major, hamstrung by the Euro-skeptics and his slim majority, looked on helplessly. Unlike the United States, where the executive and legislative branches are divided and disputes between them are expected, in Britain they are joined in the House of Commons. The public expects that the government will know what it wants to do and its supporters will fall in behind. Nothing was more damaging to public confidence than the widespread impression that John Major was a leader who could not control his own followers, and that the Conservatives were a party unable to resolve their differences on Europe.

The Parties

In January, 1997 Ladbrokes, the chain of betting shops that had confounded the pollsters and predicted the outcome of the 1992 election, was taking bets at odds of 7–2 against a Conservative win and 1–6 in favor of Labour. A *Sunday Times* poll at the end of February showed that Labour was holding its own: Labour was at 52 percent, the Conservatives were at 31 percent, and the Liberal Democrats at 11 percent.

As Labour soared in the polls, John Major seemed to be on the ropes. While the British public recognized his good qualities, the opinion grew that, try as he might, for whatever reason, things just did not go his way. It seemed that one Tory mess followed another: the ERM, negative equity, "Black Wednesday," the Maastricht debates, the tax increases of 1993, "back to basics," and "mad cow" disease. A distinguished military officer (retired) commented: "This government lives on a permanent banana skin."

Just as the election campaign got rolling, another incompetence issue arose: Gulf War syndrome. Although Gulf War veterans had been complaining for some time, the Ministry of Defence had consistently maintained that their illness was not a result of their service in the war. The armed forces minister denied that organo-phosphates, an insecticide derived from Nazi nerve gas and sometimes used for dipping sheep, had been used in the gulf. When a parliamentary committee investigated, they found that the insecticide had indeed been used. The minister had to recant, stating that he had been misadvised by officials in the ministry. Labour cried "coverup," and the Major ministry had another smudge on its record.

A similar fiasco took place when it was revealed that Douglas Hogg, minister of agriculture, had failed to follow up on a report prepared in his own department that showed low standards of sanitation in Britain's slaughterhouses. Some questioned whether a ministry dedicated to the interests of producers should be the regulator of food safety. With BSE also in mind, the Vegetarian Society awarded Hogg a certificate for his contributions to their cause.

Public disdain for the Conservatives was enhanced by continuing incidents of sleaze: the chairman of the Scottish Conservative Party resigned due to an "indiscretion," believed to be a homosexual affair with an aide; another MP resigned due to alcoholism and an affair with a mother of four; another resigned due to allegations by the *Sun* that he had engaged in "nights of passion" with a seventeen-year old nightclub hostess; another withdrew as a candidate after admitting that he took large payments to ask questions in Parliament; two others were under pressure to step down for receiving unreported cash from a lobbyist.

With an electoral victory close at hand, Tony Blair knew that he still had to prove the fitness of himself and New Labour for government. He dominated his party through his intense ambition and energy. He had reorganized the party in a way that strengthened his control of the central machinery and democratized the constituency organizations. Membership had doubled since he became leader and for the first time membership exceeded that of the Conservatives, which had fallen dramatically. He displayed the killer instinct when he shredded John Major's floundering ministry: "weak, weak, weak," he cried. "Weak, weak!" He even had nice things to say about the zeal and toughness with which Margaret Thatcher had driven her agenda.

Blair had made a tireless effort to court business. He had traveled throughout Britain, meeting owners of small businesses as well as heads and directors of large corporations. He claimed to have met ten thousand business people. His main purpose had been to reassure business about the intentions of New Labour. He promised again and again that the changes of the 1980s in business and industrial relations would not be reversed.

Even though business people might not accept Labour, they admired Blair's leadership and drive, and the way that he had taken over a run-down firm (the Labour Party) with unattractive personnel and products and turned it into a winner. Tony Blair made it respectable for business to vote Labour.

Tony Blair also realized that a Labour victory would require closing the gender gap. In 1992 the Conservatives led Labour among women by 15 percent, whereas among men the two parties were virtually even. Among women over 55, only 25 percent had voted Labour. Although women are 52 percent of the population, only sixty women were elected to the House of Commons in 1992. To win favor with woman voters, Labour required some constituencies to choose a woman candidate, a policy that later was overruled by an industrial court as gender discrimination. Nevertheless, until it was outlawed the policy seems to have worked. A poll of women in March 1997, showed Labour leading the Tories, 52 percent to 32 percent, with the Liberal Democrats at 14 percent. Tony Blair was also winning the youth vote. Among those between eighteen and twenty-seven, Labour was at 62 percent, the Conservatives were at 22 percent, and the Liberal Democrats attracted a mere 9 percent.

The Liberal Democrats were determined to maintain their own identity. They had to differ from Labour enough to keep their own members from defecting and to attract disgruntled Conservatives. At the same time they wanted to keep close enough to Labour to be part of a coalition should Labour need their support in the new Parliament. Paddy Ashdown's nightmare was a Labour landslide that would make his party irrelevant.

The Issues

The end of the Thatcher era was evident in the large number of issues where the differences between the two major parties were minimal to nonexistent. The economic principles of Thatcherism had become conventional wisdom, and the Thatcher reforms in the civil service, business, industry, and the unions were generally accepted. The polls showed that the most important issues identified by the public were health care, education, and unemployment. On these, Labour overwhelmingly was regarded as the party with the best policies. The economy and Europe were rated as of secondary importance.

On taxation, Conservative efforts to paint Labour as the high tax party were negated by the Conservative tax increases of 1993. Seeking to regain public confidence, Kenneth Clarke's 1997 budget called for tight limits on spending and a modest reduction in the income tax, with the goal of eventually reaching a base rate of 20 percent.

Replying to Conservative charges that Labour's spending plans would require tax increases, Gordon Brown, the shadow chancellor, stated that Labour would not increase personal income tax rates and promised to cut VAT on domestic fuel. The only new tax proposed by Labour was a "windfall profits" tax on the profits of the privatized public utilities, to be dedicated to reducing youth unemployment. Brown promised a two-year overall freeze on spending at the level set in Clarke's 1997 budget.

As the election approached, the Conservative Party advanced controversial proposals to privatize the Post Office (or parts of it) and London Underground. Plans were prepared for more property sales, including the massive holdings of the Department of Social Security and the Inland Revenue. Somerset House, a magnificent eighteenth-century building along the Thames in central London, could be put on the block.

Facing tight spending limits, Labour also looked favorably on the policy of selling off public assets, which would help fund its social programs. London Underground was the only public asset that was excluded. Tony Blair tipped his hat to Thatcherism when he stated that "economic activity is best left to the private sector."

Thatcherism ended the political and economic powers of the unions, and membership today is half that of 1979. To erase memories of the past, Blair made it clear that the unions would not control a Labour government. "It's our job to govern for the entire country," he said. Blair declared that he would not seek to change the union legislation of the 1980s. Despite their dissatisfaction with many aspects of New Labour, the unions supported Blair because he was committed to the Social Chapter and the minimum wage. He also agreed to a proposal that would require employers to accept a union if approved by 50 percent of the employees.

A Labour ministry, as employer, would be expected to deal firmly with public-sector strikes that affected the general public adversely. During the summer of 1996, Tony Blair had been upset by intermittent strikes in the Post Office and London Underground. He was determined that Labour's electoral prospects would not be destroyed by public sector strikes, as in 1979. Some union leaders complained that Blair "has kicked us in the teeth."

Both parties knew that Britain could not afford (or was unwilling to pay for) the welfare state as presently constituted. But neither party was willing to face up to the increased funding that would be necessary to fulfill existing commitments, apart from making it better. They emphasized getting welfare beneficiaries back to work through incentives and training:

"a hand up, not a handout" was the refrain. Pensions were also on the table, as the basic state pension became increasingly inadequate. The Tories proposed a complex and controversial plan to supplement the state pension with private insurance plans. Tony Blair indicated that he, too, intended to reform pensions, but he was noncommittal about how he meant to do it.

One of Labour's strong points with the public was its support for the National Health Service, despite John Major's efforts to overcome the distrust of the Tories engendered during the Thatcher years. Labour had no important proposals for reform, apart from promising to reduce administrative overhead and modify the internal market. The tight Conservative budget for the next two years (adopted by Labour), included negligible increases for the NHS. But Tony Blair's claim that Labour had founded the NHS and Labour would improve it carried conviction with the public.

The Tories promised to expand grant-maintained schools and to preserve the remaining 161 grammar schools. Labour described these remnants of Thatcherism as "clapped-out ideology." Tony Blair declared that his main thrust would be to improve education, not by fostering a dual system of schools but by making all schools better. Like the Conservatives, he would adopt national standards and enforce them. He would even keep Chris Woodhead, scourge of the teachers, as chief inspector of schools.

Blair encountered strong opposition from the National Union of Teachers, which demanded the dismissal of Woodhead, dismantling of Ofsted, abolition of grammar schools, restoration of grant-maintained schools to local control, an end to league tables, and a return to comprehensive schools. Teachers complained of large class sizes and excessive work loads. "We are giving Labour a year," said one union leader. "If we cannot get agreement from the new government we will do it ourselves and ballot to boycott all this unnecessary nonsense."

Labour presented ambitious plans for constitutional change: devolution for Scotland, Wales, and the English regions if they wished it; metropolitan government for Greater London with an elected mayor; a Freedom of Information Act; incorporation of the European Declaration of Human Rights into British law; and reform of the House of Lords by eliminating the hereditary members and eventually making it a partially elected body. On reform of the electoral system, Blair stated that he was "not persuaded" of the need for some kind of proportional representation but promised to hold a referendum.

John Major declared his opposition to proposals for reform of the House of Lords, electoral reform, and devolution for Scotland and Wales. He appealed for preservation of the United Kingdom as a sovereign entity within the European Union. He claimed that Labour's devolution plan would lead to the breakup of the United Kingdom, a possibility that some Scots welcomed.

The Liberal Democrats had long been committed to constitutional reform, which was the only way they could break the monopoly of the two major parties. Their major interest was an electoral system for the House of Commons based on some form of proportional representation. They also called for a written constitution, a Freedom of Information Act to break "the culture of secrecy" in Whitehall, incorporation of the European Declaration of Human Rights into British law, devolution for Scotland, Wales, and the English regions, and strengthening local government.

Constitutional reform had gained wide public acceptance. A poll conducted for the *Economist* the week before the election showed that the voters favored a bill of rights (seven-one), a Scottish parliament (two-one), reform of the House of Lords, elected mayors (nine-one), and reform of the voting system including proportional representation (two-one).

Electorally devolution for Scotland was an important issue for Labour, which had to compete with the Scottish National Party. Within the Scottish Labour Party devolution was popular, not only as a reaction against Thatcherism, but because Scottish Labour was not Blairite, retaining much of the social democratic heritage of Old Labour. Polls in Scotland showed Labour at 46 percent, the Scottish National Party at 26 percent, the Conservatives at 16 percent, and the Liberal Democrats at 10 percent. Scottish voters favored devolution (44 percent), but there was surprisingly strong support for independence within the European Union (34 percent). Only 18 percent favored the status quo.

There was no appreciable difference between the Conservatives and Labour on Northern Ireland. Tony Blair accepted the Downing Street Declaration and the Framework Document. Both parties wished to see the peace process continue, and they hoped that the province would settle down as the IRA and loyalist paramilitaries were marginalized.

The IRA participated in the election campaign in its own special way, setting off bombs both in Northern Ireland and in Britain and disrupting transportation with bomb scares. One bomb scare forced delay of the Grand National steeplechase at Aintree. Sixty thousand people were affected. As many as five thousand people were taken into homes by local families. The parties agreed to avoid making the IRA an election issue: John Major called the bombings "an insult to democracy," and Tony Blair stated that he had "an iron determination to stand up to outrages of this kind."

Relations with the European Union, and especially the single currency, was the great issue that John Major and Tony Blair, aware of differences within their own parties, preferred not to discuss. John Major attempted to maintain the "wait and see" policy against a rising tide of Euro-skepticism. Euro-skeptics saw resistance to monetary union as a favorable election issue for them. Opposition to the Social Chapter was a better issue for the Conservatives, because did not expose their disunity. The Social Chapter, which Labour accepted, could be presented to the public as responsible for the stagnant economies and high unemployment of Europe.

Tony Blair was friendly to the European Union, an attitude welcome to many businesspeople. He continued to advocate acceptance of the Social Chapter, but he promised that Labour would consult with business and the unions first. He discovered "formidable obstacles" to British participation in the single currency, and stated that British participation in 1999 was "unlikely." Blair expressed enough defiance of Brussels to make it clear that he would not be a "soft touch." The Liberal Democrats, long committed to the European project, also modified their support for monetary union. Euro-skepticism had won the day in Britain and seemed to be spreading on the continent also.

Public opinion polls continued to show voter disdain for the Conservative government and party. Party disunity and "sleaze" weighed heavily. The farmers, normally among the most loyal Conservatives, deserted in droves to show their unhappiness with Tory handling of BSE and other concerns of agriculture. Fishermen accused the Major ministry of failing to stand up for them against the fisheries policies of the European Union. The Church of England issued a report criticizing eighteen years of Conservative rule for long-term unemployment, emasculation of the trade unions, and abandonment of the minimum wage.

The Election Campaign

John Major called the election in mid-March, with voting to take place on 1 May. A campaign lasting six weeks was unusually long (British election campaigns are normally four weeks), but Major hoped to find chinks in Labour's armor or exploit opportunities that might arise. Tony Blair's main concern was that some unforeseen controversy or unguarded remark might deprive him of the victory that seemed to be in the bag. Seeking to exploit voter uncertainty about the newness of "New Labour," the Conservative slogan was "You Can Only be Sure with the Conservatives." Labour showed its commitment to incrementalism by claiming only that "Britain Can Be Better."

Blair's campaign managers had studied closely the Clinton presidential campaigns of 1992 and 1996, and they introduced techniques that revolutionized British political campaigning. The Blair campaign was tightly organized and disciplined, and controlled by a close inner circle. Campaign headquarters was set up like a war room, using modern communications and polling to track candidates, keep everyone "on message," respond quickly to attacks, and maintain the focus on the leader. The goal was no risks, no mistakes, no leaks, and no wobbles.

In contrast, the Conservative campaign was a shambles. John Major preferred to rely on his experience in office, mastery of detail, and political instincts. Negative advertising and personal attacks on Tony Blair fell flat. The differences within the Conservative Party broke wide open. More than two hundred Tory candidates threw over the traces and announced their opposition to the single currency, despite the "wait and see" policy of the ministry. Rival leaders and factions entered into an unseemly squabble about the party leadership after the anticipated political demise of John Major.

The newspapers were much less partisan than in previous elections. The *Sun* endorsed Labour, the *Sunday Times* endorsed the Conservatives, and the *Times* made no party endorsement, urging voters to support Euroskeptics of all parties. An analysis of two thousand newspaper articles showed that the press was tilted toward Labour, which had 26 percent positive articles and 31 percent negative. Articles about the Tories were 17 percent positive and 40 percent negative.

Mainly the campaign was conducted on and for television. The candidates appeared in frequent press conferences and interviews, where they faced rigorous questioning by skilled reporters and interviewers. They even exposed themselves to the questions of ordinary citizens on radio call-in shows. In Britain, purchase of television time for political purposes is prohibited. Instead, the parties are given free television time for political broadcasts. Prepared by advertising agencies, these slick presentations were perhaps more entertaining than the talking heads of the past, but their effectiveness was questionable.

Missing from the mix was American-style prime-ministerial debates, an idea supported by the leaders of both major parties and generally welcomed by the public. John Major believed that he would do better than Tony Blair in a face-to-face confrontation. When Blair raised questions about the format, the Conservatives claimed he was "chicken" and sent an actor dressed as a chicken to follow him around the country. The main obstacle to debates was Paddy Ashdown, who insisted on equal participation. The television producers believed that Ashdown's presence would disrupt the cut-and-thrust expected from John Major and Tony Blair, and neither major party wanted to give additional attention to the Liberal Democrats. So the debates did not take place.

Both party leaders toured the country in buses, while their central offices coordinated campaign rallies, press conferences, and television interviews. Other party luminaries also held rallies and press conferences, but the public showed little interest or involvement in the campaign. Election rallies, once the core of political campaigns, were poorly attended. In the constituencies, efforts of the candidates to meet the voters on the streets or on the doorstep were usually met with polite disinterest. Foreign Secretary Jeremy Rifkind was seen in a supermarket parking lot, helping shoppers load grocery bags into their cars, as a means of meeting his constituents.

The pollsters were busy tracking the campaign and trying to adjust their figures to the large number of potential voters who were undecided or unwilling to reveal their preferences. A *Times* poll in mid-April showed Labour at 48 percent, the Conservatives at 27 percent, and the Liberal Democrats at 17 percent. The final poll, taken at the end of April, was virtually identical. Polls suggested a Labour majority of 165 seats or more, with up to eight Conservative ministers failing to gain reelection. Six weeks of campaigning had not made the slightest difference.

The determining factor was the desire of the voters to get rid of the

Tories, not enthusiasm for Labour. Voters still liked John Major, but they thought he was too weak to lead his party or the government. They were willing to give Tony Blair a chance to show what he and Labour could do. The voters had decided that it was "time for a change," and nothing the politicians or their spin-doctors could do would change that.

In the last week both candidates attempted to bring "passion" into campaigns that lay dead in the water. John Major relied mainly on the "true-blue" Tory issues that his backbenchers had advocated for some time: opposition to European integration (including delay on the single currency), and staunch opposition to devolution. Major charged that Blair would not stand up for Britain in negotiations with Europe, and a Tory advertisement showed Tony Blair as a puppet sitting on the knee of Chancellor Kohl. When John Major capitulated to Euro-skepticism, Lady Thatcher came out in support of her party and hit the campaign trail herself.

Tony Blair also adopted the nationalist approach, asserting in Thatcherite terms the global view of Britain's destiny. As a power of moderate size, he said, Britain was still important in NATO, in its relations with the United States and Russia, and in the world economy. He proclaimed the importance of well-trained, well-equipped military forces to help preserve peace in many parts of the world. He hailed the importance of the English language as the global language of ideas and trade. Above all, he claimed that Labour was now the "One Nation" party, in contrast to the divisiveness of Thatcherism. "I am a British patriot," he declared.

The End of an Era

The election was held on Thursday, 1 May. The polls closed at 10:00 p.m., and as the results flowed in the nation was stunned at the size of the Labour landslide. Labour won four hundred and nineteen seats with 44 percent of the vote, which translated into an overall majority of one hundred and seventy-nine members. The Conservatives gained 31 percent of the vote and one hundred and sixty-four seats, which reduced them to one-fourth of the House of Commons. Seven cabinet members were not reelected, including the foreign secretary, whose helpfulness with shopping bags could not overcome the unpopularity of his party. Compared to the election of 1992, the Liberal Democrats doubled their number of seats (forty-six), but their 17 percent of the vote was slightly lower. The turnout was 71 percent, an all-time low for post-war elections.

Labour made huge gains in London and the surrounding counties. The Tories won no seats in the large cities and were reduced to a party of the small towns, the suburbs, and rural England. They were were wiped out in Scotland and Wales. Conservative moderates were hardest hit, leaving the party even more divided than before. In Northern Ireland, Gerry Adams and another Sinn Fein candidate were elected, although they refused to take their seats in the House of Commons.

On Friday morning John Major went to Buckingham Palace and resigned as prime minister. Tony Blair met with the queen shortly thereafter and was authorized to form a government. At forty-three, he became the youngest prime minister since Lord Liverpool in 1812. Announcements of the principal cabinet officers followed quickly and other appointments were made over the weekend. By Monday morning the Blair ministry was in business.

Unlike American elections, there was no elaborate inauguration. On election eve, as the results came in, Labour Party workers held an ecstatic party at Royal Festival Hall, along the Thames. On Friday an enthusiastic crowd of supporters and tourists gathered at Downing St. to greet Tony Blair and his wife, Cherie, as they entered No. 10. That was it!

The Labour victory in the election was anticipated, but it was astonishing in its completeness. Like the election of 1906, which ushered in "the New Liberalism," and the Labour landslide in 1945, the election of 1997 utterly changed the political landscape.

The election merely confirmed the message that the polls had been communicating for more than a year. John Major's hopeless six-week campaign served only to irritate the British public, which had already made up its mind. Continued infighting among the Conservatives undoubtedly alienated potential voters, while the steadiness of Tony Blair and the discipline of Labour inspired confidence. The negative tone of the Tory campaign backfired when placed against Labour's positive message.

The low turnout undoubtedly helped Labour and the Liberals. Many who did not vote were Conservative in their sympathies but unwilling to give the party their endorsement at the ballot box. Conservative party candidates, agents, and workers in the constituencies were discouraged by the negative reactions they received. Euro-skepticism did not energize voters; it may have had the opposite effect. An important reason for the low turnout was the verdict of the polls that the result was a foregone conclusion.

An important source of Labour and Liberal Democratic gains was their strength in local government. Most local councillors are elected on the basis of their affiliation with the national parties, but it is still important for them to win the approval and support of the local voters. In the previous few years the Conservatives had been virtually shut out of local government offices. As the Labour and Liberal parties gained strength and experience in local government, they developed a pool of attractive candidates for Parliament. Of one hundred and eighty-one new MPs (most of them Labour or Liberal Democrat), one hundred and twenty had been councillors.

Labour's landslide brought important change to the social makeup of the House of Commons. Labour elected one hundred and two women candidates out of one hundred and fifty-eight. The average age of the new Labour MPs was forty-three, the same age as their leader. They were public-sector employees, local officials, union workers (seventeen), lawyers, social workers (twenty-one), teachers or lecturers (forty-two), journalists, one was a fire-fighter and one a taxi-driver. Eight of them were under thirty. There were five Asians and four blacks.

Tactical voting contributed to the outcome. There was a widespread desire to get rid of the Tory government. In constituencies where a close vote was expected, voters marked their ballots for the candidate most likely to defeat the Conservative. The Conservatives lost heavily in marginal seats, sometimes to Labour, sometimes to the Liberal Democrats. The resurgence of Paddy Ashdown and the Liberal Democrats is primarily attributable to tactical voting, but not entirely. Some Conservatives, who could not bring themselves to vote for Labour, saw the Liberal Democrats as an acceptable alternative.

Tony Blair's claim that Labour had become the "one nation" party was confirmed. Labour's support among men and women was approximately equal. The Conservatives held their support among voters over sixty-five, but Labour's vote among young people (under thirty) was up 57 percent over 1992. White-collar workers defected from the Tories in large numbers, giving 47 percent of their votes to Labour, compared to 28 percent in 1992.

Without minimizing the contributions of Neil Kinnock and John Smith, the Labour sweep was primarily due to the leadership, personal attractiveness, energy, and realism of Tony Blair. His claim to have built a new Labour Party was vindicated by the election, although his argument that he had done so while preserving the values of the old was suspect. Blair made Labour electable by accepting the changes brought into British government by Margaret Thatcher and John Major. His victory rested on his claim that he would bring competence, moderation, and concern for ordinary people to the challenges of the post-Thatcher era.

John Major, hurt and humiliated, announced that he would resign from the leadership of the Conservative Party. "When the curtain falls," he said, "it is time to get off the stage." Michael Heseltine, who had had a heart attack in 1993, had a mild recurrence and announced that he would not be a candidate for the leadership.

The Conservatives found cold comfort in the view that their loss was the result of their previous successes. They claimed that eighteen years in office and four electoral victories had left the country ripe for a change. They complained that Tony Blair had won by adopting their principles. Although those arguments had validity, the Conservatives could not deny that their own muddle and disunity had turned a likely defeat into a disaster.

Looking to the future, the Conservatives were down but by no means could be counted out. Although they gained only 25 percent of the seats, they received 31 percent of the votes. In 1992, with a larger turnout, John Major had received more votes (14 million) than Tony Blair got in 1997 (13.5 million). Many of the Tory voters of 1992 were presumably among those who stayed home in 1997. With strong leadership and a clear message the Conservative Party could revive, especially if the Blair government made serious mistakes or his party became divided along the fault line of "Old" versus "New" Labour.

The election was not a repudiation of John Major personally. The British people continued to like and respect him. But they felt that he had failed to give his party the strong leadership that they expect in a prime minister. The electorate repudiated the Conservative Party, and John Major had to accept some responsibility for a party that had disintegrated on his watch.

The election was not a repudiation of Thatcherism, for the changes of the Thatcher-Major era—civil service reform, privatization, and limitation of union power—were generally accepted. Public unease with the Tories grew out of the Thatcherite reforms of the welfare state. While the economy was doing well, there was also a widespread sense of insecurity. The voters looked for assurance that the state would be there to help them in time of need, and they found it in Tony Blair and Labour.

The relationship with the European Union, including the single currency, was not an important issue in the election, except for the antagonisms that it sowed within the Conservative Party. The public assumed that the connection with Europe would continue, and that a leader friendly to Europe and untainted by previous conflicts could bring differences to a sensible resolution. That leader appeared to be Tony Blair.

Throughout the nation there was a sense of relief that the election was over and that the nation was making a fresh start. The *Sun* took a sentimental view of the Labour victory with a front page that showed Cherie Blair kissing her husband and the headline: "SEALED WITH A X."

9

An Assessment

Margaret Thatcher

The Thatcher and Major ministries belong together as marking a distinctive period in British history. Margaret Thatcher was the innovator who used a political and economic crisis to begin a period of radical reform. John Major was the consolidator who carried to completion most of the key items in the Thatcher agenda. With the election of 1997 the age of Thatcherism was over, in that Tony Blair had accepted the Thatcherite reforms and given them permanence.

Margaret Thatcher began the painful transition of Britain to a post-industrial economy. She was an advocate of competitive capitalism: reducing the intrusiveness of the state into the economy, controlling inflation by restraining public spending and borrowing, cutting taxes to encourage saving and investment, privatization of nationalized industries in the interest of competitiveness, and limitation of the powers of the trade unions.

During the Thatcher years the British economy turned in a new direction, although at heavy cost. Finance and trade flourished while older industries languished. Some of the privatizations were highly successful, some less so. Breaking the powers of the unions was essential to creating an entrepreneurial culture. In the process a high price was paid. Unemployment soared and remained endemic in the old industrial areas. Regional disparities increased, as much of the new wealth was concentrated in the south-east of England. Startling inequalities in income emerged: high-flyers made fortunes, the well-educated middle class prospered, and a growing pool of low-paid or unemployed people became dependent on the services of the welfare state.

Mrs. Thatcher was a modernizer who undertook to reform many of the established institutions of Britain. The civil service, local government, the schools, the universities, the National Health Service, and the social security system all felt her lash in the quest for economy and efficiency. The value of these changes remains problematical, but the Blair ministry is unlikely to reverse them to any significant extent.

The results of Thatcherism have been exaggerated, especially in the United States. Mrs. Thatcher did not reduce government spending, although it can be argued that she kept it from rising as much as it might have under a less determined leader. Nor did she cut taxes; reductions in income tax were offset by increases in VAT and national insurance contributions, which fell heaviest on low income people. She did not reduce the cost of the welfare state. The modest savings that were made by her reforms were more than offset by the high cost of long-term unemployment.

Margaret Thatcher's active foreign policy was more show than substance, although on occasion she demonstrated that a well-led power of medium rank could exercise an important influence. Her attempt to restore "the special relationship" with the United States was little more than a personal friendship with President Ronald Reagan. The dissolution of the British Empire was completed on her watch.

Although regarded as antagonistic to the European Community, she strengthened Britain's ties with Europe by signing the Single European Act and taking Britain (albeit reluctantly) into the Exchange Rate Mechanism. Her relationships with Ronald Reagan and Michael Gorbachev probably made some contribution to easing the tensions of the Cold War. Her encouragement and military support made it possible for President George Bush to form the coalition that fought the Gulf War.

Mrs. Thatcher's policies did not by themselves transform Britain, but they made it possible for Britain to fit into a world that was being transformed. In the 1970s and 1980s vast masses of capital flowed throughout the world, creating a truly global economy. Personal computers capable of complex processes first appeared in 1981; when Thatcher left office, they were ubiquitous. The world was linked by high-speed air travel, satellite communications, and huge freighters and oil tankers. New industrial competitors in Asia and Latin America challenged the supremacy of the West.

These changes would have affected Britain in any case, but the Thatcher reforms broke open the constraints of bureaucracy, socialism, and trade union power, and enabled Britain to be a leader, not a laggard, in the movement to modernity. Mrs. Thatcher's ideas were not unique, but she was the first leader of a major country to put those ideas into effect. In so doing, she blazed a trail that most of the world has since felt it desirable to travel.

John Major

When John Major succeeded Margaret Thatcher in 1990, he proved to be more than a stop-gap. Major was not a man of fresh ideas or bold leadership, but he kept the Thatcherite agenda moving along. Mrs. Thatcher's dominating ways had generated bitter personal rivalries within the Conservative Party and strong differences of opinion concerning relations with Europe. Politically, John Major was a survivor because he was able to hold his quarreling party together. He was a calmer of troubled waters and a manager of the day-to-day problems of the political process. What was not expected from John Major were his toughness and resiliency.

The Major ministry can be best understood as the concluding phase of Thatcherism. Like his predecessor, John Major had to cope with a recession, fight inflation, and struggle to control public spending and borrowing. His ministry brought to completion most of the Thatcher agenda: civil service reform, privatization of the nationalized industries, and reform of the National Health Service, education, and the social services.

Major was also a Thatcherite in his dealings with the European Union and Northern Ireland, while being less abrasive and more patient than his predecessor. His approach was to avoid crises and clear-cut decions. This form of leadership was in striking contrast to Mrs. Thatcher's decisiveness, but there is much to be said for letting the problems of Europe and Northern Ireland work themselves out gradually.

The election of 1992 showed that the electorate had changed, but the election results were indecisive. Support for the Tories was unenthusiastic. Labour was not seen as ready for government. A vote for the Liberal Democrats seemed to be a wasted vote. John Major won the election, but he did not win a reliable parliamentary majority or a broad base of public confidence. For the next five years he struggled in circumstances that made him responsible for government without the kind of parliamentary and public support he needed to lead effectively.

John Major's problems began immediately after his electoral victory in 1992, and were never satisfactorily resolved. Despite his opt-outs, the debate over the Maastricht Treaty brought out divisions within the Conservative Party that he could not contain. "Black Wednesday" was a shock to public confidence, and put the Major ministry in a financial predicament that led to unpopular tax increases and heavy borrowing. Major's Cabinet and party were quarrelsome, unpredictable, and incident-prone. John Major's problems with his own party diminished his credibility as a leader of the country.

In the meantime, Tony Blair succeeded in making New Labour an attractive alternative to the Tories. Blair was an effective and energetic speaker and debater, who performed well in Parliament and the media. He made a great effort to avoid the mistakes of his predecessors. He disavowed the principles and tactics of Old Labour and accepted the Thatcherite reforms, leaving the Conservatives no issues of their own. Tony Blair offered a fresh face to replace a government that was viewed by the public as stale and tired.

As the 1997 election approached, Britain was doing reasonably well. There was no sense of crisis, as there was in 1979 when Margaret Thatcher led the Conservatives to power. Tony Blair's acceptance of Thatcherism had made Labour electable. Under Margaret Thatcher and John Major, Britain had been transformed, and it was time for new leadership with a new agenda.

Tony Blair

The Blair ministry faces problems for which Thatcherism lacked acceptable policies. They must begin to resolve the tensions created by membership in the European Union. Widespread dissatisfaction with Britain's constitution and electoral system has led to controversial proposals for change. The communal antagonisms of Northern Ireland remain.

The main challenge facing the Labour government is social breakdown at a time of general prosperity: regional disparities, decaying inner cities, welfare dependency, single parenthood, unsatisfactory schools, crime, drug abuse, vandalism, hooliganism, ethnic and racial tensions, and a general lack of social cohesion, especially among the young. Within the welfare state, it will be necessary to establish priorities between the meeting the obligations of the past, primarily pensions and health care, and investing in the future: schools, universities, research and development, the infrastructure, and the environment.

Unlike Margaret Thatcher and John Major, Tony Blair does not come to office facing a national crisis. Britain can reasonably look forward to a period of stability that will give Blair and Labour an opportunity to fulfill their promise that Britain can be better.

Bibliographical Note

The factual scaffolding for this book was derived primarily from that useful work of reference, the *Annual Register: A Record of World Events* (London: Cartermill, 1979–1995). The first chapter of the *Annual Register*, "History of the United Kingdom," is normally about 50 pages. In addition, the *Annual Register* includes an editorial giving a broad assessment of world affairs, a chapter on economic and social developments that takes a world view but gives special attention to the economies of the United States and the United Kingdom, extensive tables of economic and social data, and the succinct "Chronicle of Principal Events," which covers the year. Most of the figures in this book concerning the public finances and the state of the economy are based on the data presented in the *Annual Register*.

The main periodicals used were the *Times* (London), the *Sunday Times* (London), and the *Economist*. All were valuable as sources of ideas and comment as well as factual information. On the election of 1997, diverse points of view were presented in the *Guardian* in its weekly edition, the *Spectator*, and the *New Statesman*.

A useful work of reference is *Twentieth-Century Britain: An Encyclopedia*, ed. F. M. Leventhal (New York: Garland, 1995). *Social Trends, 1995* (London, 1996), an annual publication of the Central Statistical Office, provided a wealth of information. Another valuable reference is David Butler and Gareth Butler, *British Political Facts, 1900 to 1994* (7th ed., London: Macmillan, 1994). For additional bibliography see the chapter notes in Bill Jones and Dennis Kavanagh, *British Politics Today* (5th ed., Manchester: University Press, 1994) and the extensive list of references in Steve Ludlam and Martin J. Smith, editors, *Contemporary British Conservatism* (London: Macmillan, 1996).

Margaret Thatcher's memoirs entitled *The Downing Street Years* (London: HarperCollins, 1993) and *The Path to Power* (London: HarperCollins, 1995), were important sources, not only for Lady Thatcher's own perspective on her life and political career, but as storehouses of factual information. They are well indexed, with useful appendices providing a chronology and lists of officeholders.

Two other memoirs were especially useful. Sir Geoffrey Howe, *Conflict of Loyalty* (London: Macmillan, 1994) tells the story of Thatcher's chancellor of the Exchequer and foreign secretary. Nigel Lawson, *The View from No. 11* (New York: Doubleday, 1993) is a full and fascinating account of the Thatcher ministry from the brilliant, willful chancellor of the Exchequer. In addition to covering financial and economic policy, the book is a storehouse of fascinating information on the vast variety of matters that are involved in the raising and spending of the public money.

Any historian relies on the works of others for general background and interesting tidbits. A useful chronological survey from 1945 through the election of 1992 is Alan Sked and Chris Cook, *Post-War Britain: A Political History* (4th ed., Penguin: London, 1993). Jones and Kavanagh, *British Politics Today*, provides topical analysis. Peter Jenkins, *Mrs. Thatcher's Revolution: The Ending of the Socialist Era* (Cambridge, MA: Harvard University Press, 1988) was an early assessment of Thatcherism. Kavanagh and Anthony Seldon have edited *The Thatcher Effect* (Oxford: Clarendon Press, 1989) and *The Major Effect*, (London: Macmillan, 1994). A stimulating book offering an alternative view of Thatcherism is Will Hutton, *The State We're In* (rev. ed., London: Random House, 1996).

Some studies of the Conservative Party are helpful. *The Conservative Century: The Conservative Party Since 1900*, ed. Anthony Seldon and Stuart Ball (New York: Oxford University Press, 1994) puts Thatcherism in perspective. *The Conservative Party*, ed. Philip Norton (New York: Prentice Hall, 1996) his as a similar purpose. *Contemporary British Conservatism*, ed. Ludlam and Smith, offers a stimulating collection of essays.

Special recognition is due to the publications of the Institute of Contemporary British History located in London. These books are written by authorities on the subject. They have good bibliographies, and many of them have valuable appendices that provide lists of office-holders or runs of data. The volumes used are: James Barber, *The Prime Minister Since*

1945 (Oxford: Blackwell, 1991); Dennis Kavanagh and Peter Morris, *Consensus Politics from Attlee to Major* (2nd ed., Oxford: Blackwell, 1994); Peter Dorey, *British Politics since 1945* (Oxford: Blackwell, 1995); Eric Shaw, *The Labour Party since 1945: Old Labour, New Labour* (Oxford: Blackwell, 1996); David Butler, *British General Elections Since 1945* (2nd ed., Oxford: Blackwell, 1995); Robert M. Worcester, *British Public Opinion: A Guide to the History and Methodology of Political Opinion Polling* (Oxford: Blackwell, 1991); Kevin Theakston, *The Civil Service Since 1945* (Oxford: Blackwell, 1995); Michael Dockrill, *British Defence Since 1945* (Oxford: Blackwell, 1988); Alec Cairncross, *The British Economy Since 1945: Economic Policy and Performance* (Oxford: Blackwell, 1995); Howard Glennerster, *British Social Policy Since 1945* (Oxford: Blackwell, 1995); Robert Taylor, *The Trade Union Question in British Politics: Government and Unions Since 1945* (Oxford: Blackwell, 1993). My figures on unemployment are based on Appendix 5: Table A5.1 of this book. Figures concerning inflation (the retail price index) and earnings are based on Appendix 5: Table A5.6.

Other useful volumes from this series are Zig Layton-Henry, *The Politics of Immigration: Immigration, "Race", and "Race" Relations in Postwar Britain* (Oxford: Blackwell, 1992); Stephen George, *Britain and European Integration Since 1945* (Oxford: Blackwell, 1995); Paul Arthur and Keith Jeffery, *Northern Ireland Since 1968* (2nd ed., Oxford: Blackwell, 1996); and John Darwin, *The End of the British Empire: The Historical Debate* (Oxford: Blackwell, 1991).

Index

About the Author

Earl A. Reitan was born in Grove City, MN in 1925. He received his B. A. degree from Concordia College, Moorhead, MN (1948) and his Ph.D. degree in history from the University of Illinois (1954). Since 1954 he has been professor of history (now emeritus) at Illinois State University, Normal, IL.

His academic specialty is eighteenth-century Britain. His first book was *George III: Tyrant or Constitutional Monarch?* (Boston: D. C. Heath, 1965). He published in scholarly journals a series of articles on the political importance of the civil list, 1689–1804 and the role of Edmund Burke in administrative reform, 1779–1783. He edited *The Best of the Gentleman's Magazine, 1731–1754* (Lewiston, NY: Mellen, 1987). He is the author of *Politics, War, and Empire: The Rise of Britain to a World Power, 1688–1792* (Arlington Heights, IL: Harlan Davidson, 1994). He is co-author of *English Heritage* (2nd ed., Arlington Heights, IL: Harlan Davidson, 1988), a textbook on English History, for which he wrote the chapters on nineteenth and twentieth century Britain.

He is a veteran of World War II, having served as a rifleman with the Third Infantry Division on the Anzio beachhead, in the landing in southern France (where he was wounded), and in the Vosges and Colmar Pocket campaigns. He has published articles on battles in which his battalion was engaged.